Legal Institutions
The Development of Dispute Set

To
David Daube
on his seventy-fifth birthday

Legal Institutions
The Development of Dispute Settlement

Peter Stein JP, FBA
Solicitor; Regius Professor of Civil Law
in the University of Cambridge

London
Butterworths
1984

England	Butterworth & Co (Publishers) Ltd, 88 Kingsway, LONDON WC2B 6AB
Australia	Butterworths Pty Ltd, SYDNEY, MELBOURNE, BRISBANE, ADELAIDE and PERTH
Canada	Butterworth & Co (Canada) Ltd, TORONTO Butterworth & Co (Western Canada) Ltd, VANCOUVER
New Zealand	Butterworths of New Zealand Ltd, WELLINGTON
Singapore	Butterworth & Co (Asia) Pte Ltd, SINGAPORE
South Africa	Butterworth Publishers (Pty) Ltd, DURBAN
USA	Butterworths Legal Publishers, ST PAUL, Minnesota Butterworth Legal Publishers, SEATTLE, Washington; BOSTON, Massachusetts; and AUSTIN, Texas D & S Publishers, CLEARWATER, Florida

© Butterworth & Co (Publishers) Ltd 1984

British Library Cataloguing in Publication Data

Stein, Peter, *1926–*
    Legal institutions.
    1. Comparative law
    I. Title
    342   K559

    ISBN Hardcover   0 406 40025 3
    ISBN Softcover   0 406 40026 1

The cover of the softcover edition shows Jean Fouquet's *Trial of duc d'Alençon before Parlement de Paris:* Bayerische Staatsbibliothek, München (call number: Cod.gall.6, f.2v).

Typeset by Phoenix Photosetting, Chatham
Printed by Mackays of Chatham Ltd

Preface

This book owes its origin to some remarks I made in a presidential address to the Society of Public Teachers of Law in 1981.[1] I was urging the need to give students of law, at an early stage in their course, a bird's eye view of the main institutions found in most developed legal systems, without concentrating on one particular system. When I gave the address I had no intention of working out my ideas in book form, but afterwards it was suggested to me by Mr James Clarke of Messrs Butterworths, egged on by my wife, that if what I had said had any merit, it was worth a fuller demonstration.

An institution is understood simply as 'something established', a recognised way of doing things. To orient himself in the law, the student should first be able to identify established ways of settling disputes and of finding and declaring the law. Secondly, he should be able to recognise established ways in which the substantive law copes with the recurring problems that face it. If he sees the same processes at work and the same devices used in the legal systems of different kinds of society, he will gain an understanding of the nature of the legal process, which he could not acquire from the study of any one system. He will find it easier to recognise what is characteristic of any developed legal system and what is the result of historical accident.

Traditionally these educational aims have been achieved through the study of Roman law. The society of ancient Rome was manifestly different from our own, yet it produced a highly sophisticated law, which has not only had great influence on the laws of continental Europe but was itself the product of an historical development strikingly similar in certain respects to that of English law. Roman law still has great educational value, but when it is presented in relation to other laws, its interest is enhanced. Anthropologists have made us more aware of similarities and differences in the laws of simple and advanced societies and legal historians have shown us why some institutions are retained almost unchanged and others adapted. I have tried to take account of their studies.

The present work is divided into two parts. The first deals with the 'external' institutions of the law: forms of dispute settlement and

1   (1982) 2 Legal Studies 1.

types of procedure and their relationship to the forms of the law itself. The second part is devoted to the substantive law. It introduces the main institutions, as they appeared in Roman law, and then traces them into French law and German law, the two main modern systems derived from Roman law, and into English law, which has remained relatively untouched by Roman influence. The emphasis is on the institutions rather than on the rules which surround and give flesh to them, but in some cases the exposition has required some discussion of the rules.

Since the treatment is elementary, the text of the second part is not encumbered with detailed references and the reader who seeks to dig more deeply into any particular topic is referred to the standard textbooks. For English law textbooks on different parts of the law are legion; for a work that looks at the law as a whole, see P. S. James *Introduction to English Law* (10th edn, 1979). For Roman law, B. Nicholas *Introduction to Roman Law* (1962) is recommended and more detailed discussions will be found in J. A. C. Thomas *Textbook of Roman Law* (1976) and W. W. Buckland *Textbook of Roman Law* (3rd edn, 1963). For a comparison between English and Roman law, see W. W. Buckland and A. D. McNair *Roman Law and Common Law* (2nd edn by F. H. Lawson, 1952). For French law, reference may be made to Amos and Walton *Introduction to French Law* (2nd edn by F. H. Lawson, A. E. Anton and L. N. Brown, 1963) and for German law to N. Horn, H. Kötz and H. G. Leser *German Private and Commercial Law* (trans T. Weir, 1982). For a comparison of French and German law, see K. W. Ryan *An Introduction to the Civil Law* (1962).

I acknowledge with gratitude the helpful comments made on drafts of the book by Professor G. MacCormack of the University of Aberdeen and Dr. B. W. Napier of Queens' College, Cambridge, and at the proof stage by Professor J. A. Crook of St. John's College, Cambridge. They saved me from several errors and obscurities but have no responsibility for those that remain. I also record my thanks to my wife Anne and my daughter Barbara, both solicitors, for advice on particular points and to Mrs Kay Lawrence for her cheerful typing of the text.

Queens' College, Cambridge   Peter Stein
February 1984

Contents

Preface   v
Abbreviations   xi

Part I   **Institutions of dispute settlement and law-finding**   1

1. **Dispute settlement in stateless societies**   3
   Mediation and arbitration   5
   Coping with wrong-doing   7
   1. Shaming and sorcery   7
   2. Ordeals   9
   3. Contests   9
   4. Retaliation and feud   10

2. **The introduction of regular courts**   13
   The classical model of the legal process   14
   Popular feeling and the courts   16
   The kin and the survival of the blood feud   18
   Conclusion   23

3. **Models of procedure**   25
   The lay model in Roman law   25
   The lay model in English law   30
   The professional model in late Roman and French law   34
   Adversarial and inquisitorial procedures   36

4. **The effects of the procedural models**   39
   Law and fact   39
   Remedies   44
   Trial by judge alone in England   47
   Tribunals   49
   Arbitration as alternative   51

5. **Criminal prosecution and civil action**   54
   Continental criminal procedure   57
   Scottish criminal procedure   59
   English criminal procedure   60
   1. Trial by jury today   63
   2. Summary trial today   63
   Civil claims in criminal procedure   66

6. Written law and unwritten law   69
Ancient Rome   70
Medieval continental Europe   75
Medieval England   80

7. Case law statute and codification   85
England   85
  The growth of statute law   89
Continental Europe   93
  Codification of the civil law   97

Part II   **Institutions of substantive law**   105

8. Public law and private law   107
Constitutional law   109
Administrative law   114
Conclusion   122

9. The institutional system of private law   125

10. Persons   130
Roman law   130
Modern law   135
1. Legal persons   136
2. Natural persons   138
3. Family law   140

11. Property   144
Roman law   144
1. Ownership and possession   145
2. Rights less than ownership   151
3. Equity   155
Modern law   157
1. Movable things   158
2. Immovable things in the civil law   164
3. English land law   165
   (a) Common law   165
   (b) Equity   168
   (c) Rights in another's land   171

12. Succession   173
Roman law   173
1. Intestate succession   173
2. Testamentary succession   175
Modern law   177
1. Civil law   178
2. English law   181

13. Obligations 184
Roman law 184
1. Contractual obligations 184
2. Quasi-contractual obligations 193
3. Delictal obligations 194
Modern law 198
1. Contract 198
2. Quasi-contract 205
3. Delict and tort 206

14. Variants of contract 209
Commercial law 209
Consumer law 213
Labour law 214

Epilogue 220

Index 223

Abbreviations

Baker	J. H. Baker *An Introduction to English Legal History* (2nd edn, 1979)
Dawson *Lay Judges*	J. P. Dawson *A History of Lay Judges* (1960)
Dawson *Oracles*	J. P. Dawson *The Oracles of the Law* (1968)
Horn, Kötz, Leser	N. Horn, H. Kötz and H. G. Leser *German Private and Commercial Law* (trans T. Weir, 1982)
IECL	International Encyclopedia of Comparative Law
Jolowicz	H. F. Jolowicz and B. Nicholas *Historical Introduction to the Study of Roman Law* (3rd edn, 1972)
Lawson, Common Lawyer	F. H. Lawson *A Common Lawyer Looks at the Civil Law* (1955)

PART I

Institutions of dispute settlement and law finding

1 Dispute settlement in stateless societies

When we think of the law of a modern state we have in mind a set of rules applied by courts provided by the state, whose decisions are enforced by agencies of the state such as the police. When a dispute arises one party 'takes the other party to court', so that the court may settle the dispute for them. If a party is unwilling to co-operate, his attendance may be compelled by state agencies. If he fails to comply with the court's decision, again he may be compelled. So-called stateless societies have neither established courts nor official agencies able to enforce the settlement of disputes in the name of the community. Yet that does not mean that anarchy prevails, or that there are no recognised ways of settling disputes. It is just that methods other than compulsory adjudication followed by enforcement of decisions have to be found. When they are found they become accepted as part of the way of life of the society and traces of them frequently survive even when a state machinery for dispute settlement is set up.

Most of the time people in a state do not think about their obligation to conform to the law: and similarly in a stateless society they do not think about their duty to follow the ways of the community. They do not think about conformity because it rarely occurs to them to do anything but adhere to what is normally done. In any society people tend to follow established practices. The usual way of doing things seems to them to be the 'right' way, and they have been conditioned from childhood to feel that therefore they ought to do the same. Adherence to the folkways of the community is an expression of their membership of that community; it shows that they 'belong' and that enhances their sense of obligation. The more homogeneous a society is, the more the bulk of its members share the same racial and cultural background, the stronger such a feeling is likely to be. The old ways appear to be the natural ways and anything different is somehow 'unnatural'.

For most of the time, then, procedures for enforcing compliance with established practices will not be needed. Even if their sense of obligation is weak, people will see that it is to their advantage to conform to those ways rather than challenge them. If they want to be accepted by others, to marry well, acquire property, achieve status in the community, they are more likely to succeed if they fit in and do not upset their neighbours by behaving in what are considered to be deviant ways.

Where there is no state organisation to remind him that he is a 'citizen', the individual's membership of subgroups within the community becomes specially important to him. For it is on their help and support that he will call when he is in need. The most prominent group in his life will usually be his kin. This is a wider circle of blood relations than his immediate family. In some societies it consists of those related only through their father (patrilineal); in others of those related only through their mother (matrilineal); in others again of those related through both father and mother (cognatic). Sometimes the kinship group consists of a large number of members who are quite distantly related but who consider themselves to be descended from a common ancestor and bear the same name in the manner of a clan. There are of course other groups to which an individual will belong, apart from his kin, for example, his hunting party or fishing crew. In each case he will feel a strong tie of loyalty to these groups and together they provide cohesion for the society as a whole.

When an individual is involved in a dispute with other members of his group, it will normally be settled within the group without any appeal to outside agencies. A wrong done by one member of the kin against another will be settled by the senior members of the group, acting either as a council of elders or as advisors to the head of the kinship group, if one is formally recognised. Anyone who does not accept the discipline of the group must face the possibility that he will lose his membership and become an outcast, forfeiting the protection which the group offers to its members. For the ultimate sanction for behaviour which is disruptive of the group is expulsion, and in an undeveloped society, there is little place for an individual who belongs to no group.

When a member of one group becomes involved in a dispute with a member of another group, each side will expect to be backed up by the other members of his group, who will try to ensure that their side obtains what he wants. It is in this situation that the peace of the community as a whole is threatened. The pressures to conform will sometimes be insufficient to prevent arguments from flaring up into quarrels which require some action by those outside the two groups involved, if the stability of the community is to be maintained. Even stateless societies have control mechanisms for dealing with such situations, and they are effective even though the society has no way of officially mobilising its force in their support.[1]

---

1.   S. Roberts *Order and Dispute* (1979) esp pp 72ff; G. MacCormack 'Procedures for the settlement of disputes in "simple" societies' (1976) 11 Ir Jur 175.

Mediation and arbitration

All stateless societies depend considerably on mediation to settle disputes. This is particularly so when the dispute is of a private character, such as over boundary lines, non-payment of bride price, and allocation of property rights generally. The essential feature of mediation is that the mediators lead the parties themselves to reconcile their differences. Often the parties are not on speaking terms and the initiative in bringing them together has to be taken by the mediators. They try to find common ground between the parties, facilitate negotiation and create the conditions for a settlement. The simplest form of mediator is a go-between who overcomes a breakdown of communication between the disputants by travelling to and fro between them in an attempt to reduce their differences. A more active form of mediator may be able to arrange a full scale meeting of the parties, supported by their respective families and friends, at which he acts as chairman, guides the discussion and suggests possible solutions. Whatever the form of mediator, he must be accepted as impartial. His interest is to eliminate the threat to the security and cohesion of the community created by the quarrel and show the parties the dangers of allowing it to remain unresolved.

'The conditions for mediation are best in cases where both parties are interested in having the conflict resolved. The stronger this common interest is . . . the more motivated they will be for co-operating actively with [the mediator] in finding a solution, and for adjusting their demands in such a way that a solution, can be reached.'[2] Sometimes the mediator may be prompted to intervene by his position as a leader of the community; alternatively other prominent people or even the parties themselves may appeal to him to use his diplomatic skills. He will usually be a senior member of the community in terms of age, family status and service to the community and if he is successful, he will gain a reputation for diplomacy which will increase his status.

The mediator thus helps the parties to reach an accommodation of their differences for themselves. The arbitrator, on the other hand, is someone whom the parties have chosen to reach a decision for them. They submit the issue to him and leave it to him to decide. Unlike the decision of a court, however, the decision of an arbitrator binds the parties only so far as they have agreed to accept it. Thus the arbitrator, to be effective, must be more concerned than a judge to find a solution that he believes will be acceptable to both sides.

2. T. Eckhoff 'The mediator, the judge and the administrator in conflict-resolution' (1966) 10 Acta Sociologica 158ff, excerpted in V. Aubert (ed) *Sociology of Law* (1969) p 172.

The judge knows that in the end the parties must accept his decision, whether they like it or not. The arbitrator, like the mediator, aims to reconcile the parties so that they will abide by his decision. In order to achieve this reconciliation the arbitrator may well have to go into matters which are not relevant to the issue that is the immediate cause of the dispute, if those matters have proved to be irritants to the parties in the past. Unless they are removed, no settlement of the main issue, however ingenious, will be accepted, because the parties will be in no mood for any settlement.

In the abstract the distinction between the mediator who assists the parties to reach agreement and the arbitrator who at their request pronounces a decision for them is clear. In practice it is often difficult to distinguish the two and anthropologists have sometimes used the terms indiscriminately. In both cases the parties must voluntarily accept the decision if it is to be effective. It cannot, as with the judgment of a regular court, be imposed on them against their will. Whether it is their decision coaxed out of them by a mediator, or that of the arbitrator, may often not be at all clear. An arbitrator sometimes has more standing in the community and can put more pressure on the parties to accept his solution than can a mediator. He may, for example, gain acceptance by stressing the criticism which an obstinate or recalcitrant party risks by rejecting a reasonable solution. A clever arbitrator will sometimes persuade the parties that they have themselves arrived at the solution that he has suggested.

Both mediators and arbitrators function by getting the parties to talk about their grievances. In most societies there are regular meetings of groups of neighbours, to celebrate festivals or to attend funerals, at which it is customary to discuss current disputes that might disturb the peace of the community, but in some societies meetings are called as and when disputes arise. Recognised leaders take a prominent part in bringing out the parties' differences and articulating the issue with a view to achieving a reconciliation. Anthropologists have been impressed by the therapeutic effect of such discussions and have seen such general meetings as the community's way of defusing what might develop into an unpleasant quarrel. P. H. Gulliver,[3] for example, has described the operation of two forms of such meetings in African societies.

Among the Ndendeuli in Southern Tanzania, when a serious dispute arises, the parties meet together with what Gulliver calls their 'action-sets'. These are kinsmen and neighbours recruited by

---

3. *Neighbours and Networks* (1971) pp 132ff (on the Ndendeuli) and *Social Control in an African Society* (1963) pp 216ff (on the Arusha), summarised by Roberts, op cit, pp 123ff and MacCormack, op cit, pp 181ff.

the parties to support them in presenting their case. Each party will try to attract influential members of the community whose opinions will carry weight with other members. Those who are not prepared to commit themselves to either side attend the meeting to act as mediators between the two opposing groups. Whether they are in an action-set or act as mediators, their standing in the community will be enhanced if they are successful either in getting their side's case approved or in bringing the parties to a settlement. In searching for such a solution, they will refer to rules and practices generally accepted in the society, but they will also make play with other arguments such as the need to maintain the existing groupings and the harmony of the society as a whole.

Among the Arusha of Northern Tanzania, the procedure is more formal. One party to a dispute refers – his claim to a prominent member of the community who will convene a meeting at which he will secure the appearance of the other party. These meetings are not open to all and sundry; rather attendance is based on kinship or on age or on residence. Thus there is a certain degree of specialisation and the parties have some choice in the composition of the meeting which will consider their case. Both parties with their action-sets confront each other at the meeting, present their cases and try to reach a compromise. The community leaders direct the discussion and suggest ways of reaching a settlement. Although the Arusha rules are more precisely defined than those of the Ndendeuli, they are used more as arguments and bargaining counters than as decisive of the outcome of the dispute.

Both the Ndendeuli and the Arusha disapprove of self-help and exert pressure on those involved in a dispute to reach an acceptable solution by talking.

Coping with wrongdoing

So far we have been considering disputes where each side claims to be entitled to more than the other side is ready to concede, and the aim of society is to reconcile the two positions. There are also situations where one party alleges that the other has wronged him, for example, by physical assault, theft of his property, or adultery with his wife, and he seeks satisfaction, but the other party does not admit the claim. Stateless societies have different ways of dealing with such cases.

1. Shaming and sorcery

Some communities favour formal expressions of disapproval. In a small closely-knit society, whose members encounter each other frequently, there is great sensitivity to ridicule and formal shaming is an effective method of bringing deviant members in line. In New Guinea a man's wrongdoing may be trumpeted abroad by public proclamation to the whole village, whose members receive the message in silence, while directing against the accused the full force of public scorn. In other communities the shaming will be less formal. People sit in the meeting place and begin to discuss the evils of the anti-social behaviour, with more or less pointed references to how the accused's conduct will make him unwanted in their community. 'Where survival is seen in terms of group membership, the threat of loneliness is unbearable and any sign of disapproval or rejection deeply feared.'[4]

Another, more serious, form of control is the invocation of supernatural forces against the deviant individual. In 1954 E. H. Hoebel, the anthropologist, put the basis for such action as follows:

> 'Every single primitive society without exception postulates the existence of spirit beings and supernatural powers. Each of them attributes emotional intelligence to the spirit beings and holds to the belief that they respond with favour or disfavour to specific acts of men. They hold that in some or most of the important aspects of life man is subordinate to the wills of spirit being and that life must be made to harmonize with their dictates. Such presumptions are universal.'[5]

Although such ideas may be universal, the extent to which supernatural powers can be harnessed by human agencies will depend on the precise character of the beliefs of each society. Certain practices harmful to the community are normally considered displeasing to the spirit beings, who are then expected to react against them by visiting illness or bad luck on the offender and, in serious cases, by bringing drought, disease or other natural disaster on the community which harbours him. The conduct in question is taboo. However what is taboo and whether taboo violations are sanctioned by the supernatural powers on their own initiative or at the invocation of human agencies vary from one society to another. Some societies will leave taboo violations entirely to the spirit beings, and deal with other deviant conduct by secular means. Other societies will treat many forms of wrongdoing as potentially taboo and will allow the recourse to the supernatural as a reaction to forms of wrongdoing which would not elsewhere be considered of interest to the spirits. Sometimes the victim of wrongdoing may be allowed to use sorcery against the

---

4. Roberts, op cit, p 88.
5. *The Law of Primitive Man* (1954) pp 260–261.

wrongdoer or his family, but sorcery is seen to be a dangerous practice that may often cause more harm than it redresses.

Like fear of ridicule, fear of the supernatural is thus an important control mechanism, but it is an unpredictable one. Such fear, however, is useful only when a wrongdoer is already identified. Sometimes the guilt of an individual may be suspected but is denied by him.

2. Ordeals

It is this situation which provides the occasion for the practice of ordeal, the referring of the question of the guilt or innocence of a suspected individual to the judgment of the gods. That judgment is usually indicated by the outcome of an experiment. It is specially appropriate where harmful sorcery is suspected. There are infinite variations of the ordeal, using fire, water, poison, redhot iron, or merely drawing lots. Sometimes the ordeal combines the identification of guilt with the punishment in that the guilty party, by failing the test, also suffers pain or even death. Among the Loma of Liberia a suspected thief has to pluck a brass ring from the bottom of a pot of boiling oil with only a paste of leaves to protect his hand. If he does this without injury, he is innocent; if he suffers burns, he is guilty and has already been punished.[6] Such ordeals can be used to determine issues of fact in most of the cases that arise in a simple society. They are used when someone is accused of an offence not capable of normal proof, such as witchcraft, or where proof is not available and the accused does not admit the offence.

The ordeal does, however, require the participation of the accused person. In a small closely-knit community pressure from neighbours will usually ensure this, but on some occasions the necessary co-operation will not be forthcoming. One way round this difficulty is to consult an oracle. For example, among the Lugbara of Uganda a man who falls sick will assume that this is the result of supernatural forces invoked by someone with a grievance against him.[7] To find who that person is, he consults an oracle and submits to it the names of persons he suspects. By a process of elimination one name emerges. Then that person discusses with the oracle how he can best make amends for whatever caused the grievance and so bring about a reconciliation.

3. Contests

Quarrels can very easily produce violence and in a society without agencies of government, violence cannot always be avoided. Some societies tolerate violence much more easily than others. But in all societies which approve of violence as a means of redressing

6. Roberts, op cit, p 65.
7. MacCormack, op cit, pp 183ff.

grievances, there are conventions which limit the amount that can properly be inflicted on a wrongdoer.

A common way of curbing violence is to channel it into a contest. This may operate, like the ordeal, as a means for delivering the verdict of the gods, who will ensure victory to the party in the right. But contests also provide a means for letting off steam, for releasing the feelings of anger and hostility which have built up during the course of the dispute.[8]

Among the Eskimo, the two disputants meet in front of an audience and buffet each other's head until one person is knocked to the ground or gives in. The Eskimo also have so-called song duels in which the disputants hurl ritualised insults at each other. The victor is the party who manages to heap the greater humiliation on his opponent. Since the Eskimo belongs to a society in which a man's status is measured by his prowess as hunter and his consequent contribution to the welfare of the group, humiliation incurred by losing a physical contest or by losing a song duel is deeply felt, and that in itself provides satisfaction for his victorious opponent.

Contests may be used even where the dispute is not over whether one party has wronged the other. Among the Ifugao of the Philippines boundary disputes in the rice-fields are settled by wrestling matches at intervals along the disputed boundary. The falls of the parties determine where the line is to be drawn. The spirits are thought to determine that the falls will be in the right places.

4. Retaliation and feud

Sometimes the wrong is felt so seriously that only actual retaliation in kind will satisfy the victim's desire for revenge, and society will recognise the distinction between an unjustified attack on another and the exercise of justified vengeance. Normally the victim will rely on his kinsmen to help him and in the case of homicide it is left to them to redress the wrong done to their kinship group by the death. Whether exercised by the victim or his kin, the vengeance has to be carried out within a certain framework of rules. The retaliatory act should normally be no more severe than the original wrong. This is the so-called rule of talion, 'an eye for an eye, a tooth for a tooth'. The community allows retaliation in kind but limits it to the amount of harm which the victim himself has suffered. The action may be taken against the wrongdoer himself or against one of his kin, but women and children are usually exempt.

Vengeance is not merely a privilege of the kinsmen: it is their duty. For example, among almost all Eskimo tribes blood revenge

---

8.   MacCormack, op cit, p 184.

executed by the kinsmen of a murder victim is expected.[9] In the few tribes where this is not so, it is optional according to the 'strength' of the surviving kinsmen. The Eskimo also have a rule whereby a murderer becomes responsible for the family of his victim and must look after them as his own. (Sometimes, of course, desire to acquire the victim's wife is a motive for the original killing, but the rule applies whether or not this is so.)

The result of this rule is that the murderer may raise as a member of his own family the son of his victim who, when he reaches manhood, may be the one designated by the victim's kin to carry out the blood vengeance on the murderer. Where memories are long, a delay of several years in carrying out the vengeance is not disapproved.

Blood vengeance by one kinship group on another leads to the feud, which may go on for generations, long after the death of those originally involved. Yet, however fierce the feelings aroused by vengeance, there are always pressures making for the settlement of the feud through the payment of money or its equivalent in, say, cattle. Most simple societies, for example, have strict rules of exogamy barring marriage to anyone within the same kinship group, so that a man is compelled to go outside his own clan to find a wife. He then acquires an interest in his wife's kinship group. As Max Gluckman puts it, 'the fact that men of a single group of agnates [those related only through males] have mothers from different other groups, and marry wives from still other groups strikes into the unity of each vengeance group'.[10] The loyalty of the agnates to each other conflicts with other customary allegiances and this encourages settlement of the feud often by the methods of mediation described above. The very possibility of an outbreak of justified violence in furtherance of the feud is a powerful incentive to reach a settlement by negotiation. Such a settlement, if it is to be effective, must provide for a penalty for the offence and also remove the feeling of resentment in the victim's group. It must represent a 'levelling of the score' between the two groups.

The amount of violence that a society will tolerate by way of vengeance varies considerably. Hunting societies, in which warrior values prevail, allow more violence than farming societies whose values stress co-operation and stability. Another factor is the possibility of alternatives to violence. The Eskimo or the Australian aborigines have few goods which could serve as compensation payable to the victim's group as the price of forgoing vengeance.

9.   Hoebel, op cit, pp 87ff.
10.   *Custom and Conflict in Africa* (1956, repr 1966) pp 13–14.

They tolerate more retaliation than societies with more available means of providing compensation.

As methods of coping with wrongdoing, ordeals, contests and feuds, although characteristic of simple societies, survive in quite advanced societies through incorporation in the system of law enforcement.

2 The introduction of regular courts

It is with the advent of some form of central authority that we can observe the beginnings of the modern legal system. Some societies seem to manage without even chiefs. In others there are chiefs and a council of elders, who take the lead in promoting the settlement of disputes in the ways we have noted in the previous chapter. They still have no power to compel attendance, to make laws and to enforce decisions. Other societies again, however, although still quite simple in terms of the level of material culture, are organised under a central authority which can define the scope of the customary rules, declare new laws, and apply them through courts whose decisions are enforced. In such societies, informal mediation, arbitration and self help through retaliation are less prominent than in the societies which lack such institutions. But these methods of dispute settlement do not disappear. They may survive as alternatives to the regular court process, or they may be incorporated into that process and allowed after a court decision to that effect. There may be a division of disputes between the new court process and the traditional methods, certain matters of particular interest to the central authorities being settled by the courts and other matters of more local or private concern being left to be settled in informal ways.

Once a central authority has been established, relations between that authority and the ordinary members of the community become more formal and impersonal than the relations between the people and the unofficial local leaders had been. The courts set up to deal with disputes will at first follow the traditional customs which have been handed down by oral tradition from time immemorial. These customs will be known in essentials to everyone, but their exact scope will never have been precisely defined. Before the courts exist, the informal procedures aim at reconciling the parties with a view to reaching a compromise acceptable to both sides. In such circumstances the traditional rules are not expected to be applied rigidly. They provide a framework of guidelines within which negotiation can take place. But that negotiation, while it takes account of the rules, cannot ignore other considerations, such as the relative status of the parties and the relative bargaining strength that they can muster. The expectations of the community are based on the realities of social life and do not require the application of the rules without respect to persons. It is assumed that there will be differences of treatment. Where the settlement of the dispute, despite strong pressures from friends and neighbours, depends ultimately on the good will of the parties themselves, similar cases will not always be settled in the same way and so the rules themselves remain vague and ill-defined.

The classical model of the legal process

A court set up by central authority, with community force behind it, does not have to reconcile the parties. To a greater or lesser degree it can impose a decision on them and enforce it whether they accept it or not. There are three important consequences of this change.

First, there is a tendency for the judgment to take the form of an either/or, black and white affair. Instead of giving something to both sides to produce a compromise, it declares the plaintiff's claim justified and condemns the defendant, or it rejects the plaintiff's claim and absolves the defendant. This kind of judgment requires a more strict application of the rules than was the case with the informal methods of settlement. So, secondly, the rules themselves tend to become more precisely defined, so that as far as possible the exact scope and limits of each rule are laid down in advance of disputes arising. Instead of being part of the general oral folk tradition of the people, they are articulated in carefully chosen forms of words, often published in writing. Thirdly, a court tends to define the issue between the parties more narrowly than the informal procedures allowed. The identity of the parties, their status in the community and their previous relations with each other are no longer relevant factors to be taken into account. Judgment should now be based solely on the application of the rules to the facts relevant to the legal issue which separates the parties.

When these tendencies are unchecked they produce what we may call the classical model of the legal process. This postulates first, that the whole law is declared in a set of known rules of reasonable precision: secondly, that they will be applied to any conceivable set of facts so as to produce decisions that can be predicted with confidence: and thirdly, that those decisions will be based exclusively on the application of rules to the 'relevant' facts and will be totally insulated from 'irrelevant' circumstances that may affect the parties.

The classical model is more suited to some types of dispute than others. Where the issue is whether or not one party has committed a given wrong against another, or which of two competing claimants is entitled to property, it is quite appropriate. In many periods of history, either through the weakness of the state machinery or because of a prevailing philosophy that the state should interfere as little as possible in the lives of its citizens, the legal process has been largely confined to settling matters of that nature. There are, however, other types of dispute which do not lend themselves so readily to resolution by the classical model. Should they be dealt with by the regular courts or in some other way? If the regular courts adhere to the classical model too strictly, the parties will not take their case to a court but will prefer private arbitration. The eighteenth-century philosopher David Hume[1] recognised this point exactly when he observed that arbitrators, who by consent of the parties are entire masters of the subject, 'commonly discover so much equity and justice on both sides as induces them to strike a medium, and divide the difference betwixt the parties'. Civil judges, on the other hand, 'are obliged to give a decisive sentence on some one side, are often at a loss how to determine, and are necessitated to proceed on the most frivolous reasons in the world. Half rights and obligations, which seem so natural in common life, are perfect absurdities in their tribunal; for which reason they are often obliged to take half arguments for whole ones, in order to terminate the affair one way or the other'.

Some societies have not wholly accepted the classical model of the legal process. They have seen the function of the legal process to be as much the reconciliation of the parties, in the light of their relationship in its totality, as the application of a rule of law to a particular issue. In his classical account of Jewish law, the great twelfth-century jurist, Maimonides,[2] says that at the beginning of legal proceedings, the judges should enquire whether the parties want adjudication according to law or settlement by arbitration. He quotes Zechariah 8.16: 'Execute the justice of . . . peace in your gates', and, asking what is the kind of justice that carries peace with it, gives the answer 'Undoubtedly, it is arbitration'. So also, in 2 Samuel 8.15, David is said to have executed justice and charity unto all his people, and again asking what is the kind of justice that carries charity with it Maimonides answers, 'Undoubtedly it is arbitration, ie, compromise'.

Even in societies in which the courts themselves do not offer arbitration as an alternative to the strict application of the law to the facts, there is still a place for arbitration. The courts may restrict themselves to dealing with certain kinds of dispute, which will be decided by law, and leave others to be decided by an arbitrator as seems fair to him. In societies with the most developed court system,

1. *Treatise of Human Nature* III, 6 (ed Selby-Bigge, 1888, p 531).
2. *The Code of Maimonides* Book XIV, 'The Book of Judges' (trans A. M. Hershman, 1949) pp 66–67.

the parties to a dispute may always remove it from the courts to an arbitrator chosen by themselves (p 51). Legal process and arbitration are complementary to each other.

In recent years the limitations of the classical model have been recognised and there has been a demand that the law should enable the courts to extend the range of matters of which they may take account and reach compromise solutions where they are appropriate. This demand has led to a renewed interest in the way stateless societies deal with disputes and in the fact that not all societies which introduced regular courts fully accepted the classical model. A number of factors have affected the degree to which it has been adopted.

Popular feeling and the courts

In some societies, the law applied by the regular state courts will be felt to be so out of touch with the needs of a particular local community that use of those courts will be confined to cases where it cannot be avoided. In other matters the obligations created by local customs which are not applied by the courts, and are therefore not strictly 'law' are felt more strongly than the obligations created by the law of the state. As a result people feel that they should not bring certain kinds of disputes to the regular courts for settlement. Examples may be found even in modern Europe. Writing of attitudes to landrights on Tory Island off the coast of Donegal in Ireland, an anthropologist reports:

> 'Underlying all these considerations is the feeling that a principle of equal shares should operate. Thus, if a man and a woman decide to marry, and the woman has a claim to a sizable piece of property, then it is right that the land of the marriage should come from her if her husband is from a family more hard pressed. "If a man gets land from his marriage", I was told, "then he has no right to take it from his brothers and sisters." He has of course an equal claim de jure, but it is felt that he has no moral right to press his claim. Because there is no land court on the island, such matters ultimately depend on pressures of family and public opinion. But as always, it is difficult to go against the custom of the island.'[3]

In other societies such alienation of the state from popular consciousness has been avoided by adopting a form of procedure which ensures a wide degree of popular control both over the

---

3.   R. Fox *The Tory Islanders* (1978) pp 124ff.

identification of what is law and over its application in particular disputes. The consequence is that disputes may be settled with a greater sensitivity to the parties' situation than is possible through the more impersonal classical model; but the law itself, being less technical and lacking professional attention, remains undeveloped and so less certain and predictable.

In ancient Athens democratic doctrine required the participation of large numbers of citizens in making and applying law. Aristotle justified such participation in this way:

> 'The people in their gatherings have both a deliberative and a judicial capacity, and in both capacities they make decisions which are all concerned with particular matters. Any individual member of these assemblies is probably inferior to the one best man. But the state is composed of many individuals; and just as a feast to which many contribute is better than one provided by a single person, so, and for the same reason, the masses can come to a better decision, in many matters, than one individual.'[4]

Every citizen over the age of 30 who was not indebted to the state and whose civil rights had not been forfeited was eligible to serve in the popular courts, which varied in size but often consisted of 501 citizens, elected by lot. To ensure that all citizens could participate, payment was made for time spent on judicial work and so there was no shortage of volunteers, especially from the poorer sections of the citizen body. The popular courts dealt with all manner of cases, offences against the state and disputes between citizens alike. Although a magistrate presided, it was the whole court (its members voting by secret ballot), which decided issues both of fact and law. In giving their verdict the citizen judges were representatives of the sovereign power of the people.

This procedure meant that the citizen body as a whole took a great interest in the law and in its application; but equally it provided little scope for the interpretation of that law by professional lawyers or for the development of legal principles in a technical way. Many issues were so complex that they could hardly be explained intelligibly to such a large court and some parties preferred arbitration as a means of settling their disputes. A single arbitrator could go into details of financial accounts, for example, in a way that would be almost impossible for a large court. In 403 BC the practice was institutionalised. Thereafter all civil cases involving substantial sums were sent first to an arbitrator. If he was unable to bring the parties to a

---

4. *Politics* 1286a, cited by Dawson *Lay Judges* p 10, on which the account in the text is based.

settlement, he heard witnesses and tried the case. His decision could be appealed to the popular court, but only on the basis of the arbitrator's record, and new evidence could not be admitted. On the other hand, where the issue was an offence against the state, it was much more suited to be tried by the popular court, which could give a yes/no verdict, and so such cases continued to be tried by that court.

The kin and the survival of the blood-feud

Another factor which may delay the implementation of the classical model is the extent to which litigants are left to compel the attendance of their opponents in court and to enforce judgments which they have obtained by their own efforts without being able to call on community force to help them. For, although parties may resort to self-help in such circumstances, there is naturally much scope for bargaining and negotiated settlements of disputes. A party who is unable to mobilise sufficient community pressure on his behalf, to compel his opponent to pay, will have to accept a lesser sum.

Sometimes the system adapts a procedure already familiar from the pre-state period. Fasting as a form of invoking the supernatural is found in various stateless societies, and survives, in a different form, even when courts have been established and the law has been put in writing. The earliest Irish law books of the Brehons, in the early middle ages, show how a form of magic was adapted to enforce judgments given in court.[5] They prescribed that a creditor who sought to enforce a judgment debt against his debtor's property had to give him ten days' notice if he was a debtor of a humble social class. If, however, the debtor was a person of distinction, such as a chief, bard or bishop, the creditor was bound, in addition to giving notice, to fast upon him. This involved going to his house and sitting at his door for a certain time without food. If he still got no guarantee of what was due to him, the debt was doubled, and the creditor could distrain (seize the debtor's property) for twice what he would have obtained in the first place. Thus a procedure originally designed to invoke God became adapted to give publicity to the claim of a poor man against a mighty debtor, with a view to shaming him into paying his debt, or at least to coming to some arrangement with the fasting creditor to get him off his doorstep.

Some societies allow a large place to the parties' kinship groups in

---

5. L. Ginnell *The Brehon Laws* (1894) pp 161–163; D. A. Binchy 'Ancient Irish Law' (1966) I Ir Jur 85.

the enforcement of the law and are prepared to tolerate a considerable degree of institutionalised violence. Ancient Germanic society combined a tradition of popular control over the legal process with a powerful role for kinship groups. In the early middle ages throughout Western Europe, assemblies of free neighbours, or folk-moots, not only established what was the customary law of the particular tribal group but also applied it in actual disputes. In each community groups of wise men were acknowledged as the guardians of the customary traditions which were transmitted orally from one generation to another. As 'lawfinders' they identified the appropriate rule applicable in a particular case and proposed a judgment to the popular assembly, but it was the assembly as a whole that gave the judgment and took responsibility for it. Gradually the burden of regular attendance at court sittings became too great for ordinary freemen and the judicial function was exercised by an official, presiding in the name of the king, and the lawfinders, as representatives of the people, with the latter meeting three or four times a year to approve what had been done in their name.

It is sometimes assumed that when such courts are introduced retaliation disappears. It is taken for granted that the first task of the authorities is to compel the acceptance of compensation, and that if retaliation is found to survive, it necessarily indicates their inability to stamp out violence. Retaliation is seen as an irrational exercise of revenge. Recent studies have shown that this approach is incorrect. The principle of compensation is as prominent as that of retaliation even in the simplest societies. They are seen as complementary rather than opposed to each other. Both of them function to restore a balance between wrongdoer and victim that has been disturbed by the commission of the offence. They both level the score between the parties.

Early statements of Germanic law allow retaliation in kind by the victim of a wrong, but later the laws purport to make the acceptance of compensation compulsory. Instead of leaving the level of compensation to be negotiated in each case, however, they prescribe in elaborate detail tariffs of the amounts which the delinquent must pay in respect of each category of injury. They lay down exactly what is payable for injuries ranging from loss of a limb to loss of a finger or thumb, and in most cases the amount also varies according to the social status of the victim. Thus everyone knows exactly what he can expect to receive for being made to give up the traditional right to retaliate in kind.

Once the parties have appeared before the court, and stated their case, the court decides the method of proof. This may be by ordeal or by battle or by oath of the parties, supported by oath-helpers (*compurgatores*) the number required depending on the gravity of the case. In the case of injuries short of death, the wrongdoer who had been found liable would normally be made to pay his victim the prescribed compensation, known as *bot*, without the need to involve the kin. Only if he could get payment no other way would the victim appeal to his kin for help. Where the victim was killed, however, the role of the kin became important. The killer's kin was under an obligation to pay compensation, known as *wergild*, to the kin of the slain.[6] Just who were the kin for these purposes? They did not constitute a precisely defined body of relatives in a particular degree of relationship to the wrongdoer or his victim. Rather they were a fluctuating group, whose composition varied according to time and circumstance. Much would depend on who was asked for support by the victim's widow and by the wrongdoer, and what following they had among their relations. The kin who were designated as heirs for the purposes of inheritance on death was not the same group as the kin who were entitled to *wergild* and the kin who were liable to pay it were different again. In many cases the precise contributions of the members of the killer's kin or the entitlements of the victim's kin would not be matters in which the community as a whole had an interest. The head of each kin would be responsible for collecting and distributing the *wergild*. How the benefits and burdens were shared out within the kin was a purely internal 'family' matter.

As society became more complex, the members of the kin tended to become dispersed, and more precise statements of liability or entitlement were required. From the various rules set out in the Salic law of the Salian group of Franks, in what is now Northern France, the following picture emerges. The primary duty to pay the *wergild* fell on the killer himself. But in deciding what assets were available to him for this purpose, a distinction had to be made between his own personal property and the property which he enjoyed as a member of the family and which could not be disposed of outside the family. The family homestead, for example, was always exempt from liability for payment. When the killer was unable to find the whole of the *wergild*, the obligation to contribute fell on his father or perhaps in some cases both parents and his brothers. If this group were unable to pay, the obligation passed to the three closest maternal and three closest paternal relatives. So far as entitlement is concerned, half of the *wergild* went to the children of the deceased and half to his close relatives on both maternal and paternal side. If there were no-one in either category, that share went to the state treasury.

The Germanic laws, in prescribing these tariffs of payments to be made to the victim of a wrong, exude a somewhat unrealistic air.

6.   G. MacCormack 'Inheritance and Wergild in early Germanic Law' I. (1973) 8 Ir Jur 143 and II. (1974) 9 Ir Jur 166.

What happens if payment is not made? Does the king's government have the resources and organisation to enforce payment? The kin could not be expected to put up with a wrong to one of its members that received no redress. In practice the blood-feud between different family groups not only existed in Germanic societies but was openly tolerated by established governments. Its survival even after the advent of regular law courts is regarded as a stage in the development from private settlements to public arbitration.

In the Frankish kingdom the feud existed even though both the king and the Church provided courts to settle disputes. In his *History of the Franks*, the sixth-century bishop, Gregory of Tours, describes a dispute between two noble families over a wife's good name.[7] The husband having had reports of her infidelity, appeals to his kin, who approach the wife's father and ask him to prove her innocence or kill her. He gives a solemn oath in church before both kins that she is innocent. The husband's kin declare the oath to be perjury and a fight breaks out before the altar. Both parties now refer the matter to the king, but he is concerned not with the breach of the peace but only with the sacrilege and sends the case to the bishop, whose jurisdiction covered sacrilege. The parties make composition with the bishop for their behaviour in church and are forgiven but the original dispute continues. However, the woman then kills herself, perhaps on instructions from her own kin who have discovered her guilt. What is interesting is that neither the king nor the bishop question the right and duty of the kin to deal with a member who may have impugned its honour, and to sort out its differences with other kins.

It must often have happened, before people grew accustomed to the idea of royal adjudication as the norm, that outraged kinship was too strong for any mediation to succeed. In other cases the pressures to accept composition would have been effective. They would not, however, have been effective if the possibility of reopening the feud had not been present in the minds of the disputants. The line separating feud from composition is a vague one.

'Always it is touch and go what will happen: it will depend on what the kins think, how extensively they or their followings are mobilizable, how rich they are or how ready to pay or receive payment, how much the bishop or the king feels disposed to intervene.'[8] Thus for a long time money composition was an alternative to, rather than a successor to, settlement by violence.

Scotland in the sixteenth century provides abundant evidence of the institutionalised feud which was accepted by the government as

---

7. J. M. Wallace-Hadrill 'The Bloodfeud of the Franks' in *The Long-haired Kings and other studies in Frankish History* (1962) pp 121ff at p 137.
8. Wallace-Hadrill, op cit, p 146.

part of the administration of justice.[9] The royal government, which had for long been relatively weak compared with the royal government in England, was beginning to assert its control over the feudal lords in the localities. Through the king's council and the local sheriff courts it was providing an expanding royal justice. It has been assumed in the past that the survival of the blood-feud was in the face of a government that wanted to suppress it but was not strong enough to do so. Recently this view has been challenged. The traditional Germanic kinship groups had been integrated into the feudal system. The feudal lord gave protection and security to his vassals, who were the tenants of his lands, and in return they gave him their services, both military and secular. In many parts of Scotland the feudal lord was the clan chief, the head of the kinship group formed by those who bore the same name, and felt a strong emotional bond with other members of his clan. A man who had become isolated from his own kinship group could attach himself by bonds of man-rent to a powerful magnate, whom he would serve in return for the protection that only the powerful could provide. The royal governments counted on the local lords to keep the peace in their localities.

Instead of trying to overturn this system, the Scottish kings tried to incorporate it into the national law, because it offered the best means of maintaining stability in the regions. So the royal courts upheld the principle that a murderer must compensate not just the dependants, but the wider kinship group of the man he has killed. That group could be relied on to provide maintenance and support for the deceased's dependants. It is sometimes difficult to distinguish kinship relationships from the feudal relationships of lord and vassal, but the Scottish kinship group remained a strong social and political force, which the legal system ignored at its peril. The threat of the blood-feud guaranteed compensation in cases of homicide.

Even in a modern state, the blood-feud may survive, where a community within the state has a sense of national identity which is stronger than its allegiance to the state. The Albanian community in the Yugoslav province of Kosovo is a cohesive group of Albanian speakers, grouped in clans. They have a traditional customary code, which not only recognises the blood-feud but requires the kin of a clan member who has been wronged by a member of another clan to take action to avenge the wrong and settle the score between the two groups.[10] The

9. J. Wormald 'Bloodfeud, Kindred and Government in early modern Scotland' (1980) 87 Past and Present 54.
10. A Franciscan monk, S. Gjekov (1874–1929), collated existing versions of the *Canon of Lek Dukagjini* (attributed to a fifteenth-century leader of that name), most of which had been transmitted orally; I. Whitaker 'Tribal structure and National Politics in Albania, 1910–1958' in I. M. Lewis (ed) *History and Social Anthropology* (1968) p 265; M. Hasluck *The Unwritten Law in Albania* (1954) pp 210ff.

customs prescribe rules for the taking of vengeance. For example, women and children are exempt; vengeance is only possible against an adult male.

This law has a stronger emotional hold on Albanians in Kosovo than Yugoslav federal law. The system is so effective that in rural districts a substantial number of adult males are in fact confined to large semifortified farms, because if they went outside they would run the risk of being killed in the course of a feud.[11] Of course the Yugoslav federal law does not recognise the blood-feud and has to treat such killings as murder. In practice, when the police investigate vengeance killings, the killer's kin sometimes nominate a youth in the family to confess to the killing, even though he was not the actual perpetrator. As a young man he will get a lighter sentence of imprisonment than an older man, whose presence in the family may be more important. While in prison the youth will at least be protected from the retaliation of the victim's kin, which he would certainly risk if he went outside the homestead and participated in the activities of the young people of the community. At the same time, by serving a prison sentence for a crime he did not commit, he will be doing his duty by his fellows in the kin, and will gain their favour for his sacrifice.[12]

In most states the pressures to accept compensation rather than resort to violence are eventually successful. This is primarily because the kin as a group becomes less of a cohesive body. With the passage of time its members become scattered over a wide area and join different territorial communities. Even in Frankish times, it was possible to leave one kin and join another. But kinship ties must inevitably have weakened and it must have become increasingly difficult to mobilise the kin to take concerted action. The Church in Europe consistently opposed bloodshed and worked to eliminate the feud, and as central governments became stronger, they could rely on their own resources for law enforcement and it was no longer needed.

Conclusion

Where for one reason or another the classical model of the legal process is not achieved, the law may be kept in touch with popular sentiment. But the price that has to be paid is the lack of incentive

11. R. Marmullaku *Albania and the Albanians* (1975) pp 86–88, observes that officially the blood-feud has been eliminated in Albania proper but among the Albanians in Kosovo, 'between 1964 and 1970, the circuit court in Prishtine tried 320 cases involving bloodfeuds'.
12. Information from Professor D. Stojcevic, Belgrade.

for the growth of a class of professional lawyers, who accept responsibility for the development of the law in its technical aspects. When there is no professional participation in the legal process, the courts may give decisions that are satisfactory to the parties, but they do not explain how they arrive at those decisions. They may take into account whatever factors they wish, but it is not known what they have considered since they do not justify their conclusions with arguments based on the law. In ancient Athens, for example, the popular courts were more likely to be swayed by the speeches of orators trained in the art of rhetoric, the presentation of a case in its most persuasive form, than by the patient elucidation of the scope and limits of the law.

Among the countries of Germanic law, the advent of professionalism was affected by the presence or absence of a monarchy with a desire to impose its authority throughout the kingdom. In England and in France, where such a political factor was present, the local courts, to which all freemen owed a duty of 'suit of court', were gradually superseded by other forms of court which included professional participation. As a result, in both countries the law was developed with a high degree of continuity. The various states in Germany, on the other hand, where a strong central authority was lacking, clung tenaciously to the principle of community participation in judicial decisions. The participation was not by large segments of the citizen body, as in Athens, but by small groups of men, known as Schöffen, who were chosen as respected members of the community to take responsibility for the application of the customary law.[13] They provided continuity but they were not professionals, and devoted the bulk of their time to other occupations. As a result the law in the German states remained undeveloped, and could not cope with the growing demands of commerce.

The advent of professionals does not require the acceptance of a single procedural model. In some systems the professionals completely displace the lay element; in others they divide the judicial function with laymen. These forms of procedure will be considered in the next chapter.

---

13.   Dawson *Lay Judges* p 97.

3   Models of procedure

In a developed legal system, the legal process involves three distinct phases, first, the identification of the parties' dispute as one appropriate for solution by that process; secondly, the finding of the rules applicable to that issue; and thirdly, the discovery of the relevant facts and application of the rules to those facts. We have noted that this analysis is not applicable to all legal systems in their early stages. There must always be some way of finding the law, such as consulting the elders who are recognised as its custodians; but the facts are not always investigated. Certain kinds of issue, when identified, may be put directly to the judgment of God, as expressed in an ordeal or battle. Such methods of trial are often called 'irrational'. But in an age of faith, when there is a general belief in the direct intervention of divine providence in human affairs, it is not irrational to think that God knows what happened better than any human and that He will indicate which party was in the right. Sooner or later, however, popular demand requires an investigation of the facts in every case.

At this stage legal systems have two alternative models of the legal process at their disposal, one giving both law-finding and fact-finding to professionals and the other using professionals to deal with the law and laymen to find the facts and give the verdict. Some systems go, early in their development, to the wholly professional model. In Roman law and English law there was a progression from the lay model to the wholly professional one. Both these systems are documented by written records for a thousand years of legal development and have shown a capacity to respond to new social conditions while maintaining a high degree of continuity.

The lay model in Roman law

The Roman Republic of the fifth century BC was a small community with few material resources, but from the beginning it showed a strong public concern for the problems of maintaining order and settling disputes. The law at that time was a set of customary practices, orally transmitted from one generation to another as part of the cultural heritage of the Roman people. The customs prescribed what was right for Roman citizens and applied only to them; civil law (*ius civile*) means originally law for citizens. Quite early in the Republic, however, a written statement of these rules was produced, known as the Twelve Tables.[1] It did not state what everyone knew and took for granted, but concentrated rather on points that had given or might give rise to dispute. In particular the Twelve Tables show a concern for the details of procedure, for precisely what a citizen could do for himself without the help of a court and what he had to do to put the state machinery for dispute settlement into motion.[2]

Although the Twelve Tables show that self-help and retaliation were still tolerated, they also show that the community was determined to 'institutionalise' them and keep their exercise within strict limits. In certain cases, such as when a thief was caught on one's premises at night, or when he resisted arrest, he could be killed immediately without more ado, but in most cases a court ruling was required before self-help was permitted. So when a thief was adjudged to have been caught in the act of stealing, he was officially handed over to the victim to work for him in forced labour. Where, however, the thief was not caught in the act, his victim had to be satisfied with a money penalty of double the value of the thing stolen. Where a court established that serious physical injury had been caused, the parties were encouraged to reach agreement on appropriate compensation, but if they were unable to do so, retaliation in kind was authorised. The possibility of such retaliation would act as a spur on the parties to reach agreement, and it would have probably been necessary to exercise it only against a delinquent whose family would not help him to find an appropriate sum in compensation. For less serious injuries, the Twelve Tables did not allow retaliation; fixed amounts of compensation were prescribed.

If the delinquent was himself a slave or a son or daughter in the power of the father, he would have no money of his own to satisfy any claim for compensation. In Roman law a child did not cease to be subject to his father's power on becoming an adult. So far as property was concerned, he remained in his father's power until the latter died. Consequently all the family property was kept together, and although adult members had no property of their own while the father lived, the resources of the family as a whole were strengthened. So a claim by the victim of theft or personal injury committed by a slave or child in power had to be brought against the family head, since, as the controller of family property, he alone was

---

1. *Ancient Roman Statutes* (trans A. C. Johnson, P. R. Coleman-Norton and F. C. Bourne, 1961) pp 9ff; Jolowicz, ch 8; post, p 70.
2. Jolowicz, ch 12.

in a position to satisfy it. The Twelve Tables provided that the family head should surrender the delinquent to the victim of the theft or to *his* family head but that he could avoid this by paying damages. Later the emphasis was reversed: the primary duty was considered to be the payment of damages but the family head could escape payment by surrendering the delinquent to the victim.

The unit with which early Roman law was concerned was thus the family group. The law was not concerned with what went on within the family. The duties owed by its members to each other were not enforced in a public court but were left to be dealt with in the privacy of the family. The family consisted of the family head (*paterfamilias*), who acted in the name of the family, and his descendants in the male line who were in his power (his agnates). (A married daughter and her descendants would be in the power of her husband or his *paterfamilias*.) The power of the *paterfamilias*, as manager of the family enterprise, was in theory well-nigh absolute. We hear little of the wider kinship group. It is mentioned as having a right to inherit property if there are no closer relatives, but it takes no part in the settlement of disputes. The reason seems to be that the wider kin usually take the initiative where the family head has been killed, but cases of homicide were treated by the Romans from early times as warranting the intervention of the magistrate on behalf of the community as a whole rather than being left to the deceased's kin to pursue a claim for compensation (p 55). Blood-feuds were therefore avoided.

When a dispute arose, the parties first appeared before a magistrate, the praetor, elected annually, who was responsible for the administration of the civil law. The purpose of this meeting was to decide whether the dispute raised an issue which was recognised by the civil law and if so how it should be decided. In very early times, before the foundation of the Republic, it is likely that the Romans had recourse to ordeals or battle or oath-taking as a means of settling disputes, and indeed oaths remained a prominent feature of Roman procedure. But by Republican times, the normal way of deciding any legal issue was by referring it to a layman chosen with the agreement of both parties. The layman, a single juryman called the *iudex*, would at a subsequent meeting look into the facts (perhaps at first relying on his own knowledge), examine witnesses, hear the parties' arguments and deliver judgment condemning or absolving the defendant.

Since the force of the state was not available to ensure the attendance of litigants and witnesses, much depended on the co-operation of those involved. It was the responsibility of the plaintiff to secure his opponent's presence before the magistrate. If, and only if, the defendant had (in front of witnesses) unreasonably refused a request to come with him, or had tried to run away, the Twelve Tables allowed the plaintiff to use force to compel his attendance. The rules go into great detail on what exactly he was entitled to do. A sick or aged defendant had to be provided with a conveyance of some kind, but it need not be a cushioned litter.

Similarly at the end of legal proceedings, the plaintiff himself had to take steps to ensure that a judgment in his favour was satisfied. If the sum which the lay *iudex* had awarded to him was not paid in 30 days, the Twelve Tables allowed the plaintiff to bring the debtor forcibly before the magistrate – this time without the necessity of asking him first. If payment was not made, or guaranteed by a surety of substance on the debtor's behalf, the plaintiff was permitted to put him in chains and keep him in confinement for 60 days. During that period he had to exhibit the debtor in public forum on three successive market days. This would give an opportunity for his family or friends to satisfy the judgment or make some compromise with the plaintiff. If even this procedure failed to produce payment, the debtor could finally be killed by creditors and cut into pieces. The Twelve Tables anticipated the arguments of Portia in *The Merchant of Venice* by carefully providing that if creditors cut more than their share it should be without liability. Alternatively they could sell him into slavery outside Rome.

As the Roman Republic progressed, the more primitive features of Roman procedure were modified. The magistrate could help a plaintiff by authorising him to put pressure on an evasive defendant through taking control of his property until he agreed to co-operate, or even exacting a penalty from the defendant for his failure to appear. The creditors of a judgment debtor were no longer allowed to kill him but had to enable him to work off the debt by his labour. Eventually an alternative form of execution of judgment was introduced, whereby the debtor was made bankrupt through the public auction of his goods for the benefit of all his creditors. Throughout the proceedings the emphasis was thus on the need for the parties to settle their dispute for themselves with the minimum intervention from the state that was necessary to secure co-operation.

Originally the first stage of an action before the praetor was stylised and technical. The plaintiff recited his claim in set words, the defendant denied it similarly, and the praetor formally remitted the issue to the *iudex*. Under this procedure, the forms of action were fixed, matters of doubt being resolved by the pontiffs, and the praetor had little scope for initiative; the most he could do was to deny an action to an unmeritorious plaintiff by refusing to co-operate in the initial ritual.

In the later Republic an alternative procedure was introduced, the formulary procedure,[3] in which the parties appeared before the praetor and made their pleas informally. The praetor then expressed the issue in hypothetical terms in a written document, known as a formula, addressed to the *iudex*, to condemn the defendant if he found certain allegations to be proved and otherwise to absolve him. The praetor could grant such a formula whenever he felt that legal policy required that a litigant should have a remedy so long as he substantiated his allegations. At the beginning of his year of office the praetor published an edict in which he catalogued the circumstances in which he would grant actions or defences to actions, with the appropriate formulae appended. Prospective litigants could obtain any remedy given in the edict on demand if they considered that it covered their case.

The new system gave the praetor considerable powers to extend the range of the law through his control of remedies. It was used to widen the jurisdiction of Roman law to cover not just disputes between Roman citizens but also those involving non-citizens, peregrines, to whom the old civil law did not apply. They had to be allowed to express their claims informally.[4] In deciding whether to grant them a remedy the praetor took into account rules which were considered to be part of the laws of all civilised peoples, the so-called *ius gentium*, or law of nations. Such remedies, given to peregrines, could not be denied to citizens.

Except in an unusual case, the first stage of an action before the praetor took very little time. In agreeing to the grant of a formula, a defendant who believed in his case would be in no way prejudiced, since if the plaintiff was unable to prove his allegations to the satisfaction of the *iudex*, the defendant was entitled to the verdict. What was time-consuming was the second stage before the *iudex*. The examination of witnesses, the perusal of documentary evidence and the speeches of the parties, or of those who represented them, required much attention of the *iudex* before he could give his decision. The *iudex* was normally a man of substance in the community, but he was not an arbitrator. He did not have a free hand to decide the issue as he thought fit. His powers were limited by the formula and his decision had to be either condemnation or absolution in the terms of the formula. If it was condemnation, and the claim was not for a fixed sum of money, he had to estimate the amount of damages payable by the defendant and the Romans recognised that, in doing that, he was exercising discretion in the manner of an arbitrator. But his main function was to answer yes or no to the question contained in the formula.

---

3. Jolowicz, pp 199ff.
4. Such claims came before a special 'peregrine' praetor, for whom indeed the formulary procedure may have been originally devised.

This system was economical of official time. It also meant that responsibility for the final decision rested with a layman who had been chosen by the parties. There was no appeal from his verdict (although there might be an action against him personally for misconduct). His decision was final in the way that the judgment of God was final.

The odd feature of the Roman administration of justice was that neither the praetor nor the *iudex* nor even the advocates who represented the parties before them were lawyers. The praetor had no legal qualification and was in office only for a year. The only contact that the *iudex* had with the law might be the case which he was picked to decide. The orators who represented the parties' case put skill in argument before legal knowledge. Like Greek advocates their expertise was rhetoric not law. But behind all of them, ready to offer advice on request, stood professional lawyers. From the third century BC the anonymous pontiffs, who had given opinions as a body, were replaced as legal experts by secular jurists, who made it their business to know the law. Popular control of legal proceedings in Greece left little scope for professionals but the formulary system came to require professionals to operate it, who were expert in its technicalities. They had no formal role to play in the legal drama, but praetor, *iudex*, and advocate all consulted them for guidance. It was the jurists who effectively controlled what remedies were available and what was the scope of each section and defence. Roman law was thus developed by a continuous succession of individuals, each generation building on the work of its predecessors, who, though they lacked an official position in the legal process, were yet intimately connected with the day to day application of the law.

The lay model in English law

English law is a form of Germanic law, of which it includes two separate strains, Anglo-Saxon and Norman. The Norman kings' success in imposing centralised government over the country they had conquered and in keeping the principal feudal lords from becoming too independent of their authority gave English law certain features which distinguish it from other forms of Germanic law. Self-help was severely restricted at an early stage in its history and the blood-feud was not tolerated.

For some time, however, disputes were brought to local courts based on the assemblies of freemen and the traditional methods of proof survived. Ordeals were used to test guilt or innocence of wrongdoing.[5] The usual form required the accused to carry a heated

5.   Baker, p 5.

iron for a certain distance or to plunge his hand into boiling water to pull out a stone. Then his hand was sealed with bandages for three nights; if it was found to be clean, he was innocent; if not, he was guilty. The ordeal was supervised by the clergy and they sometimes manipulated the result. Because of such abuses the Church itself ordered the abolition of ordeals in 1215.

Another way of deciding a legal issue, particularly favoured by the Normans, was by formal battle under strict rules. It was regarded not so much as an appeal to physical force, giving victory to the stronger, as an appeal to God, who would ensure that victory went to the party with the better right, and it was used to settle a variety of issues in early English law. 'A man could in this way prove his innocence of crime, his right to property, or right to obtain payment of a debt.'[6] It could also be used to test matters incidental to the issue, such as the truth of the evidence given by witnesses, who could be called on to defend their veracity by battle. At first the only people who could decline to do battle personally were children, women and men over 60 years of age. They were allowed to employ champions to do battle on their behalf. Then the power to appoint champions was extended even to those who could be expected to fight their own battles. Originally the champion had to assert his belief in the truth of the cause he represented and was subject to the penalties for perjury if he swore falsely. However the Statute of Westminster I in 1275 provided that champions need not swear that they had personal knowledge of the cause which they were employed to defend. By that time battle was already going out of favour. The Church disapproved of it and it was coming to be regarded as a barbaric survival. However it remained in theory as a possible means of trying an action concerning the ownership of land, or of defending a charge of murder, until its formal abolition in 1819.

Wager of law was a contest of reputations.[7] A party called on to make his law swore an oath as to the righteousness of his cause and then found a number of 'compurgators' who were prepared to swear that his oath was trustworthy and could be relied on. They did not swear to the facts, but to the character of the party they were supporting. This method was used both to test allegations of wrongdoing and to decide claims that a debt was owed or not owed. In the fourteenth century the citizens of London insisted on retaining it as a defence to debts claimed on the evidence of merchants' books, and in actions of debt it lasted until it was finally abolished in 1833.

From the twelfth century the royal court, part of the king's

---

6. W. Holdsworth *History of English Law* I (7th edn, 1956) p 308.
7. Holdsworth, op cit, p 305.

council, began gradually to supersede the local courts. The latter were not abolished but litigants tended to prefer the royal court because it offered more effective remedies. The superiority of the royal court's methods and its increasing popularity resulted in its splitting into three courts. The King's Bench originally consisted of the judges attending the king, wherever he was in England. It dealt with matters in which the king had an interest and later exercised a supervision over other courts. The Common Pleas was settled in Westminster and originally had exclusive jurisdiction in matters in which there was no royal interest. It was this court more than any other which developed the medieval English law. The Exchequer, although primarily an administrative body, had jurisdiction in all cases involving debtors to the king. Gradually all three courts extended their jurisdiction so that most cases could be tried by any of them. For example, the Exchequer entertained claims by an ordinary creditor against a debtor for payment of the debt if he stated that unless he was paid, he would be unable to pay his taxes to the king.

Every action before the king's courts involved two stages, the legal part and the factual part. Actions were begun by writ, a royal command in writing addressed to a royal official in a locality bidding him bring a certain person before the king's court to answer a claim against him. Thus everything depended on royal officials having sufficient power to do the king's will, even when it was inconvenient to local feudal lords. The parties to a dispute did not have to rely on their own efforts to get each other to court. A plaintiff obtained his writ from the royal Chancery, and so the government, by controlling the supply of writs, controlled the kind of cases they wished the royal courts to deal with and left the rest to the local courts. For example, writs would issue to settle disputes about freehold land, ie, land held on free tenure (p 164). A considerable part of the land in England was held on unfree tenure, in return for the performance of specified services for the feudal lord. Disputes about such land were left to be settled in the lord's court. Again the cause of action in the royal court had to be worth 40 shillings, a not inconsiderable sum in the middle ages. So writs were only issued where the matter was of some substance, and the government felt it had an interest in seeing it settled. There were Registers of Writs, which listed those that were granted as a matter of course, and English litigants could obtain them from the Chancery in the way that Roman litigants chose their formulae from the praetor's edict. At the end of an action, a successful plaintiff, who did not receive from the defendant what he had been awarded, could obtain a writ through which royal officials compelled satisfaction of the judgment.

The judges of the three royal courts were professionals who

specialised in the law. When the parties' representatives appeared before them, the general nature of the issue was already clear from the writ which stated what the plaintiff was claiming. At this stage, that of pleading, the judges and the parties' representatives engaged in an oral discussion designed to reduce the area of dispute to one or two facts which were asserted by one side and denied by the other. Since the facts had not yet been discovered, much of the argument was necessarily hypothetical, on the lines of 'what would be the legal position if the facts were so and so?' Finally, when the area of disagreement had been narrowed as much as possible, the case would normally be remitted for the trial of fact by a group of 12 men from the neighbourhood. To avoid the need for them to travel to Westminster, judges of the central courts travelled around the country, which for this purpose was divided into six circuits, and held assizes in the main towns.

The use of a group of neighbours to provide information of various kinds for the government is found in several Germanic societies from the ninth century onwards.[8] Sometimes, the inquest was used to find out the custom of the region on such matters as land-holding or succession. Sometimes it was used to gain information about who owned what for purposes of taxation. Much of the information in Domesday Book was collected in this way. In the twelfth century the Norman kings began to use groups of neighbours to inquire into any matter in which it was alleged that the king's peace, the public order of the community, had been broken. The members of such a group were sworn (*iurati*) to tell the truth, and became known as jurors.

At first the members of the jury were examined individually about what they knew personally, as witnesses. By the fourteenth century, however, the distinction between witness and juror was recognised and it was established that the jury's function was to consider evidence given orally by witnesses and then collectively to decide the relevant facts. They now participated in the judicial function: the judges were concerned with the law, the jury with the facts. To protect them from outside influences, once the evidence was concluded, they were confined without food or warmth until they had reached agreement on the questions which had been put to them. Majority verdicts were not allowed; unanimity was required.

Like the judgment of God and the decision of the Roman *iudex*, the verdict of the jury, deciding for example, that the plaintiff had been in possession of a piece of land at a certain time, was final: no appeal was possible. Only if there was a technical error on the record could the matter go back to the judges. The latter were therefore saved from the responsibility of examining the evidence critically. If

8. Baker, pp 64ff.

the verdict was unpopular, it was not their fault. They could concentrate their attention on purely legal matters. Indeed once the pleadings were over, the judges would often have nothing more to do with the case.

The professional model in late Roman and French law

In the highly organised state of the later Roman Empire the formulary procedure was replaced by the so-called *cognitio* procedure, in which the whole action was under the control of professional magistrates.[9] In the formulary system not only were the original summons of opponents and the execution of judgments in the hands of the parties, but so also was much of the actual proceedings. They had to agree on the terms of the formula and to select the independent citizen who was to be *iudex*. In the *cognito* system the word *iudex* meant a state official who was in complete control of the case from start to finish. The plaintiff presented his claim, known technically as a libel, to the court and it was served by a court officer on the defendant, who then prepared his counter-libel. The parties appeared before the judge, in person or by their representatives, the legal issues were debated and proof of fact was taken. After the judge had given his judgment, it was enforced by a court officer, unless there was an appeal to a higher court. For it was now possible to appeal from the judgment of a lower court through the judicial hierarchy up to the court of the Emperor himself.

The *cognitio* procedure of late Roman law was the model for the procedure developed in the church courts applying canon law and under the label of Romano-canonical procedure it eventually became the procedure of most continental countries.

In medieval France the monarchy was at first weaker than in England and only began to develop a central court out of the royal council in the thirteenth century, about a century after the similar development had taken place in England. That court, the Parlement de Paris, adopted a version of the Romano-canonical procedure which had recently become popular in arbitrations by churchmen.[10] There was no lay participation, the judges were all professionals and they were allocated to different Chambers of the Parlement according to function. Litigation began when the plaintiff submitted a written request to the king which was examined by the Chamber of Requests to see that it disclosed a proper legal issue. If it was in order, proceedings continued with a public oral debate before the

9.   Jolowicz, pp 397ff.
10.   Dawson *Oracles* pp 273ff; R. C. van Caeneghem, IECL XVI. 2. 28.

Great Chamber, in which the parties' representatives argued about the facts of the case and the relevant legal rules. They were then told to put into writing those facts which were not admitted by both sides, and the case was remitted for investigation to the Chamber of Inquests. In the absence of the parties or their representatives, to prevent their exercising undue influence on the course of the inquiry, commissioners then conducted a private proof of the matters the parties had raised by examining witnesses and considering documentary evidence. All the evidence was written down and sent back to the Chamber of Inquests, whose members (with the help of one of their number who was designated reporter) then evaluated it. Since the parties were originally not represented at this stage, their written pleas had to anticipate any potentially damaging features of the case that might be revealed and try to avoid their effect in advance. The pleadings were thus very complex and the dossier containing the evidence usually bulky. Yet the judgment delivered by the Chamber of Inquests made no specific findings of fact nor gave reasons for the decision. In the sixteenth century the parties became entitled to see the evidence which was submitted to the Chamber and to argue about its effect.

In time all French courts, even those of minor feudal lords, followed the Parlement de Paris in preferring the Romano-canonical method of establishing facts to that of the local group inquest. As J. P. Dawson puts it:

'By following the lead of the canonists in more refined methods of investigation, French courts committed themselves to a system that was likely to develop according to its own internal logic. When it was decided that witnesses were to be examined individually and in secret, a reliable examiner was needed and some record must be kept. If the examiner was to ask all the necessary questions, he would have to be prompted by a list of questions beforehand. In a case of any complexity it would be imperative that the questions be put into writing: it was natural to cast on the parties involved the burden of preparing the questions. To be sure that the draft interrogatories prepared by the parties were relevant and proper, it was convenient to have the initial statements of claim and defense put into writing. . . . There was heavy and continuous pressure, in short, to move toward a written procedure.'[11]

Since appeals were possible, the Parlement operated mainly as an appeal court from lower courts and the time of the judges was mainly occupied with rehearing cases that had already been dealt with in a lower court.

---

11. Dawson *Lay Judges* p 59.

In comparing the lay and the professional models the first point to note is the great economy of the lay model in the use of law-professionals.[12] In England from the thirteenth century until the nineteenth, the total number of judges of the royal courts, who had jurisdiction over the whole country, very rarely exceeded 15 at any one time. By contrast in France the Parlement de Paris already had 51 judges at the end of the thirteenth century and by the eighteenth this number had grown to 240. By then 12 other regional Parlements had grown up and the total membership of all the Parlements was over 1,200. During this period the population of France was about four times that of England so that, making allowance for that difference, the French needed about twenty times as many judges as the English. The reason for this disparity is not that the French people were more litigious or that the English judges worked harder; the judges in the two countries were expected to do different things. The English judges could concentrate on the purely legal aspects of the case. Like the Roman praetor, they could take the facts for granted in making their rulings. If the facts turned out later not to be as alleged, then the final decision would differ accordingly. The French judges, on the other hand, were mainly preoccupied with investigating and evaluating the facts. They were responsible for the interrogation of the witnesses and the perusal of documents, both time-consuming tasks. And the greater prevalency of appeals meant that the same facts would be considered on more than one occasion.

The small number of English judges meant that they were a tightly knit, cohesive group with shared values and a strong corporate feeling. On the other hand, it also meant that in periods when the government was inclined to interfere with the administration of justice, they were vulnerable to outside pressures. The removal of just one or two awkward judges and their replacement by more pliant colleagues could have a dramatic effect on their independence. Where there were numerous judges, acting anonymously as a college, there was a safety in numbers, since they were individually less vulnerable and the removal of one or two judges would have little effect.

'Adversarial' and 'inquisitorial' procedures

The two procedural models, which we have considered, were the forerunners of what are today often called the 'adversarial'

12.   Dawson *Lay Judges* pp 54, 70ff; P. Stein 'Safety in numbers: sharing of responsibility for judicial decision in early modern Europe' *Diritto e potere nella storia europea* (Atti IV Cong int soc ital storia del diritto) (1982) pp 211ff and [1982] Juridical Rev 186ff.

procedure, characteristic of countries following the tradition of the English common law and the 'inquisitorial' procedure, universal in countries of the Roman civil law tradition.[13]

The main feature of the adversarial procedure is a set piece trial, in which both sides confront each other before the presiding judge and the jury. Each side produces its witnesses who are first examined on behalf of the party who has called them and then what they have said is tested by cross-examination on behalf of the opposing party. The matters that are aired at the trial and the matters that are excluded are controlled by the parties. The judge does not normally initiate lines of inquiry. His role is that of an umpire; he sees that the questions put to the witnesses are proper and that the manner of questioning is fair. To prevent the jury receiving untrustworthy evidence a number of 'exclusionary' rules grew up, by which certain kinds of evidence are declared inadmissible. The most familiar example is the exclusion of 'hearsay' evidence, the statement by a witness of what someone said to him, where that someone cannot be challenged in cross-examination. At the conclusion of the evidence the judge immediately summarises it for the jury, so as to bring out the questions that they must decide, and they then consider their verdict. The adversarial procedure thus vividly dramatises the pitting of the evidence adduced by one side against that adduced by the other.

In the inquisitorial procedure there is no trial in the sense of a concentrated event at which the parties face each other with their respective witnesses. There is usually a preliminary stage at which pleadings are submitted and a hearing judge appointed. There follows a series of isolated meetings and written communications between the judge and the parties' representatives, at which evidence is produced. The judge himself conducts the questioning of the witnesses (hence the label 'inquisitorial'). In theory he can ask whatever he thinks necessary to discover the truth, but in practice he normally restricts himself to lines of questions which have been submitted to him beforehand in writing by the parties. Thus everyone knows in advance what matters are going to be investigated. An unexpected revelation by a witness has less dramatic effect than at a trial, since there can always be a further hearing at which its effect can be countered by other evidence gathered in the meantime.

Although there is no need for exclusionary rules of evidence, such as those designed to protect the jury, the inquisitorial procedure has also traditionally recognised a number of rules of evidence. Some prescribe how much evidence is required before a finding of fact can

13.   J. H. Merryman *The Civil Law Tradition* (1969) pp 120ff.

be made. They are based on the old rule of canon law that one witness is no witness (*unus testis, nullus testis*), in the sense that evidence of one witness that was not corroborated was insufficient to establish a fact. Other rules provide that where certain facts are found, they create a presumption by which the judge is obliged to infer another fact. These rules were originally designed (like the secrecy in which the French Chamber of Inquests operated) to shelter the professional judges against improper influences exercised by powerful parties, by limiting their powers of evaluating the evidence; yet substantial traces of them still survive. At the conclusion of the hearing stage the judge prepares a written record of the case and reports to the other judges (usually a panel) who consider the record, study the written briefs submitted on behalf of the parties and give their judgment.

Evidence in the two procedures is based on different psychological assumptions. In the accusatorial procedure it is assumed that a witness is unlikely to tell the truth unless he testifies in open court, so that what he says can be challenged by the party against whom he is testifying. In the inquisitorial procedure it is assumed that a witness will be inhibited by the prospect of challenge and that he is more likely to tell the truth in private to a judge who questions him from a neutral standpoint.

The accusatorial procedure has the advantage of producing greater precision about the issues. The parties have only one chance to make their points and must therefore be well prepared when they come to court. The proceedings are transacted orally (for the jury cannot be expected to study technical documents), and there is a sense of immediacy, concentration and dispatch. In the inquisitorial procedure, the issues may only gradually emerge as the proceedings continue. The fact that most of the judges who decide the case have not seen the witnesses, with the consequent need to put everything in writing, produces a bulky dossier for each case and gives a slow-moving bureaucratic air to the procedure. In some countries there are proposals to concentrate the hearings so as to give them more of the immediacy of a trial. At the same time, the impression is often given that the accusatorial procedure, being dominated by the parties, is not concerned with reaching the truth, whereas in its rival, where the proceedings, at least in form, are in the control of the judges, there is more emphasis on getting at the truth.

4　The effects of the procedural models

The choice between a wholly professional model and a model which involves both laymen and professionals has important consequences on the way law develops. This can be seen if we consider two aspects of procedure: first, the functions attributed to the court, and secondly, the remedies which the court is able to give.

Law and fact

Where the whole proceedings are in the control of professionals, there is no need to distinguish between the various functions of the court. In particular it is not necessary to make a sharp distinction between the facts of the case and the legal issue which has to be decided. A professional court can investigate the facts first and allow the legal issue to emerge as the facts become established. Indeed it was said to be a characteristic of the Romano-canonical procedure that 'the law arises out of the facts'. On the other hand, where there is a division of function between professionals and laymen, it must be clear from the beginning which tasks are being assigned to each of them. It is usual to say that in general the professionals are the judges of law and the laymen the judges of fact. In the archetypal jury action this is essentially true. The legal issues which the case seemed to throw up were first discussed by the parties' representatives and the judges. Debate would usually focus on whether the terms of the writ which the plaintiff had issued applied to the case. The discussion would then indicate how far the answer to that question depended on a particular fact or facts, asserted by one side and denied by the other. The jury would then be asked a question such as 'Was the plaintiff's father in possession of this field at the time of his death?' and the verdict would depend on their answer.

In Rome, however, the *iudex* was never restricted to questions of fact and the English jury was soon asked to decide questions which were not purely factual. The distinction between law and fact does not indicate precisely the kind of questions which are suitable for laymen to decide. Consideration both of the relationship between law and fact and of the tasks suitable for laymen is required.

The distinction between law and fact is easy to draw in general terms.[1] The existence of a rule is clearly a matter of law. So also is its interpretation in the sense of clarifying its meaning without reference to a particular case. What the parties did and said are equally matters of fact. When a witness describes what he saw, for example, that he saw the defendant holding a hammer near a house, and the question is whether his evidence should be believed, that is now called a question of primary fact. What may be inferred from the observations of witnesses is also a question of fact. For example, if one witness saw the defendant with a hammer near the house and another shortly afterwards saw that the window was broken, it can be inferred that the defendant broke the window. Such a finding would be called a matter of inferential or secondary fact. The state of mind of a person is always a question of inference, for what a man thought when he did a particular act can never be known for certain but can only be inferred from what he said or what he did. Such questions as the credibility of witnesses or the proper inferences to be drawn from observations are questions of fact because they increase our knowledge of what happened.

The difficult problems arise when rules of law have to be applied to the facts so established.[2] Legal rules, like all other rules, are expressed in general terms. They concern classes of persons and classes of actions and they prescribe legal consequences for persons and actions falling into the relevant categories. The application of the rule to a particular case, therefore, involves a decision on whether the facts of that case fall within the categories mentioned in the rule. Such a decision is strictly not a question of fact, since it does not tell us any more than we knew already about what actually happened. It establishes the legal effect of what happened; liability depends on whether or not an act is regarded as falling into the category. For example, it is a matter of inference from the way a man acts and speaks that his mind is disturbed, and that is a question of fact. Whether he is so disturbed as to be 'insane', and so not responsible for his actions, is strictly not a question of fact since it tells us no more about him or what he did but only about the legal effect of his actions. Yet it may still be a very appropriate question for laymen to answer. For that reason such questions have been loosely called 'questions of fact' when what is meant is that they are for laymen to decide, using their experience of the world rather than knowledge of the law.

In simple societies the distinction between law and fact is especially difficult to make. The notions of 'owning' something or 'being indebted' to another are legal notions, but in simple societies

1.   G. L. Williams 'Law and fact' [1976] Crim LR 422.
2.   E. Mureinik 'The application of rules: law or fact?' (1982) 98 LQR 587.

they are straightforward and have little technicality. As societies advance, however, such notions become more complex and technical. Ownership expresses a relationship between a person and a thing and indicates what the person can do in regard to it, compared with what others can do. In a simple society the owner is normally the possessor and it is clear from his behaviour whether he regards himself as owner. As the society develops, ownership becomes separated from possession, so that one person may own a thing and another person may legally be in possession of it, and even enjoy the benefit of it for life. A debt expresses a relationship between a creditor and a debtor, which entitles the creditor to sue the debtor if he does not pay what he owes. The ways in which one person may become indebted to another become more and more various as, for example, society moves from mainly cash transactions to a situation in which credit is commonly given.

For a Roman lay *iudex* in the early Republic to have to decide whether the plaintiff owned a horse was not so difficult a question as it became later. In legal proceedings such a question always depends on the plaintiff being able to produce evidence of his ownership. At its simplest that means evidence that he openly treated the horse as his, and in so doing he was not challenged. Similarly the allegation by A that B owed him money could be substantiated only by evidence of one of a few relatively simple transactions, such as that B had borrowed money and not repaid it, or that he had bought something and not paid the price. Such questions are not inappropriate for a layman who is a man of the world with property of his own. But as society and its law become more complicated, the notion of ownership and the notion of liability for debt become more and more 'legalised', and therefore more difficult for an uninstructed layman to decide without help. Although they are not restricted to questions of fact only, laymen can only be expected to decide questions that are readily intelligible and clear-cut.

In England, instead of asking the jury specific questions of fact, there was a tendency to give it the general issue to decide.[3] 'Is the defendant liable to the plaintiff's claim?' 'Is the accused guilty of the charge?' When the jury is left to decide such a general issue, it is necessarily involved in questions of law, for such issues raise the question of how far particular defences are admissible. Yet special pleas raising such defences may be too complicated for the jury to disentangle. Take, for example, an action for personal injury alleged to have been wrongfully inflicted by the defendant on the plaintiff. The jury might accept an argument that the harm was not caused

3. S. F. C. Milsom 'Law and fact in legal development' (1967) 17 Univ of Toronto LJ 1.

by the defendant, or they might think that although he had caused the harm, it was not his fault and that therefore he should not be liable for it. In either case they would decide in favour of the defendant but no-one would know whether this was because in the view of the jury he did not do the act or because they thought he should not be blamed for it. In such circumstances a question of law, such as how far accident is a defence, would be difficult to answer, because its effect would be hidden in the blanket verdict of the jury. Laymen cannot be expected to give reasons for their decisions.

Although this situation is not helpful to the development of the law as a science, it does mean that the jury's decision can take account of the general merits of the case, almost despite the legal issues. Though inexperienced in the ways of the law, the Roman *iudex* and the English jury were normally experienced in the ways of the world. When they decided the issues left to them by formula or pleading, they could ensure that the party with whom they sympathised would win the case, by finding the facts alleged by that party or by deciding the general issue in his favour. For the *iudex* did not reveal his thought processes and the secrecy of the jury room ensured that the way the jurors reached their decisions would not be disclosed.

In one aspect of decision-making laymen are in fact superior to professionals. That is the application of general standards of conduct, such as reasonableness, fairness, good faith.[4] Such standards all involve a moral rather than a legal judgment on conduct. They call not for technical knowledge exactly applied but for common sense about everyday matters. They are not formulated in a defined way but are relative to time and place and circumstances, so that over a period of time their application will vary as the public understanding of what they require changes. Laymen are well suited to express such changes.

The Romans exploited this attribute in the *iudex* by adapting the formula to allow for the application of the standard of good faith (*bona fides*) in certain contracts. If a dispute arose from, say, a contract of sale, whether the complaint was by the buyer or by the seller, the formula instructed the *iudex*, if he was satisfied as to the existence of the contract and its terms, to condemn the defendant to whatever 'in good faith' he ought to pay to the plaintiff. The phrase allowed the *iudex* to take account of any defences or counterclaims which he thought affected the claim in any way, to balance them against the claim and so to give a judgment which was

---

4.   R. Pound *Introduction to the Philosophy of Law* (revised edn, 1954) p 58; P. Stein and J. Shand *Legal Values in Western Society* (1974) pp 93ff.

not confined to the particular claim raised by the plaintiff but took account of all relevant factors. As time went on, the standards required of sellers and buyers rose as successive generations of Romans, taking their turn to act as *iudex*, reflected public opinion that higher standards were needed.

Similarly in English law, juries have been asked not only to discover what the parties did, but to evaluate it according to a standard, for example, by deciding whether it was reasonable. Would a reasonable man have foreseen that if he acted in a certain way, his conduct was likely to cause damage to another? If so, and the defendant in the case acted in that way, he was not acting reasonably and so must be liable. Again, as awareness of the requirements of reasonableness spread, so the demands of the standard increased. In attributing blame for damage that had been caused, the jury acted as a repository of the current values of society.

In the application of standards laymen have a free hand to evaluate the facts as they think fit. If a *iudex* or jury finds that in a particular case one party was acting unreasonably, that finding is binding only on the parties to the action. It is treated as 'a matter of fact' rather than of law, and facts being infinitely various, the decision cannot affect another *iudex* or jury in a later case. The decision of a professional judge on the application of a standard is different since, unlike the verdict of *iudex* or jury, it is subject to appeal to a higher court. Normally on a matter of primary fact, a higher court working on the written record will not interfere with the findings of the judge of first instance, because he had the opportunity of observing the witnesses in person, whereas the appeal court merely has a record of what they said. In the evaluation of facts, however, appeal courts will be concerned to ensure uniformity of adjudication. So in the application of standards, appeal courts may indicate the kind of conduct which, in their view, falls inside and outside the relevant category. In the interests of certainty and predictability there is continuous pressure on higher courts to give such guidance. They are able to do this more readily because a professional judge will not only give a verdict, but will also explain how he has reached it. He will state both the relevant rules of law and also the facts that he regards as particularly important in reaching his decision. Appeal courts are then invited to approve or correct such statements, and whether or not there is a system of binding precedent, such corrections will normally be followed by judges in the lower courts anxious to win the approval of their superiors. From being a 'matter of fact', the evaluation has become a 'matter of law'.

An example from Roman law may illustrate the disadvantages of this transformation.[5] In the classical period, the law regulating the

5. A. F. Rodger *Owners and Neighbours in Roman Law* (1972) pp 38ff.

conduct of neighbouring land owners to each other was dominated by the notion of reasonableness. The owner could build as much as he liked on his own land, so long as he left his neighbour with a reasonable amount of light to the windows of his house. If he wanted to build so high that his neighbour's windows were obscured beyond what was reasonable, then he had to negotiate with his neighbour for the grant of a special right, known as servitude, in favour of his own land, entitling him to build higher. If the neighbour wanted to have more than just a reasonable amount of light, and so restrict the building to a lower level, then the neighbour had to negotiate the grant of a servitude preventing the builder from building beyond the height that was specified. The rules, therefore, centred around what was a reasonable amount of light to the neighbour's windows and that was an appropriate question for a lay *iudex* to answer. The professional judges of the late Empire did not find it easy to decide what was reasonable. They wanted more precise guides, and statutory rules had to be introduced to assist them, such as the rule which attempted to solve the problem by requiring a gap of 12 feet between the builder's house and his neighbour's house. Such a rule could be applied mechanically without regard to circumstances. Precision was achieved at the loss of flexibility.

Thus the regular injection of lay experience into the legal process acts as an antidote against excessive technicality and is some guarantee that law does not diverge too far from reality. The price to be paid is that the dispute may be oversimplified and certain important aspects eliminated from consideration because they make the issue too complicated for lay judges.

Remedies

We have seen that the association of laymen in the legal process tends to limit the issue to a clear-cut question which they can readily answer without having to give reasons. A similar limitation applies to the remedies that a lay court can give. The experience of both Roman law and English law shows that the normal remedy given by laymen is the award of money damages. It is characteristic of the Roman *iudex* and the English jury that once they have made their order they cease to exist as a court. They cannot in practice remain in being to supervise what happens afterwards. So a lay court has difficulty in ordering a person to do something and ensuring that he does it, or in forbidding a person to do something and punishing him later if he does it. So also, since it is a 'one off' tribunal, a lay court is unsuited to the carrying out of a consistent legal policy in a series of cases.

In the two-stage procedure of Roman law a *iudex* who had given judgment in favour of a plaintiff could award him damages and nothing else. 'All condemnations are pecuniary'. Sometimes the formula would instruct him precisely how to assess the damages, eg twice the value of the thing stolen, and sometimes it left the sum entirely to his discretion, 'whatever in good faith the defendant ought to pay'. Even when the claim was for a thing owned by the plaintiff and wrongly detained by the defendant, the formula instructed the *iudex* to award the plaintiff the value of his property, unless at his direction the defendant restored it to the plaintiff. In assessing the value in such a case, the *iudex* could adopt the value put on the thing by the plaintiff himself, so that the damages would be generous, but they might not always be an adequate substitute for the return of his property. What the *iudex* could not do was to compel the defendant by state force to hand back the property. He did not have officials at his disposal to do that, and the magistrates were reluctant to get involved in such matters. They would help the plaintiff to enforce payment of the money awarded, by authorising him to take possession of the recalcitrant defendant's goods and, if need be, make him bankrupt but that was all.

A decision that the defendant is liable, followed by an award of damages, is not a satisfactory way of dealing with all types of case. Even when the ordinary procedure involved remitting cases to a lay *iudex*, certain types of case were either dealt with 'extraordinarily' by the praetor himself or by a special magistrate appointed to deal with a particular type of business. For example, in certain cases the praetor could, in the exercise of his discretion, cancel the legal effect of a transaction which was formally valid, if its consequences were unfair.[6] This might happen if a man was away on public service and so was unable to take the steps necessary to prevent his property being acquired by another through lapse of time; or if a young man, on account of youthful inexperience, had entered into an unwise transaction to his detriment. The praetor could order *restitutio in integrum*, which was effectively a declaration that the parties to a transaction be put into the legal position they would have been in if the transaction had not taken place. Great self-restraint had to be shown in the grant of this remedy; if given wholesale it would have undermined public confidence in the law, but to refuse to give it would have perpetuated injustice. A consistent legal policy was required and lay discretion would have been too arbitrary, so the praetor dealt with the matter himself. Similarly in cases which involved the close scrutiny of accounts over a period of time, such as in allegations of misconduct against guardians who looked after the

6. Jolowicz, pp 229ff.

property of those who were under age, a lay court was inappropriate and a special praetor was appointed who could remove an unsatisfactory guardian.

In the *cognitio* system of the late Roman Empire, the proceedings were wholly controlled by a professional judge, who was not restricted to awards of damages. He could make an order for specific performance, to compel a defendant to hand over a specific thing to the plaintiff, and if the order was not carried out, court officials would enforce it. It was this late Roman practice which formed the model for later professional procedures, as in French and German law (p 205). For them the normal remedy is an order to the defendant to do what he is legally bound to do. The award of damages is regarded as a secondary or 'substitutional' remedy, to be made only when for some reason specific performance is not feasible.

In England the typical remedy in jury trials was damages.[7] (The only significant exception was in the action to recover land, when a jury verdict that the claimant was entitled could result in a court order for the land to be restored.) Since they did not have to explain what they did, juries could award lump sums, by way of compensation for loss suffered by the plaintiff, which sometimes gave the appearance of being plucked out of the air. Some heads of loss would be specified during the trial, but other elements would be incalculable, such as damages for 'pain and suffering', and the jury was free to decide on an appropriate figure 'at large'. When motor vehicles and motor accidents first became common, the volatile character of juries and their presumed susceptibility to persuasive advocacy provoked many trials of cases which would have been settled by compromise out of court if the damages to be obtained had been more predictable.

The three royal courts, with their jury trials, were the main courts available to litigants but from the fourteenth century they were supplemented by another court which was wholly professional and which offered remedies other than damages. This was the Court of Chancery.[8] The law had become rigid and technical, juries could be tampered with, and litigants dissatisfied with the justice they received in the king's courts petitioned the King in Council for better remedies. Such petitions were handled by the Chancellor, the head of the Chancery and 'the keeper of the King's conscience'. He was free of the procedural formalities of the regular courts and saw it as his duty to ensure that justice was done as conscience dictated. Instead of letting the sheriff seise the property of a defendant who

---

7.   F. H. Lawson *Remedies of English Law* (2nd edn, 1980) pp 54ff.
8.   Baker, pp 87ff; J. L. Barton 'Equity in the medieval common law' in R. A. Newman (ed) *Equity in the World's Legal Systems* (1973) pp 139ff.

failed to satisfy a judgment against him, as happened after a jury verdict, the Chancellor and his deputies acted directly on the defendant's person. They enforced their orders by committing anyone who disobeyed them to prison for 'contempt of court'. Thus they could order that a party in breach of a contract should carry out what he had undertaken rather than pay damages and they could issue an injunction to stop the commission of an act which was wrongful or unconscionable. By granting a so-called 'common injunction' the Chancellor could even forbid a party, who had been successful in an action in the ordinary court, from enforcing the judgment in his favour, if in the circumstances it would be unfair to do so. The Chancery court could also investigate accounting practices in a way that was only possible for a professional court.

Trial by judge alone in England

In the last 50 years, except in serious criminal cases, to be considered in the next chapter, the jury has been almost eliminated as a means of trial in England, and the professional judge has taken over. This has not, however, meant the substitution of the continental professional model, with its inquisitorial procedure, for the lay model, since the accusatorial mode of trial, which was developed largely because it was suitable for juries, has been retained. Professional judges are aware of this and in carrying out the functions of fact finding, evaluation and decision making, traditionally assigned to the jury, they have sought to put themselves into the position of a jury.

A judge alone is in some respects able to perform the jury's functions more readily than the jury itself. The taking of evidence can be quicker, since it can be assumed that one who is experienced at dealing with witnesses will pick up the trend of what is being said, and assess its credibility more easily than an inexperienced group of laymen. A judge, for example, will know what a jury may not know, that a witness who testifies as to an event that he witnessed three years before, and purports to remember details, will in fact have made a statement to a solicitor a few days after the event, will have refreshed his memory from that statement immediately before going into the witness box, and will probably be able to recall only what was in the statement. Many of the technical rules about admissibility of evidence, introduced to protect the jury, have disappeared and since the Civil Evidence Act 1968, most evidence is admissible if the judge considers it relevant. This is especially important since most trials are about disputed facts rather than disputed law.

In regard to the award of damages, judges are less likely than juries to make arbitrary awards. They will know through experience the kind of sum that is awarded in similar cases, and can use that as a guide in reaching their own assessments. Thus there is more uniformity in the compensation awarded in similar cases than there was under the jury system, and that in turn leads to greater predictability in the legal process. When parties are able to foresee the outcome of an action with reasonable certainty, they are more likely to make an out of court settlement in order to avoid the expenses of litigation.[9]

All judges now have the powers both of the old common law courts and of the Chancery court so that they have a range of remedies at their disposal in addition to damages. These remedies are, however, still normally used in circumstances in which they have traditionally been used. Specific performance of a duty imposed by a contract may be ordered but only when damages are an insufficient remedy for the plaintiff. Damages are still the primary remedy.

Probably the most significant feature in the task of a modern English judge is the amount of discretionary power which has been conferred on him to decide not according to precise rules but according to his sense of fairness. Earlier in this century there was a tendency to limit judicial discretion. Appeal courts specified precisely when there was liability and when there was not, or laid it down that the presence of certain facts constituted 'reasonableness' and other facts 'unreasonableness'. Further, as a distinguished judge has put it, 'the capacity of individuals or tribunals to make a succession of value judgments without, consciously or unconsciously, constructing stereotypes is limited. . . . Nothing destroys flexibility as quickly as precedent'.[10] Recently, however, this tendency has been reversed. Parliament has responded to the popular demand for fairness by allowing judges to avoid the either/or decisions required by the classical model and to 'give something' to each party.[11]

This tendency is particularly noticeable in matrimonial cases. Problems arise today not in regard to divorce itself but in regard to payments, both of periodical sums and of capital, by one party to another following a divorce. Any set of rules capable of being applied mechanically would certainly produce arbitrary results and in effect the whole matter is left to the judge's discretion, having 'regard to all the circumstances of the case'. In reaching his decision he is told to take into account a number of factors, such as the parties' likely

9.   Cf the comparison of 'trained judges' and laymen by Lord Widgery LCJ in *Wetherall v Harrison* [1976] 1 QB 773 at 777.
10.   Sir R. Ormrod 'Judges and the process of judging' Univ of Birmingham Jubilee Lectures (1981) p 185.
11.   Ormrod, op cit, pp 193ff.

income in the future, their financial responsibilities, their ages and the duration of the marriage, their contributions to the family (including keeping house) and so on,[12] but essentially he is expected to do what he considers fair to the parties. When appeals are made in such cases the higher courts today are reluctant to interfere with the judge's discretion unless he appears to have approached the matter in the wrong way. Appeals are thus discouraged, and in cases that are appealed, the courts emphasise that the opinions they express are to be taken only as guidelines or starting points and not as rigid precedents. A similar discretion is given to judges in dealing with the claims of dependants of a deceased person to a share of his estate; in effect they can overturn a will, or even the rules of intestacy, in order to produce a distribution of the estate which is fair (p 182). As in wills, so also in contracts, courts have a discretion in certain cases to overturn contracts which are formally valid, if their contents appear to be unfair (p 202). Sometimes a particular topic has been encrusted with presumptions, or inferences which a court is bound to make from the existence of certain facts, and in order to increase the judge's discretion these have had to be removed. Rights of parents in regard to the custody of their children, laid down in a series of precedent rulings, were an area much affected by such presumptions. But they were swept away in a case in 1970 which laid down that, however the parents behaved, the judge was to be guided solely by what he considered was for the child's welfare.[13]

One of the most striking illustrations of the tendency towards discretionary fairness in judicial decisions is to be found in regard to limitation of actions. Most legal systems have rules which require actions to be brought within fixed periods of time and English law has long had periods of limitation for different classes of action. These periods were fixed and had to be applied rigidly. A defendant who showed that the plaintiff was out of time was *entitled* to have the action against him dismissed. The Limitation Act 1975, after stating the periods, then allows the court to override them if in the particular circumstances it would be equitable to allow the action to proceed, notwithstanding that the periods have elapsed.

Tribunals

So far we have been considering situations in which the law now allows the judges of the regular courts to decide cases not by fixed rules but by their ideas of what is just as between the individual

12. Matrimonial Causes Act 1973, s 25(1).
13. *J v C* [1970] AC 668, HL.

parties. In some situations, which are of more general concern, and where there is a need for a quick and expeditious settlement of the dispute, the practice has grown up of removing the cases from the regular courts to special courts, always described as 'tribunals', whose members normally include both a professional lawyer and laymen. They deal with a large range of disputes, concerning such matters as rent assessment, unfair dismissal, social security benefits, compensation for compulsory purchase and immigration. The procedure is informal and the parties often present their own case.

Much of the work of these tribunals involves the application of standards. For example, the assessment of what is a fair rent is a matter that not only affects a particular landlord and a particular tenant, but also others whose premises may be very similar to those directly affected by the decision. Rent assessment tribunals will be familiar with the conditions in the locality and can build up a special experience and expertise. Whether an employer's dismissal of his worker is unfair is again a matter which may affect many others in a similar position and an industrial tribunal will take into account the conditions of the industry in question (p 218).

These tribunals contain a substantial lay element but they are different from juries in that the lay members are not involved only on a 'one-off' basis but sit regularly and build up a semi-professionalism. Their discretion is not formally limited, but in deciding what is fair and just in the circumstances of a particular case, they take account of what they know to have been decided in other analogous cases, so that stereotype situations are present in their minds. There is normally an appeal from such tribunals to a higher tribunal but such appellate bodies are not expected to substitute their own idea of what is fair for that of the tribunal which first heard the case. If they lay down too many detailed guidelines for the tribunals to follow, they will unduly restrict the discretion of a largely lay tribunal to apply standards. For example, if the issue is whether a particular departure from normal industrial practice is so serious as to make the dismissal of an employee unreasonable, and so unfair, they will try to avoid categorising types of behaviour as reasonable or unreasonable. On the other hand, if they provide the tribunals with no guidance on how to approach the question of what is reasonable industrial practice, there will be no uniformity between the various tribunals throughout the country and similar behaviour may be held to be reasonable in one area and unreasonable in another.[14] In general the appeal body will not interfere with the decision of a tribunal applying a standard unless it considers that it approached the question in the wrong way and so

---

14. Cf the remarks of Browne-Wilkinson J in *Grundy (Teddington) Ltd v Plummer and Salt* [1983] IRLR 98.

reached a 'perverse' conclusion. Complaints about the procedure of such tribunals, as opposed to appeals against decisions, may be taken to a watchdog body, the Council on Tribunals.

Arbitration as an alternative

Those involved in disputes do not always wish to have them settled by the process of law, whether in an ordinary court or a specialised tribunal. They may be put off by the publicity attendant on a trial, which might lead to the revelation of facts that might embarrass them. They may want to avoid time-consuming procedural formalities and the need to explain to the judge many background features of the case which would be familiar to anyone involved in the relevant milieu. A further reason might be the all or nothing, win or lose aspect of legal proceedings and the fact that they can only be concerned with the strictly legal issues. Or it may be that the sheer expense of legal proceedings makes them seek some alternative. One alternative is arbitration, the use of contract to exclude the law courts.

In an arbitration the parties agree to refer their differences to a private individual, without official status, and so long as he keeps within the terms of the agreement, his award will be final. Most legal systems recognise the institution of arbitration but to preserve its utility they have to strictly limit their control of it. For a party who has agreed to arbitration and does not receive an award which satisfies him may be tempted to try to revert to the law, with a view to upsetting the award or releasing himself from its terms. By recognising arbitration, the law must restrain itself from interfering in such a situation. But it cannot ignore it altogether.

In Roman law an agreement to submit a dispute to an arbitrator was known as *compromissum*.[15] It was not of itself binding on the parties, but they could make it binding by giving mutual promises in which each party promised to pay the other a penalty if he failed to obey the arbitrator's award. Arbitration interacted with the law at two points. First, the praetor could be asked to compel a reluctant arbitrator who had accepted a reference but later tried to avoid acting. He would allow the arbitrator to be excused on grounds such as conflict of interest, illness and election to public office. Secondly, the praetor could be asked to grant a legal action to recover the penalty payable if the award was not obeyed. The only interest of the law was that the arbitrator should decide the question put to him and decide it according to his real opinion. It was not concerned with

15.   P. Stein 'Arbitration under Roman law' (1974) 41 Arbitration 203.

the kind of decision he reached. The parties had conferred unlimited discretion on him by their agreement, and so his award bound them irrespective of its merits. The parties could disobey the arbitrator only if he stepped outside the terms of their agreement. He might do that either in his conduct of arbitration, such as summoning the parties to meet at an unsuitable place or time (in one example an arbitrator summoned the parties to meet in a brothel), or by trying to decide questions other than those submitted to him. It was possible to have more than one arbitrator, though parties were advised to have an odd number who could decide by a majority.

The attitude of modern law to arbitration is essentially similar. English law first gave it statutory recognition in 1697, and the rules are now set out in the Arbitration Acts of 1950 and 1979. In certain contexts, particularly in trades and professions, parties to a contract bind themselves to submit any dispute that may arise out of the contract to an arbitrator chosen by themselves or, failing agreement, by a third person, such as the president of the relevant trade association or professional body. Such a clause is frequently included in leases between landlord and tenant and in insurance policies.

A reference may be to more than one arbitrator, with provision for an umpire to settle a difference should two arbitrators fail to agree. Although most arbitration arises from the agreements of parties, certain statutes provide for disputes arising out of their provisions to be referred to arbitration. Examples are the Agricultural Holdings Act 1948 and the Lands Tribunal Act 1949. A court itself may refer a case to arbitration if the matter is highly technical, though in this case the arbitrator is chosen by the court and has a more official status than a normal arbitrator. A small claim, where the sum involved is less than £500, will be sent by a county court for arbitration unless the issues are shown to be such that only a formal trial would be appropriate. In such a case the parties do not need a lawyer and can assert claims without risk of heavy legal costs. In the case of industrial disputes, there is a government backed Central Arbitration Committee, which can function only if both sides agree.

To be valid and enforceable an arbitration award must be within the scope of the agreement and must deal with all the matters referred to the arbitrator. If it complies with these conditions, it is final. The only circumstances in which it can be challenged in court are if the arbitrator misbehaved, for example by failing to give each side a proper opportunity to present his case, or if he made an error of law. (His findings of fact cannot be questioned.) Even on these limited grounds appeal to a court can be excluded by prior agreement. In the absence of any such grounds for challenge, the award can be enforced in the same way as the judgment of a court. In some countries, such as France, it is customary to authorise arbitrators to act as 'amicable compounders' (*amicables compositeurs*), which gives them greater freedom to decide 'equitably' and excludes appeal based on error of law.

Arbitration has the advantages of certainty and finality. The parties know that they will get a settlement of their disputes in a reasonable time without the possibility of appeals to higher courts, and with a consequent saving of expense. The actual proceedings are informal and private, they can be arranged at short notice and they can be conducted wherever the parties choose, with visits to view the site readily arranged as they are needed. In particular the arbitrator can be expected to know the background to the dispute. On the other hand, since arbitrators work in isolation from one another, there is sometimes less predictability in the way they reach their decisions, and if they are not legally trained, they may be less able to assess the weight of legal arguments than lawyers for whom it has become second nature. They do not have the same powers as judges to compel good conduct, for example by penalising a party who resorts to delaying tactics. If it is desired to bring a third party into the proceedings, that party cannot be made to enter an arbitration as he could be made a party to legal proceedings. For most people who resort to arbitration, however, unless they have signed a contract containing an arbitration clause without bothering to read it, these are minor blemishes in an institution which in many areas has ousted the regular process.

5 Criminal prosecution and civil action

As the state becomes stronger and better organised, it tends to take over some of the functions previously carried out by kinship groups. Such a transfer of function from the kin to the state produces a distinction between civil action and criminal prosecution. A civil action is brought by the party who has been wronged and aims at compensating him for what he has suffered, whereas a criminal prosecution is brought by the state and is designed to penalise those who offend against public order.

As we have seen, in societies in which the state is either non-existent or exists only in a rudimentary form, the victim of wrong, supported by his family and friends, proceeds against one who has caused him wrong with a view to obtaining a solution which offers both compensation for himself and at the same time punishment to the wrongdoer. The pressure of the community favours the acceptance of money payment as the appropriate form of compensation, but the amount payable will often be more than the actual loss suffered by the victim and so will include a penal element. Payment is secured by the threat of retaliation in kind or a potential blood-feud, if it is not made. At this stage there is no procedural distinction between action aimed at punishment and action settling a dispute between citizens.

A new situation arises when the state and its officers wish to proceed against those who have wronged the community as a whole. Such an action does not aim at the payment of compensation by the wrongdoer. In some cases its purpose may be the elimination of the wrongdoer, by his exclusion from the community or his death, with the consequent forfeiture of his property to the state. In less serious cases it may result in his temporary loss of liberty or some form of corporal punishment or merely the payment of a fine to the state. Such a fine, however, is not compensation based on the amount of damage that he has caused, but is considered as a penalty marking the state's disapproval of what he has done. At this stage the state is taking over from the kinship groups the responsibility for the maintenance of good order in the community.

The manner of this transfer of function varies considerably from one society to another. The form of the procedure by which offences against the state are judged will often depend on the political organisation of the state. In a radical democracy, there will be considerable popular control, and the officers of the state will be restricted in their powers. In an autocratic state the officers of the state will act with little, if any, control except from within their own hierarchy. As illustrations we may consider at one extreme Republican Rome and at the other imperial China.

The Romans of the early Republic were reluctant to develop a criminal jurisdiction because they did not wish to give too great a power of prosecution to the state officials. So personal assaults and offences against property, such as theft, were not at first the subject of state action and were treated purely as grounds for private action by the victim. Although in form civil, the action in such cases was considered to have a penal purpose and the damages payable by the wrongdoer would often be a multiple of the victim's loss (p 195). For example, in ordinary cases of theft, damages were twice the value of the thing stolen, even when the thing was recovered. If this seems unrealistic, in view of the fact that thieves are usually not worth suing for simple damages, let alone a multiple, it should be remembered that thieves would often be either slaves or else freemen in the power of their family head. The victim of the theft would sue the slave's owner or the family head and he would be obliged either to pay the damages that would have been payable if the delinquent were free or to hand over the slave or son to the victim.

Where the wrong consisted of the killing of the victim, the state, through its officers, had either to prosecute for the murder or leave the matter to the victim's kin, with considerable risk of a blood-feud. For otherwise it would have been safer to kill than merely to injure. In early Rome the state did take action for murders but precisely how is a matter of dispute. Probably the killer was declared an outcast and expelled from the community. In the case of certain offences against the community, such as treason and breaches of public order, where there was no identifiable victim who could sue, the principal magistrates could proceed against the accused and, after investigation of the circumstances, punish him.[1] They acted with little in the way of procedural rules to restrain them. But from the beginning of the Republic any citizen accused of a serious charge had a right of appeal to the popular assembly (the so-called *provocatio*), before he was finally condemned. Thus, although the popular assembly had nothing to do with civil matters, in which area citizen participation was confined to the activity of the single *iudex*, it could exercise its sovereign power whenever a citizen was threatened with death or exile. In practice, a convicted offender was usually allowed to go into exile rather than be put to death, with the proviso that if he returned from banishment without permission, he could be summarily done away with.

1. Dawson *Lay judges* pp 15ff; Jolowicz, pp 305ff.

In the later Republic, special criminal courts with lay judges were set up by statutes of the popular assembly to deal with particular crimes. The first such court dealt with charges of extortion brought by provincials against their Roman governors. The idea of having such a standing court was extended piecemeal to a number of other crimes but was never made general. In Cicero's time the courts consisted of from 51 to 75 citizens, who sat under the chairmanship of a magistrate and decided the case by majority vote of the whole membership. In effect, by establishing these standing courts, the popular assembly delegated its powers of decision-making, previously exercised on the *provocatio* procedure, to groups of laymen. By so doing, the assembly also limited the power of the magistrates to deal with such crimes by direct action against the offender.

The reluctance of the Romans to give their magistrates unrestricted powers to keep good order ended with the Republic. Under the Empire magistrates were granted wide discretionary powers to deal with crimes, both those that were covered by statutory courts and those that were not. Gradually the statutory courts were displaced by the new procedure in which the magistrates proceeded inquisitorially and were controlled only by their superiors in the imperial bureaucracy.

In contrast with the early Roman preference for civil remedies over criminal prosecutions is the attitude of imperial China. It shows that a well-organised state with a strong government can effectively make all disputes into matters of criminal law. Traditional Chinese society did not favour the legal process, in the sense of independent fact investigation and application of rules by a court, as a means of settling disputes. The Chinese regarded humans as an organic part of the universe, and human society as governed by natural forces, so that any action by man that was anti-social was also a violation of the total cosmic order. The all-pervading ethics of Confucianism prescribed certain accepted modes of behaviour, and those who deviated from those norms were subjected to a variety of pressures to make them conform. These pressures came from kinship groups, or community elders, or workmates. One turned to officialdom only as a last resort when a dispute could not be settled in any other way.

If the parties could not settle their differences themselves, the party at fault, being impervious to social pressures, had to be punished. Thus, if a dispute involved two individuals, individual A did not bring a suit against individual B. Rather he lodged his complaint with the authorities, who then decided whether to prosecute individual B. Since the law was thus exclusively penal, 'matters of a civil nature were either ignored by it entirely (for example contracts) or were given only limited treatment within its penal format (for example property rights, inheritance, marriage)'.[2] What mattered, in the Chinese view, was not the official protection of the individual's rights but the maintenance of the harmony of the social order.[3] Indeed those who did seek the magistrate's aid, quite justifiably, were often regarded as troublemakers. The Emperor K'ang Hsi, in the seventeenth century, tried to discourage the use of the legal process, declaring; 'law-suits would tend to increase to a frightful amount, if people were not afraid of the tribunals, and if they felt confident of always finding in them ready and perfect justice . . . I desire therefore that those who have recourse to the tribunals should be treated without any pity, and in such a manner that they shall be disgusted with law and tremble to appear before a magistrate'.[4]

Continental criminal procedure

Continental European systems have experienced dramatic changes in the procedure of criminal trials. In early medieval Europe the procedure normally contained an element of popular control. In France, after the disappearance of ordeals and trial by battle, this took the form of a group-inquest. The king's officers came to the localities and made a select group of local inhabitants answer questions on oath about wrongdoing in the neighbourhood. In Germany the community was represented by the *Schöffen*, who formed a permanent lay court of about 12 to 15 members. In both cases proceedings were accusatorial and the responsibility for initiating proceedings lay with the victim of the wrong. However, everywhere on the continent courts of professional judges were set up, using a variant of the Romano-canonical procedure, with a private investigation of the allegations. Proceedings were usually begun by an official representing the Sovereign.

The application of the inquisitorial procedure to criminal prosecutions involved the introduction of the elaborate law of proof developed by the canonists. In principle the evidence of two witnesses of the commission of the crime was required for conviction (the *unus testis nullus testis* rule). In the absence of two witnesses the court could convict the accused only if he confessed. Circumstantial

---

2. D. Bodde and C. Morris *Law in Imperial China* (1967) p 4.
3. In certain non-intentional homicides, although the proceedings were in the form of a prosecution, the sum due from the killer was paid to the victim's family.
4. Cited by H. McAleavy 'Chinese Law' in J. D. M. Derrett (ed) *An Introduction to Legal Systems* (1968) p 115, from S. van der Sprenkel *Legal Institutions in Manchu China* (1962) p 77.

evidence, the so-called *indicia*, however compelling, was not a basis for conviction. But where there was 'half-proof', in the form of one eye-witness, or compelling circumstantial evidence, amounting to a substantial case for the accused to answer, the court was permitted to torture him with a view to obtaining a confession.[5] Torture was supposed to be used in such a way as to obtain not just a bare admission of guilt but the revelation of details which no innocent person would know. The aim of these rules was to limit the element of discretion in the professional judge and to ensure that proof of the commission of the crime by the accused was as certain as possible. The judge should not convict on the basis of his own impression but only on a firm basis of objective evidence.

In France the professional judges excluded laymen from criminal procedure altogether until the Revolution, but in Germany the *Schöffen* maintained at least a formal presence at criminal trials. In 1532 the Emperor Charles V required the presence of two *Schöffen* at criminal inquisitions, and of four when judgment was given. This number rose to seven when the death penalty was imposed.[6] Thus at least the principle of lay participation was maintained.

In the nineteenth century, often under the influence of English institutions, lay participation returned to continental criminal procedure, at least in the trial of serious crimes. In modern French law, proceedings are begun by a public prosecutor (*procureur de la République*), who receives reports from the police and decides whether the case should proceed.[7] If so, the case is then investigated by a professional 'examining magistrate', known as the *juge d'instruction*, whose function is to collect and examine, in private, all the evidence in a particular case, including the (inquisitorial) examination of the accused, and to decide whether a case should be sent for trial and, if so, in which court. Less serious cases then go to a court of professional judges (other than the *juge d'instruction*); more serious cases are sent to a *chambre d'accusation* and if its judges so rule, are tried in a *cour d'assise* consisting of three professional judges and a jury of nine laymen. Jurors must be 30 years of age, be literate and not have forfeited civil rights (which happens on conviction for certain serious offences).

At the conclusion of the trial, the jury are told that the law does not require them to say by what means they are convinced nor does it lay down rules by which they must assess the sufficiency of the evidence. It merely requires them to consider what impression the evidence has made on them and answer the question, 'Are you thoroughly convinced?'

---

5.   J. H. Langbein *Torture and the Law of proof* (1977) pp 5ff.
6.   Dawson *Lay judges* pp 109–110.
7.   A. V. Sheehan *Criminal procedure in Scotland and France* (1975) p 185.

The jury and the judges deliberate together both on the verdict and on the sentence. The court may decide by a majority of its 12 members but at least 8 votes are necessary for a verdict of guilty. This rule ensures that the opinion of the lay jurors must prevail: If the verdict is guilty, the court decides the sentence by a simple majority. This compromise is thought to allow the jury its independence, and at the same time let the judges help the jurors to interpret the evidence in complex cases and counteract any inexperience on their part.

In Germany most crimes (apart from petty offences) are tried by a mixed court of professional judges and laymen.[8] Less important cases are heard by the *Schöffengericht*, composed of one professional and two lay judges, while more serious cases go to the *Grosse Strafkammer*, consisting of three professional and two lay judges. Proceedings are initiated by the public prosecutor (*Staatsanwalt*), a state official who does much of the preliminary investigation that in France is done by the *juge d'instruction*, and prepares the pre-trial dossier. At the trial the presiding judge (always a professional), having studied the dossier, examines the accused and takes the evidence. All the judges sit as a single panel and deliberate together. For verdicts of guilty and the sentence, a two-thirds majority of the members of the court is required. Thus in the *Schöffengericht* the laymen can overrule the professional, and in the *Grosse Strafkammer* they can force a verdict of acquittal but not of guilty against the views of the professionals.

Scottish criminal procedure

Scotland's criminal procedure is based on the right to a trial by jury in serious cases, but it has several special features derived from continental procedure.[9]

All crimes are investigated by a public prosecutor, known as the procurator-fiscal, who receives reports from the police, instructs them to make investigations and in appropriate cases prepares the prosecution. Procurators-fiscal are employed by the state and under the directions of the Crown Office, headed by the Lord Advocate, who is a member of the government. While less serious cases may be tried by a professional judge, known as a sheriff, alone, serious crime is tried by so-called solemn procedure, before a professional judge and a jury of 15. The jury is composed of adult residents in the area with a minimal property qualification. For each trial 30 jurors are

8. J. H. Langbein *Comparative Criminal Procedure: Germany* (1977) pp 62–63.
9. Sheehan *Criminal Procedure* pp 97ff.

listed and their names drawn out of an urn until 15 are chosen. Each accused may challenge up to 5 jurors without cause and more with cause, such as relationship or enmity.

The trial is accusatorial in form, the witnesses being examined and cross-examined by the parties' representatives rather than by the judge. After hearing the evidence and the judge's directions on the relevant law and the standard of proof required, the jury retires without the judge to decide whether the accused is guilty or not. This verdict may be by a majority, at least eight votes being needed for a guilty verdict.

Scottish rules of evidence are much influenced by the rules developed in the Romano-canonical procedure and there is still much emphasis on the need for corroboration of evidence. The burden of proof is on the prosecutor to provide corroborated evidence when it is required. If he produces two witnesses, one of whom is believed by the jury but not the other, the jury, instead of giving a verdict of 'not guilty' may bring in a verdict of 'not proven'. The legal effect of such a verdict is the same as that of not guilty, but a certain stigma naturally attaches to one in whose case the jury have given a verdict of not proven. Once the verdict has been given, the jury's function is over; sentence is purely for the judge to decide.

English criminal procedure

We have noted that a feature of medieval England, in comparison with other European countries, was the strong centralised government introduced by the Norman kings, who demonstrated their control by establishing effective courts and causing the virtual disappearance of the blood-feud. Some of the disputes brought before the king's courts were of concern primarily to the parties concerned, such as which of them owned freehold land. Others were concerned with wrongs done to the complainant. Serious wrongs which not only injured a private citizen but also the public order of the state, the so-called 'king's peace', were designated felonies.[10] Anyone convicted of felony was hanged, his personal goods were forfeited to the king and his land reverted to his feudal lord (by 'escheat'). Originally the victim of felony could himself bring an action against the wrongdoer by 'appeal of felony' but there were disadvantages in this remedy. The designated mode of trial was by battle, with the attendant risks to the appellant; and even if he succeeded in obtaining a conviction, he received no compensation, because the felon's property was already bespoken either to the king or to his lord.

10.   Baker, pp 413ff.

Although hardly profitable to the victim of felony, actions for felony brought considerable profit to the king, and his officials initiated proceedings by a formal accusation called 'bill of indictment'. In this case the mode of trial before 1215 was by ordeal of water. Later an accused who pleaded 'not guilty' could ask to be tried 'by God and the country', which entitled him to be tried by a jury of his peers, and since then anyone accused of crime on indictment has had the right to be tried by jury. Until 1772, if he declined a jury, he was pressed to death slowly with heavy weights, but at least he died unconvicted so that his property was not forfeited and could pass to his family.

Since the category of felonies extended well beyond heinous crimes, like murder and armed robbery, this regime would have been very severe if it had not been mitigated in practice. The main device for avoiding the consequences of conviction for felony was 'benefit of clergy'. Traditionally clerics were exempt from the jurisdiction of the king's court and were dealt with by their own church courts. The test of whether anyone was a cleric came to be the ability to read a passage from the psalms, so that literate felons were allowed to escape death. Later the system became regularised and the benefit was withdrawn from the more serious felonies.

The victim of felony thus had no chance of obtaining satisfaction from the wrongdoer. Everything went to the state or to the feudal lord. If the victim tried to bring a civil action before the criminal prosecution, he was told that the king had priority over the claims of private individuals and so his action was stayed until the criminal prosecution had been completed, by which time, of course, it was too late to get any satisfaction. His evidence was often crucial to the success of the prosecution, but if he tried to negotiate a settlement with the accused before the prosecution was brought, he was himself guilty of the crime of 'compounding a felony'.

The responsibility for preparing the prosecution case against the accused fell upon the justices of the peace, socially prominent men in the localities who were responsible for much of the administration of local government. By a statute of 1361 they were given the duty of identifying and punishing certain types of offenders and from the sixteenth century they conducted preliminary investigations into suspected felonies to decide whether the accused should be committed for trial. Before the development of organised police forces in the nineteenth century, these justices effectively did the kind of preparatory work of a prosecution which in France would have been done by the public prosecutor.

The actual initiation of proceedings was the presentment of the accused by a 'grand jury', which came to number 23, who decided whether there was a 'true bill' (of indictment), ie, a case for the accused to answer. It was possible for anyone to bring an indictment before the grand jury, but most indictments were against those committed for trial by justices of the peace. The case was then brought for trial before a 'petty jury' of 12 men either at Quarter Sessions, the quarterly meeting of the justices of the peace of the county, or at Assizes, when a judge came on circuit to deal with the more serious felonies. The petty or trial jury was drawn from a panel of householders occupying premises of a certain minimum value, and therefore could be regarded as socially superior to most accused. Traditionally the accused could challenge up to 35 jurors without giving any reason and more if he could show good cause, such as a conflict of interest.

The procedural rules governing the trial before the jury were weighted against the accused. He had no right to be legally represented by a lawyer; he could not compel the attendance of witnesses who might give evidence favourable to him, in the way that the prosecution could compel the prosecution witnesses to appear; and he was debarred from giving evidence on his own behalf. Despite these defects, which were all corrected in the nineteenth century, the fact that no-one could be convicted of felony without the verdict of a jury of laymen has always been regarded as a safeguard of individual liberty. The jury had to be satisfied of the accused's guilt beyond reasonable doubt and had to be unanimous in their verdict. If, after making every effort, they could not agree, the judge could discharge them and there would be a new trial before a fresh jury. At one time juries which were reluctant to convict an accused might be bullied into submission, even by imprisonment, if the verdict appeared to the judge to be perverse. By the end of the seventeenth century, however, it was established that a jury's verdict of not guilty, however surprising in the face of the evidence, could not be challenged, nor could the jurors be penalised for it. A verdict of guilty could be challenged only if the judge had misdirected the jury on what they had to decide. The death penalty was removed from many felonies in the nineteenth century and forfeiture abolished in 1870. Since then, the judge, who has always been solely responsible for sentencing after conviction, has had much more discretion than before.

Felonies were not the only crimes; less serious crimes were designated misdemeanours. They could be tried on indictment like felonies, but minor misdemeanours were normally dealt with summarily by the justices of the peace without the participation of a jury. Conviction did not involve death or forfeiture.

The Criminal Justice Act of 1967 abolished the distinction between felonies and misdemeanours, but there are still two forms of criminal procedure. Serious crimes are tried on indictment in the

Crown Court by a jury instructed by a professional judge; less serious crimes are dealt with summarily; and there is an intermediate group which may be tried by either procedure, the accused having the right to opt for jury trial. Since the latter is more elaborate and expensive, there have been several moves to remove the right to jury trial in as many crimes as possible, but they have always met strong resistance from those who regard the jury as the bastion of individual liberty, particularly in cases where there is an allegation of dishonesty.

1. Trial by jury today

The trial of serious crime today is not essentially different from the traditional mode, although there has been some streamlining of the procedure. The preliminary hearing before the justices of the peace (now usually called magistrates) has since 1967 become in most cases a mere formality, at which no evidence is given, and both parties consent to the matter going to the Crown Court for trial. It is still possible, however, for the accused to demand an 'old style committal', which can be conducted by a single magistrate, at which evidence is given and a decision made as to whether there is a sufficient case against the accused to justify sending him for trial.

At the Crown Court there is a professional judge, usually a Circuit Judge or Recorder, who may sit with up to four lay magistrates. The professional judge presides, and the magistrates only participate at the sentencing stage, if the accused is found guilty. At that stage the judge and the magistrates decide by a majority. The decision as to guilt or innocence is taken by a jury, which now includes women, and since no property qualification is now required for jury service, is composed of people from all social classes. At the conclusion of the case the judge sums up the evidence and explains to the jury what they have to decide and what standard of proof they must apply. In various ways he may hint at his own view of the case, but he must not take over the jury's task, and since he does not retire with the jury when they consider their verdict, they are free of his influence at the crucial moment of decision. To deal with the situation created by one or two jurors who refuse to go along with a verdict agreed by the rest, the Act of 1967 allows the judge to accept a majority verdict, when the jury has deliberated for a least two hours, and, if there are not less than 11 jurors (as may happen when a juror becomes ill in the middle of a case), when at least 10 of them agree on the verdict.

2. Summary trial today

Well over 90% of all crimes today are tried summarily. In most countries, such crimes are dealt with by a professional judge, sometimes of relatively junior status. In England and Wales a single professional judge known as a stipendiary magistrate, deals with summary cases in London and certain large cities. But the bulk of summary trials come before lay magistrates. Although these are the justices of the peace of old, their character and composition have changed radically since the Second World War.

Magistrates shed most of their administrative duties in the nineteenth century, and their functions became more strictly judicial. But appointment was still most frequently made as a reward for political services, and benches often did not convey the impression that they were able to approach their judicial duties in a proper spirit of impartiality.

In recent decades great efforts have been made to ensure that in each locality the magistrates' bench represents a cross section of the community, socially, politically and in other ways.[11] Local advisory committees advertise for applicants and make recommendations to the Lord Chancellor, who makes the appointments. The result has been a considerable reduction in public criticism of magistrates' courts, a corresponding increase in the amount of work they have to do, and a rise in their numbers. In 1983 there were 25,934 magistrates in England and Wales, of whom 15,606 were men and 10,328 were women. They receive no remuneration for their work but are entitled to claim allowances for actual financial loss. They have to undertake to sit at least 26 half-days each year, but to obtain an even distribution of the work of the bench, they usually sit more frequently.

Lay magistrates normally sit as a bench of three and decide by a majority; they can adjudicate with only two, but then they must agree on a guilty verdict. Unlike a jury, they decide not only the guilt or innocence of the accused but also the sentence. They are given preliminary training on court procedure and on the nature of their own duties, so that they will be seen to be acting in a judicial manner. But they are not expected to know the rules of substantive law. To advise them on those rules and particularly on the extent of their powers, they have a professionally trained clerk. The clerk is not part of the court, but acts in an advisory capacity and has a duty to intervene if the magistrates appear to be about to do something that is outside their powers.

The fact that magistrates are lay judges means that, like juries, they are not expected to give reasons for their verdicts. In certain preliminary matters, such as the question of whether an accused person awaiting trial should be in custody or on bail, magistrates may have to give their reasons for their decisions. The law now gives an accused a right to bail except for good reasons and so requires

11.   Sir T. Skyrme *The Changing Face of the Magistracy* (2nd edn, 1983).

magistrates, if they refuse bail, to specify their reasons for so doing. But in the substantive issue of guilt or innocence they normally would not do so, if only because, being laymen, they might make a mistake which would justify an appeal. The chairman merely announces that they find the accused guilty or not guilty. In every case an appeal is possible to the Crown Court, with a judge and magistrates from a different bench (but no jury) and the whole case is reheared.

Like juries, magistrates have to deal with mixed questions of fact and law. The difference between juries and magistrates is that juries' experience in dealing with such questions is limited to one case in unfamiliar surroundings, whereas magistrates inevitably become familiar with commonly recurring cases and develop at least a semi-professional attitude to them. Experience indicates the kind of witness that can be believed and the kind that cannot, and the circumstances in which a plea is genuine or not. For example, cases of theft by shop-lifting may be tried either by a jury in the Crown Court or by magistrates summarily. A common defence to such a charge, is that the accused put the goods in his basket inadvertently, in a fit of absent-mindedness, and therefore lacked the dishonest intention which is an essential element in theft. Another common defence, where the accused is a middle-aged woman, is that she was suffering under stress caused by the menopause, which was sufficient to negative the dishonest intention. A jury's attitude to such pleas is unpredictable. Much will depend on the way the evidence is presented. Magistrates, on the other hand, are familiar with such defences. This does not mean that they will assume that a defence of this kind is not genuine, but rather that they will look out for certain pointers which will suggest whether it is genuine or not. For example, they will be alert to identify what steps, if any, the accused took to conceal the goods that were not paid for, so that they would not be seen at the check-out. Or their experience might suggest that a busy general practitioner who has treated the accused, would not be prepared to wait to be called as a witness, and then testify, from his knowledge of her medical condition, that she could well have been under such stress that her mental state was affected, unless the defence was sufficiently substantial to throw doubt on the guilt of the accused.

Magistrates may not in general impose a sentence of more than six months' imprisonment on any one occasion, unless there are two or more proved charges against the accused, in which case consecutive terms to an aggregate maximum of 12 months may be imposed. Normally, however, magistrates impose non-custodial penalties, such as probation orders, community service orders, and especially, fines. In many cases fines have to be paid by instalments and a minimum periodical payment must be fixed. Non-payment will require the offender to appear before an arrears panel of the magistrates, who may commit him to prison for culpable non-payment.

No case is exactly like any other, but with many minor offences, such as those arising from traffic, the cases seem to be so similar that magistrates are concerned that similar offences should receive similar treatment. The membership of the bench sitting on any particular day is quite fortuitous. To avoid the impression that the penalties imposed for, say, speeding or illegal parking reflect the personal prejudices of the magistrates who happened to be sitting on a particular day, tariffs of agreed fines for each category of offences are applied unless circumstances are exceptional. For many traffic offences, the attendance of the accused is not required if he admits his guilt in writing.

Civil claims in criminal procedure

It may seem obvious that one who has suffered injury through another's crime should be able to establish civil liability. But during the last century many forms of conduct have been made technically into crimes, because the only practical way of enforcing compliance with a particular rule is by an action in the name of the state. They may not necessarily injure any particular individual, and if they do, the injury may be only incidental. The most convenient form of procedure for dealing with such matters is the criminal prosecution. Sometimes when Parliament creates what it is customary to call a new 'offence' (thus reserving the word 'crime' for the traditional forms of wrongdoing), it indicates in the relevant statute that there is also to be civil liability, as for example in the Deposit of Poisonous Wastes Act 1972, s 22. Sometimes the statute says expressly that there are to be no civil proceedings, as in the Race Relations Act 1968, ss 19 and 22. But often Parliament does not say whether a civil remedy is available or not, and the courts are left to decide what Parliament intended about a matter it did not mention.[12]

Even if it is clear that the commission of a crime has also created civil liability in the wrongdoer, the prospect of having to mount a separate action in a civil court may deter the victim from suing. In most continental legal systems the victim of a crime can attach his claim to the criminal prosecution. For example, someone involved in a collision between two cars through another's careless driving may have his claim in respect of his injuries and the damage to his car

12.   T. Weir *A Casebook on Tort* (5th edn, 1983) pp 149ff.

dealt with in the same proceedings as the criminal prosecution, and the court will give judgment on the claim at the same time as it decides the guilt or innocence of the accused. This procedure is very economical.

> 'All the legal consequences of a single transaction or occurrence are litigated in a single proceeding; one set of lawyers and one court suffice where there would otherwise be two. For the victim there is the further advantage that he may take a "free ride" of sorts on the prosecution case. Since the prosecutor must in any event investigate and present evidence to the court, the victim is spared having to cover the same ground in a separate civil action.'[13]

Procedure of this type is usual in France, where the victim has a choice of either bringing a separate action or intervening in a criminal prosecution as a 'civil party'. In the former case the civil action must wait until the criminal proceedings are over, so that contrary findings of fact are avoided. Where the proceedings are joined together, in all but the higher courts civil damages cannot be awarded unless the criminal prosecution succeeds.

In England, before 1972, it was hardly ever possible to use a criminal prosecution to obtain civil damages, and this meant that small claims, which did not justify the expense of a separate action, were in practice not enforceable. Now, however, a criminal court may make a compensation order of up to £400 against anyone convicted of an offence for any 'injury, loss or damage resulting from that offence', except where they arise from a road traffic offence.[14] Such a compensation order does not bar a separate civil action but any damages already awarded by the criminal court must be taken into account by the civil court.

The new rules about compensation orders, which may be made even when no compensation has actually been claimed, have had a quite dramatic effect on the way magistrates' courts dispose of cases of theft and criminal damage. At first the compensation order had to be subsidiary to the penalty. Magistrates, however, tend to look on such offences from the point of view of the victim, and try to ensure that he will get compensation for what he has suffered. In a period of economic recession, when the guilty party may well be unemployed or on short time working, the amount that he can be ordered to pay by weekly instalments is limited. Since magistrates are required, in imposing a fine, to take into account the means of the person on whom

13. J. H. Langbein *Comparative Criminal Procedure* p 111.
14. Now the Powers of Criminal Courts Act 1973, ss 35ff, on which see P. Atiyah, [1979] Crim LR 504.

it is imposed (Magistrates Courts Act 1980, s 35), an order to pay a fine and compensation cannot be made which will take several years to satisfy. As a result the compensation order was frequently much larger than the fine. As many offenders more readily recognise their obligation to compensate the person they have wronged than to pay a fine to the faceless 'them' who constitute the community, the logical next step was taken by the Criminal Justice Act 1982. It provides that a compensation order can be a sentence on its own. After a conviction a criminal court may 'dispose' of the case by ordering compensation to the victim of such an amount as it considers appropriate in the circumstances, without requiring strict proof of the value of the property lost or damaged or of the injury suffered. When it does that, and imposes no penalty, it performs a purely civil function.

Although criminal courts can now compensate as well as punish, they are confined to dealing with cases in which a crime has been proved to have been committed. They have no power to make declarations about the possible criminal effect of certain acts, nor can they issue injunctions to restrain the commission of crimes. The complexity of the modern law sometimes makes such warnings desirable but they raise procedural problems. Until 1972 only the Attorney-General, on behalf of the state, could apply to a civil court for an injunction to restrain a breach of the criminal law and the power was rarely used. In that year local authorities were given the power to bring such proceedings in the interests of local inhabitants and since then it has been widely used to stop practices which have been made criminal offences, especially by planning and public health legislation. The problem is that the defendant may be put into double jeopardy. If an injunction is issued and he ignores it, he can be punished by the civil court for contempt of court and also prosecuted for the offence in the criminal court. In civil proceedings proof is on a balance of probabilities whereas in a prosecution it must be beyond reasonable doubt. Furthermore, in a serious case the defendant in contempt proceedings would be deprived of his right to trial by jury. Thus criminal prosecution and civil action must remain distinct.

6 Written law and unwritten law

We have seen that when courts are first established they apply customs and practices generally accpted in the community which are handed down orally from one generation to another. Such practices are part of the distinctiveness of the nation, and contribute to its self-consciousness as a group, and so the groups of wise men charged with maintaining the continuity of the national tradition have a heavy responsibility.

When writing becomes available, the question arises whether the customary laws should be written down. Committing the laws to writing has certain consequences. It is useful to have a record of what is understood to be the law, so that reference can be made to it in any dispute. Before it is written the custom is usually declared only when the need arises and therefore any statement of it is coloured by the facts of the case which has created the need for the statement. Writing down the laws detaches the statement from the facts of any case and so makes it more generalised and abstract. The function of the wise men now changes. Instead of declaring the law in the light of a particular fact situation, and in terms that will resolve that situation, they now have to decide whether or not a rule previously declared in writing applies to the fact situation that has arisen. If they try to put forward an alternative formulation of the rule, it may be regarded as slanted to favour one or other of the parties, so that the formulation adopted in writing tends to become fixed and authoritative, even when the original writing was made privately by someone who had no special authority to do so. Unwritten law provided guidelines which the parties could follow in reaching a settlement or which the court could use in arriving at a judgment. But it allowed a good deal of flexibility and discretion which was restricted by the advent of writing. The parties can now insist on 'the letter of the law'.

The very existence of a text of the laws offers scope for analysis and interpretation which did not exist when the law was unwritten, and this fact encourages the growth of a new class of experts ready to advise litigants individually on the scope of the law. Previously the wise men gave their opinions anonymously as a body to the parties indifferently. Now individual professionals may give differing views to each party, suggesting how the law may be understood in the way that best favours them. The law tends to become more technical.

In some societies there is resistance to putting the laws in writing. When the laws have been taught formally by the older generation of an elite custodian group to the younger, the transmission itself has an educational function. This is lost when the laws are committed to writing to be consulted as occasion arises. The Hindu Brahmins in India opposed the writing of laws on the ground that people would have less incentive to learn them by heart and so would tend to become indolent. In European societies, on the other hand, as a result of the influence of Roman law, laws have usually been evidenced in writing at an early stage in their development.

Ancient Rome

The history of Roman law well illustrates the interaction of written and unwritten law. In the early Republic the citizen body was divided into two social groups, the patricians, a relatively small group of propertied families of noble birth, who enjoyed the dominant position in the state, and the plebeians, the have-nots, numerically larger but in various ways disadvantaged. The custodians of the traditional civil law were the pontiffs, the priests responsible for the maintenance of the state religious cult, and they were exclusively patrician.

Roman historians present the movement to have the laws written down as part of the struggle of the plebeians to gain equality of treatment with the patricians.[1] The pontiffs, as the authorities on custom and court procedure, were ready to pronounce on the validity or otherwise of particular acts and forms in individual cases. But in view of the pontiffs' social origins, the plebeians naturally suspected that such pronouncements were not always entirely disinterested. They argued that if the civil law could be written down in advance of cases, it would be to their advantage. In most situations they would then know what their legal position was without having to consult the pontiffs, whose powers of interpretation would be restricted by the text of the laws. The result of this plebeian agitation was the preparation of the collection of rules known as the Twelve Tables. It was then formally proposed to the popular assembly and approved.

When the assembly gave its approval to the magistrate's proposal, it had no sense that it was making new law to replace old law in the manner of modern legislation; rather it was establishing what was law.[2] Law (*ius*) was regarded as a set of customs and practices which

1.   Jolowicz, pp 108ff.
2.   P. Stein *Regulae iuris: from juristic rules to legal maxims* (1966) pp 4ff.

had existed from time immemorial but which were not fully revealed. When they were formally approved by the people, they became *lex* (from *legere*, to read out), but *lex* was not distinct from *ius*; it was the declaration and publication of what was *ius*. It was not until the later part of the Republic that the idea that the assembly could actually create new law made itself felt. In fact after the Twelve Tables there were very few republican enactments dealing with the law governing the relations of citizens.

For most of the Republic, the major part of *ius* remained unwritten in the sense that it was not stated in an accepted authoritative text generally applicable to all citizens. Individual citizens could establish law, just for themselves, by agreement and the same word, *lex*, was given both to a public declaration by the assembly, and to private agreements which fixed what was law as between the parties to them. In most cases, however, the law applicable to a given situation was left to be declared, after the event, in the course of litigation. A written record of such declarations might, of course, be kept, but the law so declared was not 'written law', since the text was in no way fixed and the same law could be reformulated in somewhat different terms in other cases. When the praetor granted an action he was implementing the existing law, and usually the action was based on well-recognised practice. But the praetor was entitled to grant an action whenever he thought there should be one and not just in everyday situations in which the law was well known. What if he conceded a formula in a situation in which the traditional law offered no guidance? Officially he was not making new law. His function was to declare the law (*ius dicere*) and he was merely granting a remedy to enforce what he took to be the law. In fact new remedies created new law, but since the new law was presented as an application of old law, the novelty was disguised.

When, however, the praetor promised in his edict that he would grant a remedy in certain circumstances, the law thus revealed became generalised. Each praetor was responsible for his own edict and it applied only during his year of office; but in practice the bulk of the edict was taken over by each praetor from his predecessor, and by the end of the Republic it had become stabilised. At that point, the edict had become written law in the sense that it was treated as an authoritative guide to what actions and defences were available, and as such was studied by jurists, when giving advice, with the same care that they devoted to the text of the Twelve Tables.

When the Republic gave way to the Empire, the emperors began to bring the means of law making under their control. The popular assemblies ceased to pass laws, and the praetorian edict was put into permanent form. The emperor could legislate directly by edict but his influence was greatest through rescripts, written answers given in his name to questions or petitions sent to him either by his own officials or by private citizens. Most of these rescripts were prepared by prominent jurists whom the emperor made members of his council. Their aim was to clarify the existing law rather than to make substantial changes but on occasion they would modify it to eliminate injustice. All statements of the law given in the emperor's name, imperial constitutions, were naturally authoritative and were collected and studied. Such legislation came to be called *lex*, since it took the place of the statutes enacted by the republican assemblies and had similar force.

Roman law reached its peak of technical development in the so-called classical period, roughly the first and second centuries AD. At this time, the written law included the enactments of republican assemblies, the praetorian edict and imperial constitutions, supplemented by private statements, found in contracts and testaments, of what was law for the parties in a given situation. The common feature of all these kinds of legal statement was that the resolution of any problem depended on the interpretation of a fixed text, and a number of specific techniques were developed for this purpose. Should the letter of the law prevail or the spirit? To what extent was the intention of the author decisive and how should that intention be discovered? Where the law was still in unwritten form, the jurists used a different technique. They had a freer hand in expounding those parts of the law which were accepted in general outline but were not formulated in a particular text.

Whether based on written *lex* or unwritten *ius*, Roman law was mainly developed by juristic debate and the jurists' opinions were collected together and published. Some of these opinions related to actual cases which had occurred in practice, but in the classical period the jurists increasingly engaged in teaching law and many of their reported opinions related to hypothetical sets of facts, devised in the schools for the purpose of fixing the exact scope of particular actions. The vitality of juristic debate in the early classical period was enhanced by the existence of two sects, the Proculians and the Sabinians.[3] The Sabinians tended to justify their decisions in the traditional way by an appeal to practice and to the authority of earlier jurists rather than by rational argument. They sought justice in the individual case even at the expense of logical consistency. When interpreting a text, they did not mind if the same words were given

3. P. Stein 'The two schools of jurists in the early Roman principate' (1972) 31 (1) CLJ (Jubilee Issue) 8; 'Logic and experience in Roman and Common Law' (1979) 59 Boston Univ LR 433; A. A. Schiller *Roman Law: mechanisms of development* (1978) pp 327ff.

one meaning in one text and a different meaning in another. The Proculians favoured strict interpretation of any text, whether of statute, contract or testament, insisting that the words must be given an objective meaning. They viewed the unwritten law as a coherent system of rules, logically related to each other. They looked for the rationale lying behind the detailed rules, with a view to extending the ambit of the rules by analogy. Whatever their affiliation, however, the Roman jurists did not favour broad general principles, not because they were unable to formulate them but because they did not consider them useful. They preferred cautiously to generalise the effect of their decisions, testing each reformulation of the rules by applying them to real or imaginary sets of facts. Their mode of reasoning was casuistic or 'problem-based'. Their development of the law relied on the comparison and distinction of fact-situations; but it did not depend on the actual adjudication of disputes nor did they cite judicial decisions. They paid great deference to the opinions of earlier jurists, but they did not hesitate to correct them when they considered that they were wrong.

The classical period ended in the third century AD and was followed by nearly three centuries of decline in the level of legal science. The formulary procedure gave way to the *cognitio* procedure, in which state-appointed judges had charge of the whole case. These judges, although 'professional', were of low technical competence and needed simple guides through the accumulations of imperial constitutions, now known collectively as *lex*, on the one hand, and of juristic writings, now known as *ius*, on the other. In the fifth century an official collection of constitutions, the Theodosian Code was issued and five of the later classical jurists, who had summarised the work of their predecessors, were picked out in a 'Law of Citations' as being specially worthy of respect.

In the later fifth century, the Roman Empire in the West was taken over by Germanic peoples who set up so-called 'barbarian kingdoms'. Like the Romans of the early Republic, they followed the personal principle in law and so did not at first apply their own Germanic customs to their Romanised subjects.[4] Certain of their kings provided basic collections of Roman legal materials for the use of those subjects, of which the most important was the Roman law of the Visigoths, published by Alaric II in 506. This was the main source of knowledge of Roman law in Western Europe in the early middle ages. It consists of selected constitutions from the Theodosian Code and some simplified summaries of classical jurists' works, and reflects the adaptation of the classical law to meet the practical needs of the Western provinces of the Empire.

4. Jolowicz, pp 466ff.

The Roman Empire of the East continued, largely Greek speaking, until 1453. In 527 Justinian became emperor and embarked on a programme to restore the ancient glory of the earlier Roman Empire. There had been a revival in the academic study of law in the Eastern law schools and he was able to order his minister, Tribonian, to organise a codification of the law, based on the classical law of three centuries earlier.[5] The most ambitious part of the work is the *Digest*, sometimes known by the Greek title *Pandects*, an anthology of extracts from the writings of various classical jurists, but especially the five identified in the Law of Citations. They are collected into titles, each title being devoted to a particular topic, and the titles arranged in 50 books. These extracts represent about a twentieth of the mass of writings used by the compilers, very little of which has survived except in the Digest. The compilers were told to head each fragment with an inscription giving its source, but at the same time they were to ensure that there was no obsolete matter, no contradictions and no repetitions in the work, and they could make such changes as were necessary to achieve these ends. Most of these 'interpolations' were probably made for purposes of abbreviation but their identification has been a major problem for scholars. Within each title there was little attempt to arrange the fragments in a coherent order.

The other main part of Justinian's compilation is the *Code*, a collection of imperial constitutions based on the Theodosian Code but with much later legislation, including many constitutions promulgated by Justinian himself to settle oustanding juristic disputes which the work on the Digest had brought to light. The constitutions are arranged in chronological order in titles, and the titles in 12 books. Although the Digest provided a summary of *ius* and the Code of *lex*, they were too difficult to put into the hands of students, and so Justinian ordered that they be supplemented by the *Institutes*, a students' manual in four books based on a second-century manual of the jurist Gaius (p 127). Justinian continued to issue constitutions until his death in 565, and these *Novels (novellae constitutiones)* were collected together and added to the other three parts of the codification to form what later came to be called the *Corpus Iuris Civilis*, the body of the civil law, by contrast with the canon law of the Church.

The material out of which the *Corpus Iuris* was fashioned was partly written law, the imperial constitutions, and partly unwritten, the discussions of the jurists, but the codification reduced it all to written law, and all parts (even the Institutes) were henceforth to have the same legal force. No reference was to be made to the earlier

5.   Jolowicz, pp 478ff; T. Honoré *Tribonian* (1978) pp 139ff.

authorities and commentaries were forbidden. Observing modestly that one who corrects what is not stated exactly deserves more praise than the original writer,[6] Justinian made the whole work his own and gave each part his authority.

When it was published, Justinian's codification made little impact, being largely inaccessible in the Latin speaking West and unintelligible in the Greek speaking East. By harking back to the classical law of three centuries earlier, much of it was ill-suited to the conditions of sixth-century Byzantium. Manuscripts survived, however, and 500 years later, in the eleventh century, it began to be studied in Italy, particularly at Bologna. Those who studied it, however, the Glossators, took little notice of the historical development of the material in it and treated it all as an imperial statute[7]. Despite the appalling arrangement of the Digest, they made themselves familiar with all of the texts, and attempted to reconcile the contradictions which they contained, despite Justinian's assurances to the contrary. In doing so they treated the texts as sacrosanct and applied to their interpretation techniques similar to those used in relation to the texts of Holy Scripture. In the later middle ages Justinian's law became 'the written law' par excellence. But it was written with an air of detachment from the needs of contemporary practice. The classical jurists had placed an indelible academic stamp on Roman law, and this feature was maintained both by Justinian's compilers, of whom the most active were professors from the thriving law schools in Beyrout and Byzantium, and by the professors at Bologna. The texts could not in fact be of practical use without the aid of the glosses and commentaries which explained them. Indeed, the Great Gloss to all parts of *Corpus Iuris*, produced by the Bolognese teacher Accursius in the first half of the thirteenth century, acquired equal authority with that of the texts themselves. 'What the Gloss does not recognise the court does not recognise' became a legal maxim.

Medieval continental Europe

In the early middle ages many efforts were made to record the customs of the various Germanic peoples in writing. The initiative usually came from the king and the purpose was to give the community greater certainty in the application of the traditional law. A written record of the custom provided unequivocal evidence of what the law was. It gave precision to matters which had formerly

6. Introductory Constitution *Deo Auctore*, 6.
7. Dawson *Oracles* pp 124ff.

been left to the discretion of the lay judges in the local courts and saved them from unwelcome influences. When the rules on such matters as *wergild* and payment for wrongs were stated categorically in a written text, the court could resist pressure to declare the law in terms which favoured one party by citing its duty to obey the text.

Often these early written collections of customary law record the steps taken to ascertain that law and their subsequent approval by the popular assemblies.[8] The prologue to the Salic Law (of the Salian Franks) states that four chosen men discussed the original practices in particular situations with the presidents of the local folk-moots and then collected them together to be presented to the general moot. Since they were the product of agreement between the king and all the people, such compilations were sometimes described as agreements, as in the *pactus legis Salicae*. Gradually, however, as their authority became more secure, the Germanic kings claimed the power to legislate unilaterally in the name of the people as a whole. But the law that they enacted still purported to be a correct statement of what had always been the law, although previously not correctly declared. Many such laws are attributed to a particular ruler, in order to attract the authority of his name, but in fact contain material found in similar collections from other nations. There was a common stock of rules dealing with such matters as *wergild* or right of asylum, and the compilers of one nation's customs had little hesitation in borrowing from another's collection if they found what seemed to be an appropriate statement of what their law ought to be and therefore what it should be stated to be.

As long as the Germanic peoples still adhered to the personal principle in law, each set of their customs applied only to those who belonged to a particular nation. As they were usually written in Latin, many of the terms that were used already had a technical meaning in relation to Roman law and some of that meaning was taken over into the interpretation of the customs.

In the later middle ages the personal principle was abandoned. Where peoples of different racial origin had become settled in a particular area, a territorial customary law, based on the dominant tribal law of the area, was applied by the local courts of freeholders, or the *Schöffen* who represented them, to all those resident in the area, irrespective of their nation. The rise of the feudal system turned many freemen into vassals of the most powerful local magnate, who became their lord (p 164). Each lord held a court for his tenants in which he applied the same law irrespective of their origins.

8. E. Jenks *Law and Politics in the Middle Ages* (1919) pp 7ff. C. C. Turpin 'The Antecedents of Roman-Dutch Law: an historical survey' [1963] Acta Juridica 5ff.

Knowledge of Justinian's *Corpus Iuris,* expounded by the Glossators of Bologna, was becoming widespread, even in Northern Europe. If local law did not offer any guidance on any problem, there was a tendency, among those who knew Latin, to turn to the only available body of law that could assist them, so that it became a common residuary law for the whole of Europe. In Germany and Northern Italy recourse to Roman law was sometimes justified on the ground that Charlemagne, in setting up the Holy Roman Empire, made himself and his successors the heirs of the old Roman emperors, so that Roman law was applicable by virtue of its authority as imperial law. But more and more the justification for referring to it was less its formal authority in relation to the Holy Roman Empire and more its technical superiority in substance over any possible rival. Its doctrines were regarded as the only rational ones – 'reason in writing'. It was the only secular law taught in European universities, alongside the canon law of the Church, from which it was distinguished as the 'civil law'. Consequently a university trained lawyer was of necessity a Roman lawyer, and the learned lawyers of all countries shared a common legal culture based on it. The only possible rival to the civil law, as a general secular law, was the feudal land law. The standard collection of feudal customs, the Books of Feus (*Libri Feudorum*), was made by Italian scholars in the twelfth century and the civil lawyers carried out a neat takeover by incorporating them into the *Corpus Iuris* by adding them to the Novels.

The movement by which the civil law largely superseded the local laws and became a kind of common law for all the countries of Europe, except England and Scandinavia, is known as the Reception. It took different forms and occurred at different times from country to country, but always it was associated with the development of a learned legal profession and courts of professional judges.

From the thirteenth century onwards there was continuous interaction in most European countries between the customary law and Roman law, which was variously called the written law, the imperial law, the common law (*ius commune*) or the civil law. The Italian city states recorded their individual local laws in a series of compilations, usually distinguishing customs, deriving originally from oral tradition, and *statuta*, legislative enactments of the local assembly. The Glossators, who were the first to comment on Justinian's law, had held that such local laws must yield before the Roman law, which was common law for the whole Empire, and if there was a conflict, the latter should prevail. However, the cities insisted on being masters of their own legal destinies, and maintained that a specific custom or statute must override the

Roman law. For, as one local law put it, 'human nature constantly expresses itself in new forms and more situations occur than are covered by the words of the written law'.

The Commentators, who succeeded the Glossators as authoritative exponents of the written law, were more concerned to adapt it to the needs of the time and accepted this view. Their leading figure, Bartolus, justified his modification of the previous position by reference to a Digest text (D.1.3.32), in which the jurist Julian explains why local custom is law (although in Roman doctrine this could only be where there was *no* general rule to the contrary).[9] Julian says that written laws bind us because they have been accepted by the people; so it follows that those things which the people have approved without any writing will also bind us. For what does it matter whether the people declare their will by express vote or by conduct? Finally the text asserts that written laws may be abrogated not only by vote of the legislator but also by the tacit consent of everyone through 'desuetude', in effect, by their taking no notice of it. Although Bartolus was prepared to reverse the Roman position and allow an express local law to override the imperial law, he gained acceptance for the principle that a local statute must be interpreted according to the *ius commune*. Since the imperial law was generally applicable, the local laws were given as narrow an application as was consistent with their language.

In France, the southern part, known as the country of the written law, *pays de droit écrit,* already recognised the barbarised 'Roman law of the Visigoths' as the main element in its regional customs and the new learning derived from Bologna was readily received to supplement those customs when they were lacking. In the north, the *pays de droit coutumier,* Germanic custom prevailed, but here also the lawyers were prepared to cite a rule of Roman law as a source of general legal wisdom, often not in its original sense, but in order to confirm or to prove some opinion of their own.

In Northern Europe there were no official collections of local laws on the Italian model until the sixteenth century, but in the thirteenth century private individuals, usually judges, made efforts to reduce the laws applied in the courts with which they were concerned to some kind of order. About 1280 Phillipe de Beaumanoir, *bailli,* or judge, of the Count of Clermont's court in Beauvaisis, wrote an account of the Custom of Beauvaisis.[10] Although written without any special authority, it was widely read in other regions by those

9.   P. Stein 'Bartolus, the Conflict of Laws and the Roman Law' *Multum non Multa: Festschrift für Kurt Lipstein* (1980) p 254; Schiller *Roman Law* p 560, n 3; Dawson *Oracles* p 128.
10.   P. Vinogradoff *Roman Law in Medieval Europe* (2nd edn, 1929, repr 1968) pp 80ff.

seeking a reliable guide through the wilderness of local customs. Although he does not include any substantive rules of Roman law, Beaumanoir is clearly influenced by the technical terms and notions of Roman law, which he uses as a kind of cement to bind together the slabs of customary law.

In the absence of such an account, the content of any custom whose scope was disputed had to be discovered by a local inquiry, or inquest (*enquête par turbe*). Since this was time consuming and expensive, the French kings in the mid-fifteenth century ordered the recording of all local customs. The procedure devised for this proved very successful.[11] It combined the three elements of royal authority, professional expertise and popular acceptance. The introduction of the written Romano-canonical procedure had produced a class of trained lawyers. The king's government, having determined to attain its goal, was able to send professional lawyers, usually members of the Parlements, to preside as royal commissioners over meetings of the local assemblies called for the purpose of codifying the customs. The assemblies determined the content of the customs and approved their formulation in detail. Since the customs were submitted to critical scrutiny, the opportunity was taken to reform any rule which appeared to be working unfairly. As discussions became more technical, the professional lawyers, both the presiding commissioners and lawyers who belonged to the assemblies, tended to take control of the proceedings and dictate the final outcome.

In Germany, a loose confederation of principalities and free cities, there was no comparable movement for codifying the local customs, which were established, as required, by group inquests (*Weistümer*), similar to those used earlier in France. Neither the royal concern for codification nor the professional expertise that ensured its achievement in France was present in Germany. The German rulers did not have the political authority of the French king. Power was ostensibly divided between the Holy Roman Emperor, whose court, the *Reichskammergericht*, formally adopted the Roman law of the Italian Commentators in 1495, and local princelings still in the process of establishing their independence. The *Schöffen* courts had used an informal oral procedure which had not fostered a professional class, and most of the professional lawyers in Germany were churchmen concerned primarily with canon law. Where the matter was too technical for the *Schöffen*, the parties tended to submit it to arbitration by such churchmen.

The result of these differences between France and Germany was that whereas the Reception of Roman law in France was a gradual

---

11.   J. P. Dawson 'The Codification of the French Customs' (1939) 38 Michigan LR 765.

and voluntary process extending over several centuries and was prevented by the codification of the customs from becoming too great, the Reception in Germany was relatively sudden and dramatic. In the large centres of population during a short period around 1500, professional judges, produced by the newly-established universities and ready to apply Roman law, took over much of the work that had been done by the *Schöffen* or by arbitrators.[12] The demand for a technically superior law and a written procedure seems to have come from litigants, particularly from prosperous middle class citizens, and the change produced protests from the 'lower orders', who equated the technical language of Roman law with chicanerie. The *Schöffen* courts had been in the habit of asking advice from a few superior courts of great prestige and this deference to expert authority continued with the practice, adopted by the professional courts, of seeking opinions on points of law thrown up in litigation from university law faculties. Thus the written law increasingly ousted the Germanic customs and became the common law (*gemeines Recht*) of German-speaking states.

Medieval England

At the Norman conquest England, like other European countries, had many local customs applied by local courts, but the success of the Norman kings in establishing the authority of their government and of their courts was not paralleled in other countries. Because of the superiority of the procedure of these courts, and of the enforcement of royal writs, litigants were attracted to them rather than to local courts. Their writs were available to anyone, whether of Norman or of Saxon stock, and no matter where they happened to live. The judges traversed the country to hear cases locally as well as in Westminster. It was thus in the jurisdiction of the royal courts that the common law of England was founded.

The substance of that law was created by the judges of the royal courts through their decisions. Until the fourteenth century these judges were often clerics who made a career in the royal service. It was usual to appoint new judges from those who had served as clerks to earlier judges, and so the judges of the royal courts were professionals. Their clerical training had given them some knowledge of canon and civil law which they used to eke out the deficiencies of the English customs. The victory of the national law thus created over the local customs was gradual. The king's courts

---

12.   Dawson *Oracles* p 180; W. Kunkel 'The Reception of Roman Law in Germany: an interpretation' in G. Strauss (ed) *Pre-reformation Germany* (1972) ch 7.

applied their own common law unless it was proved that a local custom governed the matter, but as late as the end of the fourteenth century, a defendant in the court of Common Pleas could argue that the common law did not apply to his case since it was covered by the custom of the small Yorkshire town of Selby.

The first literary exponents of the law were judges or royal officials. Two early treatises 'on the laws and customs of England' (*De legibus et consuetudinibus Angliae*) were produced in the late twelfth and early thirteenth century. The earlier, written by or in the name of Ranulf de Glanvill, is in effect a commentary on the main forms of writ used in the king's courts. The later, bearing the name of Henry de Bracton, had the same aim as the roughly contemporary work of de Beaumanoir in France. It is however a more elaborate work, based on the writs and making considerable use of cases decided in the king's court, but also incorporating a good deal of the Roman law of the Glossators. Bracton could have set out the writs and the relevant case law without the help of the general notions that were articulated in Roman law. But then the work would have had little structure and would have been less widely understood. Furthermore one of his aims was to persuade foreigners that, despite its outlandish appearance, English law had an internal rationality comparable to that of other countries' laws. The defensive attitude adopted by Bracton, and by Glanvill before him, suggests that certain clerics, familiar with the new Roman law coming out of Bologna, had been sneering at the presumption of English lawyers in claiming that their law was worthy of comparison with the authoritative texts of the *Corpus Iuris*. It is true, they admit, that almost all countries respect the written law and only England uses unwritten custom. But it will not be absurd to use the term 'laws' for that custom, even though it is not declared in authoritative texts.

The common law was not declared only in the context of litigation. The Norman and Angevin kings enacted a series of laws, known variously as Assises, Constitutions and Provisions, with a view to establishing what was law.[13] The judges of the king's courts, through their attachment to the royal council, often drafted such laws for emission in the king's name, and drew no distinction between a declaration of law applicable to the parties in a case, with which they were concerned judicially, and a more general statement of the law for a wider audience, which was formally circulated throughout the kingdom. The text of these laws had not been debated and discussed in a parliament or assembly and the judges felt free to give effect to them according to their personal knowledge of what the king's council had intended.

13. Baker, pp 177ff.

In the later middle ages the character of such enactments changed and statutes, as they are now called, came to be expressed as the product of a tripartite co-operation of King, Lords and Commons and required the concurrence of all three parties to be valid. The judges were no longer associated with the making of the statutes and a distinction gradually appeared between making the law, the function of Parliament, and adjudication, the function of the judges. The judges began to pay strict attention to the text of statutes, so that they should interfere as little as possible with the ancient practices that constituted 'the common law'. That phrase acquired the connotation of unwritten law of customary origin, by contrast with the written law of the statutes. Parliament made new law and abrogated old law; the judges declared what in theory had always been the law.

In the fourteenth and fifteenth centuries the common law of the king's courts became increasingly rigid and technical. The judges no longer included ecclesiastics, with a knowledge of other systems of law. They were now appointed by the king from the ranks of those who practised in the courts for a living. The records of the pleadings and decisions were contained in the plea rolls preserved by the clerks of the courts and lawyers kept a note of useful precedents to cite to a court in a similar case in the future. But the plea rolls gave no hint of the arguments on issues raised by the pleadings or the grounds for the decisions. From the end of the thirteenth century, unofficial notes began to circulate of the oral debates between judges and the professional advocates, which were conducted in Norman French, with a view to providing students of law and practitioners with a knowledge of forensic tactics. By studying these so-called 'year-books', they could learn 'the possible moves in the recondite games of legal chess played by the pleaders in open court'.[14] The plea rolls and the year-books provided written evidence of the common law, but it remained unwritten law in the absence of any fixed statement.

The professional practitioners of the common law organised themselves in Inns of Court, originally hostels in which they could enjoy a collegiate life, but which came to accept responsibility for educating aspirants to the Bar in the rudiments of the law. It was the systematic exposition of the common law in the four Inns of Court, under the control of professional practitioners, that distinguished it from the regional customary laws of the continent. Since Oxford and Cambridge, the only English universities, followed the general pattern of continental universities and taught only the Roman civil law until the eighteenth century (and the canon law until the Reformation), the Inns of Court effectively formed a legal university which became the centre of a flourishing cultural life in London.

14.   Baker, p 153.

The teaching of the common law there gave it a greater scientific structure than any of the other Germanic customary laws.

At the end of the middle ages England had national courts, with professional judges and a well-established procedure ensuring lay participation, and a highly technical body of national law developed by an insular but learned profession. It is true that the common law was limited in its scope and in the range of remedies that it offered but it had been supplemented by the body of rules known as equity, administered by the Court of Chancery. This court had no juries; its professional judges were prepared to receive evidence by written deposition and favoured a written procedure not unlike the Romano-canonical procedure, with an appeal structure. It functioned in the areas where the common law was ill-suited to operate – supervising the accounts of those, such as guardians, who looked after the interests of others, compelling parties to carry out certain types of agreements, interpreting settlements of land. Although at first guided by conscience rather than law, the Chancery judges adopted many ideas, for example, principles of inter-pretation, from the civil law (pp 46–7).

England was not immune to the civil law but needed less of it than other countries. Elsewhere national states set up professional courts to take over important business from the local courts. These courts universally adopted a variant of the Romano-canonical procedure, but they only adopted the substantive civil law to the extent that the existing law was inadequate for modern needs. Scotland provides an example. At the beginning of the sixteenth century it had a customary law of Germanic origin similar to that of England but less developed. The King's Council had spawned no regular professional court and there was no guild of professional lawyers to foster the study of the law. A permanent central court with professional judges, the Court of Session, was set up in 1532, and it followed the usual continental pattern by adopting the written Romano-canonical procedure. As far as possible it applied traditional Scots law but where that law offered no guidance, the professional lawyers turned to the *ius commune*, both in litigation and in legislation.[15] An Act of the Scots Parliament in 1583 (cap. 98) refers to a civil law rule as 'the disposition of the common law', and Lord Stair, the first great expositor of Scots law, recognised that the civil law was a common law as 'in some sort common to many nations', and stressed that it was 'not acknowledged as a law binding for its authority, yet being, as a rule, followed for its equity'.[16]

---

15. P. Stein 'The influence of Roman Law on the Law of Scotland' [1963] Juridical Rev 205.
16. *Institutions of the Law of Scotland* (1681) I. 1.11,12.

It is sometimes suggested that the civil law was imposed by princes who saw Justinian's law, with its emphasis on the legislative powers of the monarch, as an expression of the superiority of the state over local interests. Certainly a written law that contained such statements as 'the will of the prince has the force of law'[17] could hardly be anathema to princes. But the law that was received was the detailed private law and there was, in fact, no other accessible body of law which could provide answers to the problems that the courts were now facing, when the customary law was lacking.

7 Case law, statute and codification

England

At the end of the middle ages, Roman law was replacing the local customary law in most European countries, its reception being in inverse proportion to the strength of the local law. In England alone the customary law had become a common law for the whole country; it was expounded by a small, elite group of professional judges, with a strong sense of their duty to develop the law in a manner in keeping with its traditions, and it had received some systematic structure through the teaching in the Inns of Court. The influence of Roman law in England was therefore confined to the Church courts, which dealt with questions of status, marriage and succession to movables (p 135), the Court of Admiralty, which dealt with maritime matters, and to some extent the Court of Chancery.

The English common law, not being formulated in fixed texts, was necessarily declared only when the occasion required, which was in the course of litigation, and so it was essentially case law. Every legal system has case law in the sense that the scope of the rules is illustrated by their application to sets of facts, real or imaginary, and a record of such application is of value in forecasting how the rules are likely to be applied in similar cases in the future. But in those systems which have little written law in the form of authoritative statements of general rules, declarations of the rules relevant to particular cases are of greater importance, since they constitute the principal means by which the law is declared. The medieval year-books record many discussions and arguments in the royal courts between the judges and the bar on precisely what was the law on particular topics and they demonstrate a common desire to hammer out agreement on the rules, and a reluctance to make decisions until such agreement has been obtained. The judges did not see their function as the imposition of their view of the law, but rather as leadership in a joint enterprise of discovery. The records of such debates constituted evidence of what was the law but no more.

From the sixteenth century onwards, there was increasing emphasis on the precedential value of the actual decisions reached by the courts. Where the law is still in a formative stage there are dangers in requiring that precedents be followed in later cases, for the later judge is absolved from having to work out the law for himself. Philippe de Beaumanoir in thirteenth-century France argued that a judge who had participated in the decision of a case should be barred from ruling in a similar case in the future, on the ground that he would be biased in favour of his earlier ruling.[1] On the other hand, when the law becomes established, justice requires that similar cases should be decided in the same way. When a judge follows an earlier decision, he may do so from laziness, or from lack of confidence in his own opinion, or from a desire to please his superiors in the judicial hierarchy; or he may feel that he is under an obligation to follow previous decisions. The special feature of the English doctrine of precedent is that it came to have a strongly coercive character.[2] The judges came to accept that they had to follow the decisions reached in earlier cases, whatever their own feelings on the matter. Before such a strict doctrine of precedent could operate, however, it was necessary to have a regular hierarchy of courts and a reliable system of reporting important decisions, and these two conditions were not satisfied until the mid-nineteenth century. Until then the position had for long been as described by William Blackstone in the eighteenth century, when he declared it to be 'an established rule to abide by former precedents', unless they were 'contrary to reason', or 'flatly absurd and unjust'.[3] Such was the state of the privately produced law reports in Blackstone's day that there must have been many decisions which, as they were reported, were flatly absurd or unjust. In the interests of consistency and certainty and predictability, it was agreed that earlier decisions ought generally to be followed, but the strength of the obligation left some discretion to the judges.

The establishment of a semi-official series of law reports in 1865 improved the standard of reporting and the Judicature Acts of 1973–75 reorganised the courts into three tiers, the High Court, with a single judge, the Court of Appeal, with usually three judges, and the House of Lords, where cases are usually heard by five judicial Lords. The late nineteenth century saw the recognition of the doctrine, known as *stare decisis*, that even a single decision has a binding force in later cases. Not only did the decisions of higher courts bind lower courts but the Court of Appeal and House of Lords decided that they were respectively bound by their own previous decisions. This was a rule which the judges imposed on themselves, on the ground that changes in the law should not be

---

1. *La coutume de Beauvaisis* s 1880, cited by Dawson *Oracles* p xv.
2. R. Cross *Precedent in English Law* (2nd edn, 1968) pp 19ff.
3. I *Commentaries on the Laws of England* 69; C. K. Allen *Law in the Making* (7th edn, 1964) p 229.

made by judges but should be left to legislation by Parliament. In practice it is difficult to find time for piece-meal changes in the law by statute, especially in the more technical parts of the law that lack popular appeal. So in 1966 the House of Lords announced that while in general it would continue to treat past decisions as binding, it would in particular cases feel free to depart from a past decision when it thought it right to do so.[4]

The idea that the law is essentially custom reposing 'in the bosom of the judges', and waiting to be declared by them, can produce two contrasting lines of thought. On the one hand, customary law can be treated as something which has constantly been preserved unchanged as part of the national heritage. This view was set out by the seventeenth-century Chief Justice, Sir Edward Coke, in his Institutes. A master of year-book learning, he assumed that the common law was the only law that had ever prevailed in England, that it was law because it was immemorial custom and that it constituted an 'artificial reason' which only the judges were qualified to expound. One of Coke's contemporaries, Sir John Davies, argued that the common law was 'so framed and fitted to the nature and disposition of this people as we may properly say it is connatural to the nation, so as it cannot possibly be ruled by any other law'.[5] On the other hand, customary law can be regarded as something which – just because it is not formulated in fixed texts – is capable of being adapted to new social conditions more readily than the law set out in written form. This flexibility of the common law has been proclaimed by a number of reformist judges, of whom Lord Mansfield in the eighteenth century and Lord Denning in the twentieth are perhaps the most prominent.

Up to a point the two views can be reconciled by the use of certain techniques of handling precedents. Whether or not an earlier decision is a precedent is decided by the judge in the later case, and it will only be a precedent for him when the 'material facts' of the two cases are the same.[6] When they are different the earlier case is not binding on the judge in the later case, so that if he finds a relevant difference in the facts of the two cases, he can 'distinguish' the earlier decision, and so ignore it. The finding of similarity and difference in the material facts is thus the key step in the development of a rule at common law. When he wants to widen the scope of a rule applied in an earlier case, the later judge will treat as 'not material' some fact which the earlier judges thought to be important; when he wants to narrow the rule, he will emphasise some fact in the earlier case which was considered unimportant by the judges in that case.

4. *Practice Statement* [1966] WLR 1234.
5. Preface to *Irish Reports* (1612).
6. E. H. Levi *An introduction to legal reasoning* (1949).

Assuming that the facts of the two cases are similar, the judge in the later case must decide what was the rule which emerges from the earlier decision.[7] He must take account of the reasons adduced by the earlier judges but he must decide for himself what is the *ratio decidendi*, or binding rule, of the earlier case, and he may ignore *obiter dicta*, incidental comments on the law made by the judges which were not necessary for their decision. The earlier judges' statement of the rule that they are applying is not necessarily the *ratio decidendi*. In appellate courts it frequently happens that the judges, even when not dissenting, give separate judgments with different reasons for coming to their decision. So the later judge has to formulate a rule wide enough to cover both his case and the earlier case, knowing that his statement will itself be subject to reformulation in a subsequent case. Such statements are usually couched in narrow categories just wide enough to turn the particular decision into a rule. Thus the individual defendant who has been held liable may become 'a manufacturer of products', or 'a seller of goods' or 'an occupier of premises'.

When a common law rule is modified by judicial reformulation, it is accepted that the judges are making new law. But in theory they are merely declaring what has always been the law, although nobody recognised it. They declare not only what will be law for the future but also what was law in the past. As Sir Henry Maine put it in 1861:

> 'When a group of facts come before an English Court for adjudication, the whole course of the discussion between the judge and the advocate assumes that no question is, or can be, raised which will call for the application of any principles but old ones . . . It is taken absolutely for granted that there is somewhere a rule of known law which will cover the facts of the dispute now litigated, and that, if such a rule be not discovered, it is only that the necessary patience, knowledge, or acumen is not forthcoming to detect it. Yet the moment the judgement has been rendered and reported, we slide unconsciously . . . into a new language and a new train of thought. We now admit that the new decision *has* modified the law.'[8]

In reviewing a line of earlier decisions in search of the appropriate rule to apply in the case before him, the judge will tend to discuss them chronologically so as to present the rule as being gradually revealed through successive decisions, as if a cover under which the rule has been lurking has been bit by bit removed.

When a higher court overrules a decision of a lower court which

7. R. W. M. Dias *Jurisprudence* (4th edn, 1976) pp 181ff.
8. *Ancient Law* ch 2 (Everyman edn, p 19).

has been generally accepted as representing the law, judges do not say that they are changing the rule; they say that the earlier case was wrongly decided. It follows that all cases decided in accordance with the earlier decisions have also been wrongly decided. If it were not for procedural rules which restrict the time within which appeals are possible, this theory would be very inconvenient.[9] In certain areas of law, such as claims for personal injury or damage to property, no harm is done. But where property rights are involved it does not work well, because transactions will have been carried out on the assumption that the earlier decision was correct, and if it is now treated as incorrect, the validity of those transactions will be thrown in doubt, and many people who justifiably thought that they were entitled to property may find that they are not. In such situations, therefore, higher courts will very rarely overrule earlier decisions of which they disapprove, and merely recommend that Parliament change the law for the future by statute. The United States Supreme Court has assumed the power of doing what the House of Lords will not do, namely, to overrule earlier decisions prospectively only, thus sacrificing theory for convenience.

The growth of statute law

The common law, having grown up from case to case by a cautious testing of analogies and by statements made as the occasion arose, has never been promulgated as a system. Common lawyers do not believe in anticipating future cases and decide only what is immediately necessary. They recognise the difficulty of precisely formulating general principles and prefer to appeal to the authority of past examples rather than engage in abstract reasoning. Sometimes, however, a general rule is required to introduce a change in the law or to lay down a simpler or more general set of rules than those that have emerged from the cases. This is done by legislation. In medieval times there was no sharp distinction between the legislative functions and the judicial functions of the king's council, and statements of law in statutory form, emanating from the council as a whole, were treated no differently from statements made by the judges of the council in the course of an oral debate in court. It was when Parliament came into its own as the source of new law under the Tudors that legislation in the modern sense began. There was a dramatic increase in the amount of statutes enacted by the King in Parliament, most of them proposed by the king's government and accepted in some form or other by the Lords and Commons. This

9. P. Stein and J. Shand *Legal Values in Western Society* (1974) p 41.

parliamentary supremacy in law-making was forcibly expressed in the statutes which imposed the Reformation on the country. 'The changes wrought by Parliament in the Tudor period were no more significant than those effected by the courts, but they were definitely seen as changes, the work of humanist legislators confident in their ability to improve things by the right use of power.'[10]

Some judges were reluctant to admit that it was their duty to give effect to whatever Parliament laid down, however misguided it might appear, and Coke went so far as to claim that 'the common law will control acts of parliament and sometimes adjudge them to be utterly void',[11] if, for example, they were contrary to reason or impossible to be performed. However this view was decisively rejected and the judges came to accept that they had to apply what Parliament had formally enacted in a statute, however repugnant it might be to them, and that only Parliament could change what was contained in such a statute. The limitations on the powers of the king, which followed the Glorious Revolution of 1688, and the replacement of James II by William and Mary, enhanced the position of Parliament. The common lawyers had supported Parliament in its opposition to the royal claims, which precipitated the Revolution, and they had to accept the result and acknowledge the supremacy of Parliament. Legal theorists were making a sharp distinction between the legislative and the judicial functions in the state and it now appeared to be improper for the judges to usurp the functions of the legislature by doing anything with its enactments but obediently apply them.

For nearly a century and a half after 1688 Parliament, in fact, made little effort to legislate in the matters which were of prime concern to the courts and left the common law and its procedures relatively untouched. In the second quarter of the nineteenth century, however, Parliament, now itself reformed to become a more representative body, began a sustained bout of legislation, much of which was designed to do away with some of the more antiquated features of the common law, no longer useful but still cherished by lawyers. Until then 'the law' had been thought of as essentially the common law declared by the judges. Parliament could certainly change it but the judges had treated statutes as exceptional and assumed that Parliament intended their impact on the traditional doctrines to be as small as possible. Now, as a result largely of the writings of Jeremy Bentham, 'the law' came to be thought to be essentially what the legislature ordained. Bentham totally rejected the traditional view enshrined in the works of Blackstone, that the

10.   Baker, p 180.
11.   *Dr Bonham's Case* (1610) 8 Co Rep 114 at 118.

common law as expounded by the judges was the perfection of reason; for him it was imaginary law made up by the judges, indeed dog law: 'When your dog does anything you want to break him of, you wait till he does it and then beat him for it . . . this is the way the judges make law for you and me.'[12] Through Bentham's influence, reform through legislation became the order of the day, and the judges were faced with a series of statutes making radical changes in what they had considered to be the foundations on which the common law had stood for centuries.

For the last century and a half statutes have been used to achieve a number of aims that, in practice, could not have been attained in any other way. They establish new courts and new procedures to remedy grievances that were previously not adequately dealt with; they confer benefits on some groups and subject others to burdens such as taxes; they establish regulatory agencies to control particular kinds of activity. The bulk of them are concerned with public bodies and their powers, and only a small fraction deal with the traditional criminal law and private law. The government has always played the major part both in initiating and in planning the content of legislation and the role of the two Houses of Parliament has been to refine the details and point out difficulties in what the government proposes. Increasingly, as party discipline has become tighter, the government in office has come to rely on achieving its aims, and Parliament merely legitimates what the government has proposed. But all legislation requires interpretation, and when the meaning of a statutory provision is disputed only the courts can give an authoritative interpretation.

The function of a judge in such cases is to give effect to the intention of Parliament as expressed in the words of the statute. If the words used clearly apply to the facts of the case, the court must apply them, whatever the result. Equally if the words cannot be given a meaning, which it is known from other evidence was Parliament's intention, the courts may not give effect to that intention. It is therefore vital that statutes should be drafted in such a way that the words used do reflect that intention. Much of the expertise of the government draftsmen, the Parliamentary Counsel, is devoted to ensuring that statutes have the desired effect and no other effect. In the past there was much mutual suspicion between Parliament and the courts over the application of statutes to particular cases, Parliament accusing the courts of perversely twisting its clear statements and the courts replying that with such slovenly expressions of intention it was impossible to know what Parliament would have intended about a situation it probably never contemplated.

12. *Works* (ed J. Bowring, 1843) V. 235.

The courts have developed certain principles of interpretation to justify their preference for attributing one meaning rather than another to statutory texts.[13] One of the oldest is the so-called mischief rule which allows the court to interpret a text in such a way that it will be effective against the mischief which it was designed to suppress.[14] The mischief is to be discovered from the statute as a whole but the judges are not allowed openly to refer to other evidence of Parliament's intention, such as what was said in the debates on the Bill which became the Act in question. But this mischief rule was traditionally applied only if the words of the statute did not clearly apply to the facts of the case. For the courts have always preferred to apply the literal meaning of the words used, since they saw their role in relation to statutes as much more mechanical than their function in dealing with prior decisions. In view of the fact that the bulk of a judge's work now involves the consideration of statutes, the judges have come to accept that they should pay more attention than they have done to the aims and purposes of a statute in relation to its social background and in relation to the rest of the law. They may, for example, look at the reports of commissions on which the statute was based in order to discover more about its purposes than emerges from the statutory text itself. Although the courts are still not as much at home with statutes as with cases, the doctrine of precedent is as applicable to statute law as to case law and lower courts are bound to follow the meaning attributed by a higher court to a word or phrase in a statute when that meaning is raised as an issue in a subsequent case. It is admitted, however, that words do not necessarily have precisely the same meaning in every context, so that a judicial interpretation of a word in one statute does not have to be adopted when it occurs in other statutes.

No legislature can foresee all possible sets of facts that may arise in the future. A method of drafting which attempts to detail all the situations which a rule is intended to cover is much more likely to leave a *casus omissus* than a method which attempts to formulate a broader rule. On the other hand such a rule, being expressed briefly in general terms, although it may be clearer and may cover cases that the legislature did not contemplate as well as those that it had in mind, is likely to be less precise. It seems that clarity can be achieved only at the expense of precision and precision can be achieved only at the expense of clarity. A general rule leaves more discretion to the judge who applies it than a narrow one and traditionally the draftsmen have tried to reduce judicial discretion. In the past the existence

13.   D. R. Miers and A. C. Page *Legislation* (1982) pp 176ff.
14.   *Heydon's Case* (1584) 3 Co Rep 7.

of discretion in the application of the common law has been masked partly by the fact that final decisions were actually made by lay juries and partly by the doctrine of precedent which the judges imposed on themselves.

The gradual accumulation of reported cases and of detailed statutes led to great complexity in the law. In 1965 the government of the day pointed out that the English law then in force was contained in 3,000 Acts of Parliament and over 300,000 reported cases. As a result it was difficult for anyone without special training to discover just what was the law on a given topic. The Lord Chancellor argued that 'English law should be capable of being recast in a form which is accessible, intelligible and in accordance with modern needs'.[15] So Parliament established the Law Commission, an official body charged with the responsibility of tidying up the statute law by consolidating a series of Acts into a more coherent form, of suggesting reforms of both statute law and common law, where appropriate, and of codifying sections of the law. The aim is ultimately to transform English law from a system of law that is essentially unwritten to a system of written law, but it is accepted that the process will be a long one. Before that process can be accelerated, the practice of detailed drafting, which makes English statutes so difficult for the layman to understand, must be modified by the adoption of broader and more general rules. Only then will the judges be able to adapt a statutory rule to new social and economic needs without the need for continuous amendment of the rule by Parliament itself. But before that can happen, the draftsmen must come to trust the courts to apply the law less restrictively. Both draftsmen and judges may learn something from the practice of civil law countries.[16]

Continental Europe

By the sixteenth century the national states of continental Europe had established professional central courts which applied the *ius commune*, in the sense of Justinian's law as adapted and explained by the Commentators, together with as much of the local customary law as had survived. The decisions of these courts were reported and printed in large numbers, and were used by practitioners to assess how each court would treat a particular case with which they were concerned. The collections of decisions took many forms, some giving elaborate statements, taken from the court records, both of

15. *Proposals for English and Scottish Law Commissions* 1965, Cmnd 2573, p 2.
16. J. A. Clarence Smith 'Legislative drafting: English and Continental' [1980] Statute Law Rev 14.

the facts that had been found and of the legal arguments presented by the parties.[17] Others reduced a decision to a single sentence summarising its effect. The style that became standard – and which can still be observed in the printed reports of the one state in Europe that still applies uncodified *ius commune* (the Republic of San Marino) – has certain features which distinguish case law in systems based on the civil law from case law in a common law system.[18]

First, there is much less interest in the facts of the actual case which gave rise to the decision. Sometimes they are only reported in sufficient detail to explain the point of issue, and sometimes, where the issue can be detached from the facts, they are not reported at all. In the common law, as we have seen, what is of precedential value in a case is the decision of the court in relation to the material facts, and it is the decision which constitutes the law. In the uncodified civil law it is the written law of the *Corpus Iuris*, as currently understood, which is authoritative and the significance of the decision is to illustrate how that law is currently applied. What matters is the opinion of the court, and so the facts are of secondary importance.

Secondly, the arguments are based not on what was said in earlier cases but on the written law and its authoritative exponents. In the common law it is the opinions of the judges which are regarded as authoritative. The views of academic writers have no such authority, although their comments may be useful in indicating the present state of the law and in urging how it should develop or how it should be altered by statute. The civil law, on the other hand, is largely the creation of academic writers and they have maintained their role as its authentic expositors. The role of the judge is formally to choose what he considers the best opinion and apply it. Thus an argument or a judgment will attempt to marshal the texts of the *Corpus Iuris* in such a way as to bring out a rule which may not be stated expressly anywhere but is said to be implicit in it. To prove the existence of this rule statements may be cited from all parts of the *Corpus Iuris*. They may be plucked out of context and taken from titles dealing with matters quite different from those raised by the case. The views of academic writers on those texts are cited, from the Accursian Gloss, through the Commentators, such as Bartolus, to the most recent writer. But they are not cited historically with a view to showing how the rule has gradually developed. Since the rule is presented as being latent in the written law, the view of any writer, of whatever period, is as relevant as that of any other. Even though

17.   Dawson *Oracles* pp 213ff.
18.   A. Watson *The Making of the Civil Law* (1981) pp 39ff. Although the Roman-Dutch law of South Africa, cited there, is an example of uncodified civil law, the court procedure and in particular the position of the judge owe much to English practice.

there may in fact have been a development of the law, it is rarely admitted even as a progressive revelation of the truth.

As governments strove to assert their authority in their states, they initiated legislation in the form of statutes, but at first the courts in many countries were strong enough to ignore them or to give them but limited effect and frequently the same rule is found re-enacted several times in a series of statutes. As the law applied came to vary from court to court, it was accepted that there were local variants of the *ius commune*: Roman-Dutch law, Roman-German law and so on.[19] Although the views of individual earlier judges were not authoritative, the actual practice of the court, as evidenced in reported court decisions, became increasingly significant. When that practice ran counter to the law in the texts, it was justified on Bartolist principles as a local custom that had received popular approval and so overrode the imperial law (p 78).

From the middle of the seventeenth until the end of the eighteenth century, the laws of the states of continental Europe were subject to two contrasting movements. On the one hand, there was a tendency to emphasise national differences and to move towards specifically national laws, so that Roman-German law became German law (when it was not even more narrowly identified as Bavarian law or Saxon law). On the other hand, there was a tendency, particularly among academic commentators, to stress the common elements of the different systems and to point out that, although national forensic practices had moved away from Justinian's law in significant respects, they were moving in the same direction, so that there was a common 'modern use of the Digest' (*usus modernus Pandectarum*), which was generally followed in most countries. This concept was fostered particularly by commentators in the great law schools of the Netherlands, which attracted students from several other countries.

The abundance of authoritative texts and commentaries, with case law showing different forms of court practice superimposed on them, enabled courts to find authority for almost any decision they wanted and were thus an embarassment for litigants and their advisors. Demands began to be made for restatement of the law in a simpler, more rational and logical way. Seventeenth-century philosophers popularised the notion of a natural law, based on certain general principles which could be inferred from man's nature as a social animal living in communities with others. These principles were conceived of as universal and binding on all men, irrespective of the time and place in which they lived, and in particular they could be regarded as governing the relations between

19.   K. Luig 'The Institutes of National Law in the Seventeenth and Eighteenth Centuries' (1972) 17 Juridical Rev 193.

states, and so formed the basis of an international law. They were axiomatic and had the same certainty as mathematical propositions. The writers on natural law frequently invoked the mathematical analogy and tried to produce systems of law that were as logical and categorical as a theorem in geometry, starting from general self-evident principles and proceeding down to the particular rules. If natural law, an ideal law promulgated by philosophers, could be presented systematically in this way, was it not possible to do the same for the positive law that was actually applied in courts?

Academic writers, influenced by humanist notions of order and coherent arrangement, had made explicit the distinction between substantive rules, which set out the rights and duties of individuals, and procedural rules, which laid down the steps to be taken to enforce the substantive rules. In the common law, as in the classical Roman law, such a separation was difficult, as the extent of a man's rights could only be indicated in terms of the different forms of action that were available to him. If there was no remedy, there could be no right. But once lawyers began to think in terms of rights, the procedural aspects of the law became a secondary matter (p 128).

The idea of restating the substantive law as a system of rights and duties was especially attractive in France, where the codification of the local customs had preserved literally hundreds of separate legal systems so that, as Voltaire vividly put it, a traveller changed his law as often as he changed horses. Between 1667 and 1681, Colbert, Chancellor of Louis XIV, produced a series of Ordinances which applied to the whole country and thus provided a unifying element, which counteracted the centrifugal effect of various customs.[20] They did not deal with the private law, which was the prime concern of the customs, but with civil procedure, criminal procedure, criminal law, and particularly commercial law that applied to relations between businessmen (p 211). These Ordinances were direct legislation by a powerful government that expected to be obeyed, but they were carefully prepared and constructed in accordance with the most enlightened views of the age and they were admired and copied outside France. About the same time a French jurist, Jean Domat, demonstrated what could be done with the ill-arranged texts of the *ius commune* by producing *The civil laws in their natural order*,[1] in which the traditional material was rearranged to show its logical coherence as a system.

---

20.   W. Johnson *Chapters in the History of French Law* (1957) reprinted in J. G. Castel *The Civil Law System of the Province of Quebec* (1962) pp 48ff.

  1.   *Les lois civiles dans leur ordre naturel* (2 vols, 1689–94) (English translation by W. Strahan, 1722).

Codification of the civil law

These developments led to the idea that the basic private law also could be stated in a code.[2] The optimistic philosophers of the eighteenth century enlightenment persuaded the rulers of the time that the whole law could be stated simply and rationally and that all that was needed was the will to do it. They believed that in every situation there was one right way to behave and that it could be discovered by the exercise of reason. Enlightened despots, such as Frederick the Great of Prussia or Maria Theresa of Austria, felt that once the right way had been discovered it should be made compulsory for their subjects, who should be forced to be good citizens even in spite of themselves. The rulers also saw codification as a way of curbing the independence of the courts which had aroused the distrust not only of rulers but of the public in general, often through their attempts to interpret the material at their disposal in an equitable way. The courts had made the law confused, and 'God protect us from the equity of the courts' was a common saying in France. The doctrine of the separation of powers into legislative, executive and judicial, as popularised by Montesquieu, led to the conclusion that the judges should be confined to the mechanical role of applying the law rather than making it.

The movement for codification of the law had everywhere similar motives – to state the law simply, to impose uniformity in place of diversity, to curb the power of the judiciary – but it produced different results. Frederick the Great ordered a codification of Prussian law which would cover all aspects of the law and would be sufficiently detailed to cover all possible fact situations that might arise. It would have both an educational purpose, to make his subjects better people, and a political purpose, to preserve the status quo in Prussian society. The General Land Law (*Allgemeines Landrecht*), eventually promulgated in 1794, is an enormous work of about 17,000 articles. It aimed to be completely comprehensive and dealt with many matters which would today be regarded as quite inappropriate for legal regulations, such as the precise duties which husband and wife owe each other in regard to sexual intercourse (II.1.178–80). It has no less than five articles dealing with the position of hermaphrodites whose sex is in doubt (I.1.19–23). The parents are to make an initial categorisation as male or female, but on reaching full age the individual may make a personal decision as to sex, unless a third party's rights depend on that decision, in which case the third party can require an examination by a medical specialist. The judges were told to ignore both the views of academic

2.   Watson, op cit, n 18, pp 99ff.

writers and previous court decisions and apply only the code, which dealt with every conceivable situation. If they were really faced with a problem which was not covered by the rules of the code, they were not to attempt to decide it for themselves but were to adjourn the case and refer the matter to the legislature for a ruling (Introduction 46–50).

The French code of 1804 is entirely different in tone. The enactment of a code was one of the declared aims of the French Revolution. There was a desire to sweep away the legal structure which was supporting the *ancien régime*, and replace it with a brand new set of simple rules which would express the revolutionary aspirations of liberty, equality and fraternity. The imposition of such a code would at the same time place all Frenchmen under the same law, for under the *ancien régime* not only were there regional variations but also different laws for different classes of people, nobility, clergy, merchants and so on.[3] Furthermore the same individual might be subject to different systems of law in different kinds of activity: canon law in regard to his marriage and testamentary acts, Roman law in regard to his contracts, and customary law in regard to the rest. The judges of the Parlements were distrusted as favouring the interests of the aristocracy, and a code was needed to curb their discretion. However the Ordinances had been a success and few people wanted to undo Colbert's work, so it was specifically to the civil law in the sense of private law that the Constituent Assembly directed its attention. Criminal law, commercial law, and procedure, all of which had been dealt with in Ordinances, were excluded, as was any matter involving the state as such. What mattered was the law that affected the ordinary man in the street and for the first time he was to have a set of simple rules which he could carry in his pocket and on which he could plan his conduct.

The Constituent Assembly of the Revolution rejected a first draft of 697 articles as too long, but then turned down another draft with only 297 articles as too short.[4] In 1799 Napoleon seized power. He took a personal interest in the codification project, which he saw as a means of perpetuating his own memory, in the way that Justinian had done with his codification. He appointed a commission of four jurists, two from the regions of the customary law in the north and two from the area of the written law in the south, and instructed them to prepare a code which would preserve the most practical

---

3.   J. Maillet 'The historical significance of French codifications' (1970) 44 Tulane LR 681.
4.   K. Zweigert and H. Kötz *An Introduction to Comparative Law* (trans T. Weir, 1977) I. pp 78ff.

rules from both systems. Although in its form the code was to show many of the features desired by the Fathers of the Revolution, in substance many of the rules were based on the pre-Revolution law.[5] The compilers relied considerably on Domat and even more on the voluminous writings of R. J. Pothier, a conspicuously unrevolutionary professor and judge from Orleans, in the middle of the eighteenth century. He had compiled treatises on all branches of private law, drawing attention both to the common features shared by the regional customs and to their similarities with the Roman law, and often suggesting formulations which neatly reconciled the diversities.

The order of treatment was based first on the distinction, derived from Justinian's Institutes, between persons and things. The treatment of things was influenced by a treatise on the common elements in the customary law by Bourjon, a contemporary of Pothier, who subsumed the rules under 'the methods by which things are acquired' and 'the modifications of ownership through the creation of rights in others'. The code was completed in four months and is in 2281 articles, divided into three Books of uneven size, the first being devoted to persons, and the second to things and modifications of ownership. The third (articles 711–2281) is ostensibly on different ways of acquiring ownership but is in fact a rag-bag containing all rules that cannot be put into the other two books. Napoleon himself, then aged 34, despite his duties as head of state, attended more than half of the meetings of the commission, and his influence was felt especially on the language of the code. Constituting himself as the representative of the man in the street, he rejected any draft which he could not himself understand.

Even though it was confined to private law, the task of compressing all the law into such a small compass could only be achieved by the use of broad statements of principle, made up of general categories. Paradoxically, therefore, given that the code was supposed to restrict the judges' discretion and that they were not to refer back to the earlier law, the code relied heavily on their good sense in applying its provisions to fact-situations.[6] Portalis, the spokesman of the drafting commission, recognised this when he stated in his Preliminary Discourse that to be clear, the code had to be concise, and that it was its function to fix the basic principles of the law, which would be 'fertile in consequences', and not to descend into the details of the cases that might occur in regard to each topic. Rather it was for the judge and jurist, so long as they

5. A. J. Arnaud *Les origines doctrinales du code civil français* (1969).
6. A. Tunc 'The grand outlines of the code' in B. Schwartz (ed) *The Code Napoleon and the Common Law World* (1956) p 19.

were imbued with the spirit of the laws, 'to direct their application' in particular cases. Portalis envisaged that court decisions would fill in gaps in the law and at the same time exemplify how the principles were being applied to circumstances which could not have been foreseen by the draftsmen. As social circumstances changed, so, within the limits of the words used, the principles of the code would be applied in different ways.

In the nineteenth century most countries in the civil law tradition adopted codes on the French model. Among German-speaking states, Prussia already had the code of 1794 and in 1811 Austria adopted a short code of 1502 articles, based on enlightened principles and conforming more to the French than to the Prussian model.[7] Like the French code it is still in force. The idea of a common code for all German-speaking lands was put forward about the same time but it was rejected by the Historical School of jurists, who argued successfully that a nation's law should not be codified until it had evolved through its own inner working forces to a certain stage of technical development.[8] So many parts of Germany retained the uncodified *ius commune*. However the creation of the German Empire towards the end of the century created a demand for an all-German code. The commission set up to produce one relied on the work of the so-called Pandectist school of academic writers, who had reworked the *usus modernus Pandectarum* into a highly conceptualised system, organised in the manner of the systems of natural law. The result was the *Bürgerliches Gesetzbuch* (BGB) which came into force on 1 January 1900.[9]

The BGB differs considerably in style and arrangement from the Code Civil. It is expressed in much more technical language and is addressed not to the man in the street but to the professional lawyer. It is arranged in the manner of a Pandectist textbook and the reader is directed in stages from the general to the particular. Its most prominent feature is the General Part which precedes the four books of private law, devoted respectively to Obligations, Things, Family Law and Succession. The General Part sets out rules common to all kinds of legal transaction, and places great emphasis on the notion of 'act in the law' (German, *Rechtsgeschäft;* French, *acte juridique*).[10] This product of nineteenth-century concept building indicates any expression of will by which a person intends to produce a change in his legal position. So an offer to make a contract, the making of a testamentary disposition, a notice to terminate a lease, the

7. Zweigert and Kötz, op cit, I. pp 156ff.
8. P. Stein *Legal Evolution: the story of an idea* (1980) pp 51ff.
9. Zweigert and Kötz, op cit, I. pp 143ff.
10. Lawson *Common Lawyer* pp 164ff.

acceptance of the guardianship of a child, all are 'acts in the law'. To a common lawyer they are so different from each other that they have practically nothing in common save that they all have legal effects; but to a civil lawyer it is more logical to deal with such questions as the capacity to carry out transactions, and the effect of mistake or fraud on different kinds of acts, in a single place than separately in relation to each kind of act. The French code stops short of too high a degree of generalisation but the German code seems to carry it to the maximum possible extent.[11] The disadvantage is that in order to find the rules of the German code relating to a particular kind of transaction, one may have to look in several places in descending order of abstraction. The sale of a tin of beans is first an act in the law, then an obligation, then a contract and finally the particular contract of sale.

Although the form of both the French and German codes reflects the preoccupations of the lawyers of their respective periods, the materials out of which they were constructed are of similar origin and their Roman character is readily discernible. Over the centuries academic exposition of Roman law had detached many of its rules from the social circumstances in which they arose and had generalised them to the point where they were applicable to societies very different from that of ancient Rome. Nevertheless, the problem with every code of private law is that, like a still shot taken from a moving picture, it permanently displays the features of the period in which it was produced. The industrialisation of the nineteenth century and the development of modern capitalism produced a need for legal institutions that could hardly have been anticipated by the draftsmen of the Code Civil. That code reflected the values of a pre-industrial society, whereas the BGB reflected the individualistic attitudes of middle class citizens who wanted to encourage entrepreneurs to increase the wealth of society, with as few legal restrictions to their activity as possible.

The extent to which the judges can not only apply the code's provisions to unforeseen fact-situations but also adapt them to fundamental changes in society's attitudes depends partly on how the judges see their role and on how tightly the provisions of the code are drafted. It is now recognised that in applying the code, civil law judges, through their decisions, create a distinct body of law, known in French as *jurisprudence*, subsidiary to the law of the code.[12] Important decisions are reported, studied and commented on and are

11. F. Schmidt 'The German Abstract Approach to Law' (1965) 9 Scandinavian Studies in Law 131.
12. O. Kahn-Freund, C. Lévy and B. Rudden *A Source Book on French Law* (2nd edn, 1979) pp 116ff. B. Nicholas *French Law of Contract* (1982) pp 12ff.

normally followed in later cases. However, the first duty of the court
is to apply the law of the code, which in theory is the only true law
and which includes all the law applicable in its field. In their
judgments, which are written in a highly stylised form, French
courts 'motivate' their decisions only by reference to the articles of
the code and the highest court (*Cour de Cassation*) never cites
previous court decisions.[13] Yet the annual editions of the French
code, still in the traditional pocket size format, print references to
the relevant jurisprudence after each article. In the reports of
decisions, a judgment is usually followed by a 'note', often written
by an academic jurist, which explains critically the significance of the
decision in relation to other decisions, with a view to plotting the
course on which the law appears to be set. Thus the court issues the
decision as the mechanical application of the code, and then the
academic jurist, performing his traditional civil law function of
developing 'doctrine', indicates its relevance. In Germany, the
judges have been readier to acknowledge their law-making role and
the form of their judgments and of the reports has facilitated the use
of precedents in argument and in doctrine.[14]

Whether or not the judges are openly credited with a law-making
function, it is always limited by the meaning which the text of the
code is capable of bearing. In a codified system, the judges must fit
the facts of every case into a box built by the legislature. But the
generality of the rules stated in the codes and the theory that
decisions merely exemplify their application mean that they can treat
many matters as fact which the common law would regard as matters
of law. In the common law, decisions in regard to particular sets of
facts must be followed in later cases in which the same material facts
recur, and so a new rule in regard to such facts is created. Where the
facts differ, the decision may be different, and then a further rule is
created. Thus the common law favours the proliferation of a network
of narrow rules. A code article, on the other hand, being expressed
in general terms, typically attaches legal consequences to certain
types of behaviour. Whether that behaviour is present in a particular
case is a question of fact, and if the question arises in another similar
case, it is still a question of fact. Where the issue is one of fact, each
court must decide, on the basis of the evidence before it, whether the
fact-situation prescribed by the code is present. This difference gives
the court in the codified system a wider discretion in certain
situations than that enjoyed by a common law court.

In certain areas, such as the law of contract and tort, the judges

13. Article 5 of the Code specifically forbids judges to give decisions so as to make
    general rules or precedents for the future.
14. Horn, Kötz, Leser, pp 60ff.

have been quite successful in adapting the general provisions of their respective codes to new social conditions without the need for substantial legislative changes. In other areas, such as family law, twentieth-century ideas have moved so far from the values enshrined in the codes that large scale replacement of the old articles by new legislative provisions has been required. But to replace the code as a whole with a new code, more in tune with the needs of the times, has proved too daunting a task for the lawyers in both France and Germany. They have preferred to make piecemeal amendments rather than face the public debate that an entirely new draft code would provoke. Frenchmen in particular have an emotional attachment to their code, doubtless attributable to the straight-forward language in which it is couched, and they like to think that their behaviour is still governed by the original Code Napoléon.

Not only is a code rather more difficult to change than other kinds of law, it also tends to fix permanently the scope of a given area of law, so that no newly emerging branch of law can be admitted to it but must be dealt with in a separate code. From the beginning the French had a separate commercial code, criminal code and codes of civil procedure and criminal procedure. More recently there have been added also a labour code, a company code, a tax code, a social security code, a transport code and so on. Their drafting is more detailed than that of the Code Civil and they resemble more the large consolidating statutes of common law countries. The man in the street who thinks that he has the law that affects his conduct at his disposal, when he has the Code Civil in his pocket, is sadly misled. Increasingly the law that concerns him in his everyday life is to be found in these later codes rather than in the Code Civil.

Institutions of substantive law

8 Public law and private law

In considering the institutions of substantive law, we must first note the distinction between public law and private law. The principle behind this distinction today is a matter of controversy, but its existence is beyond dispute. Essentially it divides those problems which involve the state and its agencies from those problems which concern purely private individuals. The distinction was drawn in these terms by the Roman jurist Ulpian.[1] He was expressing what had for long been a tacit understanding on which Roman law as a set of developing rules had rested, namely that lawyers were concerned with matters which concerned private individuals, and that in matters involving the state and its interests there was little place for law. In the Republic, the officers of the state were allowed very wide discretion in carrying out their duties, but were constrained by the knowledge that their term of office was short, usually one year, and that after it had expired they could be called to account for their administration. In general it was felt that political sanctions were more effective than legal sanctions in ensuring good government. In the Empire the emperors increasingly assumed unlimited power and where the interests of the state were concerned, their will was law, and little scope was left for the application of rules. Yet in matters in which the state interest was not involved, the emperors tacitly accepted that they should not interfere but should leave innovation to the experts.

This separation of private from public matters explains why during a considerable part of the classical period of Roman law (roughly the first two centuries AD), when private law reached its highest peak of technical development, Rome was governed by emperors of the most despotic type, who accepted no formal limits on their powers over the citizens. Under such governments there was no possibility of a public law, in the sense of a body of rules applicable to the state and its agents, which could be applied to the resolution of disputes between the government and a private citizen. An aggrieved citizen may well have got justice in a particular case but he received it as a matter of imperial grace and favour rather than as the application of a set of rules. Matters of private law, on the other

1. Digest, 1.1.1.2; H. F. Jolowicz *Roman Foundations of Modern Law* (1957) p 49.

107

hand, were outside the area of state interest and the Roman jurists were left alone to develop the rules without executive interference. So ingrained was the acceptance of the distinction that even when litigants in a private dispute appealed to the emperor for an authoritative ruling on a point of law, they normally received a reply, drafted by the jurists of the imperial civil service, which was strictly in accordance with the established law. There was no constitutional impediment to these jurists taking the opportunity to state a new (and better) rule, which could be issued in the emperor's name, but they very rarely availed themselves of that opportunity. They felt that, in matters of private law, the emperor should explain, clarify and interpret the existing law, but that he should be reluctant to legislate.

As the bureaucracy of the imperial administration increased, there was a tendency to lay down rules for subordinate government officials to follow and such rules grew into a kind of public law. At the time when Ulpian formulated the distinction between public and private law in the early third century AD, the existence of public law in the sense of rules controlling the acts of government officials was still more of an aspiration than a fact. For centuries the law of Rome had been exclusively private law, but it came to be realised that the practices of the state religion and its priests and the functions of the officials in charge of fire prevention, sewage or maintaining public order were also subject to rules which, since they could be enforced, could also be called law.

The seed thus sown was cultivated by the continental lawyers of the middle ages, who used the expression public law to describe not so much enforceable rules of law as principles of government and of public administration. Many of their ideas were actually taken from the context of the old Roman private law. For example, in the debates about representation of the people in the state assemblies, a frequently cited maxim of public law was 'what touches all should be approved by all'. This is indeed derived from Roman law but appeared there in the context of a situation where there were several guardians of the same ward and the question was the need to obtain the approval of all of them for certain transactions on behalf of the ward.[2] In the original context it explained and justified a rule of private law; in medieval thought it was rather a maxim of good government.

In the areas of relations between one state and another and in relations between the Church and the state, some progress was made in the early modern period in developing a true public law. But so far as the relations between the state and its subjects were concerned,

2.   Code 5.59.5.2; cf G. Post *Studies in Medieval Political Thought* (1964) pp 163ff.

there was strong resistance in most continental countries to the idea that the state and its representatives were bound by legal rules. Efforts by courts to decide cases arising out of the actions of state officials were strongly opposed by governments, who considered that such control by the courts was an unacceptable interference with the business of government, which ought to be outside any legal control. In the eighteenth century the principle of the separation of legislative, executive and judicial powers among different bodies was accepted. On the one hand, this principle curbed the power of the judges by laying down that their function was to apply the law not to make it. On the other hand, it made it clear that the judges and the executive were independent of each other. One of the first enactments of the French Revolution claimed to be furthering this principle when it prohibited the courts from interfering with the executive and from hearing any cases to which the executive was a party.[3] Henceforth there was no doubt that the ordinary courts were restricted to dealing with matters of private law.

When the French civil code came to be enacted in 1804, it was assumed to be limited to governing the relations between private individuals and therefore not to apply to any matter in which the government was a party. In France the executive was then, as indeed now, considered to have an inherent power to do any acts which were necessary to ensure good government, even if they infringed the rights of individuals. But after the upheavals of the Revolution it was realised that the executive could not be allowed to act without any external control. Legal principles had to be devised which would allocate power between legislature, executive and judiciary and would safeguard both the essential needs of government on the one hand and the interests of individual citizens on the other. Such principles, however, were seen to be of a different character from those of private law and could not be applied by the ordinary courts which administered private law.

The two branches of public law which emerged in the nineteenth century were constitutional law and administrative law. The first allocates the functions of the different organs of the state and limits their various powers. The second controls the relations between the state and the individual.

Constitutional law

The prominence of this area of law in relation to other areas depends in particular on the way the powers of the state are divided up between the

3. R. David *French Law: its structure sources and methodology* (trans M. Kindred, 1972) pp 101ff.

different organs. There may be a sharp separation of powers as between the executive, the legislature and the courts, and all these powers may themselves be shared between the central authorities of the state and the regional or provincial authorities.

Whether the state is formally a federal state composed of a number of individual states, such as the USA, Australia and Germany, or is a unitary state with substantial devolution of power to the regions, as in Italy, the division of power between central and regional or state governments is always set out in a basic constitutional document. Since the constitution specifies the form of state for the country in question, it is normally the product of a specially formal procedure, involving much consultation and elaborate canvassing of different interest groups. It lays down which matters are to be dealt with by the central government, legislature and courts and which are the province of their local counterparts. In some countries it is the powers of the regions which are precisely set out and the central authorities enjoy all the remaining powers; in others specific powers are assigned to the central authorities and the residuary powers lie with the component regions.

Disputes about whether a particular matter falls within the powers of the central or the regional authorities have to be decided by a court. The problem may turn on whether a statute enacted by a particular legislature was within its powers. The special character of such problems marks them off from the problems decided by the ordinary courts that administer private or criminal law, and in some countries, such as Germany and Italy, they are dealt with by special constitutional courts, which deal with problems arising out of the interpretation of the constitution. They can declare legislation to be invalid if it goes beyond the powers allotted by the constitution to the legislature, central or local, which purported to enact it. In common law countries, however, it is the practice for the same court to handle constitutional problems as handles other legal issues. This is so in the USA, Canada and Australia, all of which have federal constitutions. The US Supreme Court is the highest court in all matters within the sphere of the federal law and matters of conflict of jurisdiction, and it may also declare legislation, whether of the federal Congress or of a state assembly, invalid if it infringes the constitution of the United States. This power of the Supreme Court to control the content of legislation was first declared in 1803 and the techniques of control of legislation elaborated by the Supreme Court have been copied by the courts of other countries, and not only those within the common law tradition.

The existence of a written constitution does not necessarily imply such judicial control of legislation. France has a written constitution which specifies how power is divided between executive, legislature and judiciary. There are no regional legislatures and all local government is subordinated to the central government, so that the problems of a conflict of powers between the centre and the localities do not arise. Legislation of the French Parliament is vetted by a Constitutional Council before it comes into force, but there is no court which can invalidate legislation on the ground of its content after it has come into force.

In Britain there is no single fundamental document which contains the constitution. It is to be found partly in a number of Acts of Parliament, such as the Act and Treaty of Union between England and Scotland (1705), the Act of Settlement, the Parliament Act, the Representation of the People Acts, the Judicature Acts and so on, and partly in certain unwritten conventions based on custom and practice. The Acts may be changed or repealed in the same way as any other statutes and have no special sanctity. In Britain, therefore, the constitution is in the hands of Parliament which can alter it at will. This is the position also in New Zealand, where there is a formal written constitution, but it can be amended by the legislature in the same way as any other kind of legislation. On the other hand, in countries such as the United States, Canada and Australia, where the constitutions are the result of special procedures and cannot be amended by the legislatures, the supreme courts have the final say on the allocation of power between the organs of government, until the constitution has been formally amended through an appeal to the people in a special amendment procedure designed to ensure maximum involvement. In a federal state, where there is rivalry between the component states and the federation, there is obviously a greater need to scrutinise the activities of the various legislatures, even when they are all democratically elected, since one of the aims of the confederation would normally be to ensure that the interests of the weaker components of the confederation are not swamped by those of the stronger.

The distinction between the two forms of constitution becomes specially important in relation to the protection of the individual citizen. Administrative law is concerned to secure his proper interests against the government. Constitutional law tries to secure his basic democratic rights, such as free speech, freedom of association and of public meeting. In a written constitution of the United States type, these rights are embedded in the constitution and can be altered only by the process of constitutional amendment, involving maximum publicity. Any statute which appears to interfere with those rights can be challenged on the ground that it is unconstitutional. In the United States the fifth and fourteenth Amendments to the constitution prohibit any interference with the individual's life, liberty or property 'without due process of law', and many statutes, both of the United

States Congress and of the state legislatures, have been challenged before the Supreme Court as infringing these rights. This has not always worked to the advantage of individuals. In the latter part of the nineteenth century and the beginning of the twentieth, the Supreme Court considerably restricted the enactment of social legislation dealing with such matters as workmen's compensation, minimum wages and hours of work, on such grounds as that they infringed the individual's right to enter into whatever contracts he pleased and so infringed the clause in the constitution that 'no state shall pass any law impairing the obligations of contracts'. Judges will necessarily interpret the constitution according to their own ideas, and such ideas may not always accord with those of the bulk of the population, but the legislatures which passed the statutes in question were democratically elected, whereas the judges were appointed.

In France, which has a written constitution but where it is thought to be not part of the judicial function to review the validity of legislation, there can be no fundamental rights in the American sense. This is so also in Britain where there is no fundamental document guaranteeing individual rights which is binding on Parliament. There are of course civil liberties, which are applications of the general rule that everything is lawful which has not been expressly made unlawful. So the individual may do whatever he pleases so long as he does not infringe the particular rules of law which govern that activity. 'The right to personal freedom is a liberty to so much personal freedom as is not taken away by law.'[4] How much personal freedom is taken away by law is left to Parliament to determine in its legislation. Since Parliament is supreme in the sense that its statutes, whatever their content, are not subject to review by courts, the control of legislation which is considered to impair civil liberties must be political rather than legal. Opposition to such legislation must take the form of mobilising a political attack on the law in Parliament rather than the initiation of a legal action. Thus many issues which are legal issues in the United States are political issues in Britain or France.

A British citizen can, however, challenge legislation indirectly by making a complaint to the European Commission of Human Rights in Strasbourg, on the ground that it infringes the European Convention on Human Rights, 1953. Britain is a signatory of the convention but has not made its provisions directly binding by incorporating them into an Act of Parliament. If the Commission decides that the complainant's allegations justify further investigation, it will ascertain the facts, and then try to produce a settlement, failing which a report is made to the Committee of

---

4.   W. I. Jennings *The Law and the Constitution* (3rd edn, 1943) p 243.

Ministers of the Council of Europe. The Committee may decide that there has been a violation of the convention, or it may refer the case to the Court of Human Rights for a definitive judgment on whether there has been a violation. The execution of such a judgment, which may include an award of damages to the complainant, depends on the force of public opinion. The government will repeal the offending law or pay damages, not because it is legally bound to do so, but because it is politically desirable.

For example, article 11 of the convention guarantees the right of freedom of association. In a recent case[5] some railwaymen were dismissed by British Rail, after British Rail had entered a 'closed shop' agreement with the railway unions, because they refused to join the relevant union. They claimed that this was a breach of article 11, since freedom to join a union includes freedom not to be forced to join one. The European Court of Human Rights held that there was a breach of article 11 and eventually fixed the damages payable to the claimants. The decision also significantly influenced a subsequent change in the British legislation relating to the 'closed shop'.

Since 1 January 1973, Britain has been a member of the European Community, and as such is subject to laws which Parliament can neither amend nor repeal and which are interpreted conclusively by a court outside Britain – the Court of Justice of the European Communities in Luxembourg. Some rules are contained in the Treaty of Rome, which originally established the Community, and they have been incorporated into English and Scots law by the European Communities Act 1972. That Act also recognised that Community Regulations, which had been or would be made for the Community as a whole, had direct effect in member states. There are also Community Directives which are directly binding on member states, but each member state is left to decide the best way of implementing them within its own territory.

Where it conflicts with the domestic law of a member state, Community law overrides it and its existence thus restricts the power of Parliament to legislate. However Community rules do not range generally over the whole of law, being limited to certain specific areas, such as agriculture, free movement of labour and capital, transport, and restrictive trade practices. All domestic courts have power to refer a case to the Court of Justice for a ruling on the effect of Community law. The Court of Justice has adopted for itself and has commended to the courts of member states a more purposive method of interpreting Community law than that used by English courts in relation to English statutes. In particular the courts should

5. *Young v UK* [1981] IRLR 408.

fill gaps in the law in the light of the aims of the legislation in question and of the objectives of the Community as set out in the Treaty. It may be that such a 'civil law' approach, if adopted by English courts in regard to Community law, will have an effect on their attitude to domestic legislation (p 92).

Administrative law

In this area France was the leader, the instrument of French administrative law being the *Conseil d'Etat* (Council of State), set up in 1800. In the course of the nineteenth century this court successfully established its independence of the executive. In the first place it gained acceptance for the idea that its judgments must be enforced even when they were not to the taste of the government of the day. Secondly, it decided that its jurisdiction extended over every act of the government and its agents and that in every matter in which its jurisdiction was disputed, the decision as to whether or not there was jurisdiction lay with the *Conseil d'Etat* itself. As the pinnacle of a whole hierarchy of administrative courts, it has made itself responsible for the development of French administrative law.[6]

This law is not codified in the manner of the civil law. Indeed it consists of rules not laid down by the legislature and is largely the product of case law. The *Conseil d'Etat* has stated and restated the principles applicable to disputes between the state and the individual in a way that strikes a balance between the public interest and the private interest of the individual affected by government action. The legislature can be confident that a proper balance will be achieved by the *Conseil d'Etat* and does not feel the need to spell out in detail precisely what the government can or cannot do. French public lawyers pride themselves on having a different ethos from that of the private lawyers. They see themselves as readier to take account of extra-legal considerations which would be regarded as irrelevant by private lawyers and they see public law as more adaptable to the challenge of new situations and generally more dynamic than private law.

This adaptability of the public lawyer is not always an unmixed blessing. The idea of administrative law applied by specialist courts with specialist lawyers is now found universally in continental countries. In Germany under the Nazis it was not difficult for the public lawyers to follow the principle that the interest of the individual citizen must always be subordinated to that of the state as

6.   L. N. Brown and J. F. Garner *French Administrative Law* (3rd edn, 1983); David *French Law* pp 103ff.

a whole. Nazi Germany is doubtless an extreme case and in recent decades, it is true, the tendency in most Western European countries has been to favour the individual. Nevertheless one can easily conceive of political situations in which administrative courts could be under great pressure from the executive to give more weight to what was conceived to be the 'common good' as against that of a single individual.

The French *Conseil d'Etat* has long been able to annul administrative acts which the official concerned had no legal power to do, or which are the result of some procedural irregularity, but it has gone further. By developing the idea of misuse of power (*détournement de pouvoir*) it is able to review cases where the act is within the official's legal powers but is exercised for a purpose different from that for which it was conferred, ie, where the official has a discretion and has 'abused' it. The *Conseil d'Etat* had no specific authority to do this but drew on certain general principles enunciated in such documents as the Declaration of the Rights of Man in 1789, which were considered to be part of French republican tradition. The remedies offered by administrative courts are now comprehensive. They can not only annul acts of officials which they decide fall outside the law, but can also award compensation to those who have suffered loss as a result of those acts.

Administrative law covers a wider field than the control of the acts of administration. In France if one of the parties to a contract for the supply of goods is a public body, such as a town council, the contract may still be an ordinary civil contract, governed by the rules of private law. But if the purpose of the contract is that the other party shall perform a public service, or the terms of the contract in some way reflect its public character, the contract is an administrative contract.[7] In that case it is not governed by private law rules and any dispute must come to the administrative court, which will apply different rules that allow it to take account of the public interest. So also when an official causes loss to a private individual in circumstances which would make a private individual liable to pay compensation, the official's fault may be regarded as purely personal, in which case he is liable in the ordinary courts according to the rules of private law. Alternatively it may be a 'fault of service', in which case he is not personally liable but the state or public body employing him is liable in the administrative courts. These examples show how easily conflicts of jurisdiction may arise between the courts administering private law and those administering administrative law. In France such disputes are settled by a special *Tribunal des Conflits*, composed of an equal number of judges from the administrative courts and from the ordinary courts.

7.   B. Nicholas *French Law of Contract* (1982) p 24.

The English common law traditionally accepted no distinction between public law and private law. It was assumed that the same body of rules applied to relations involving the king and his officers as applied to relations between private individuals. In the thirteenth century, Bracton wrote that the king – and by implication also the king's government – was 'under God and under the law' (I. viii). This principle was, however, of little practical value as long as the king could not be sued in his own courts and the legality of acts done in his name could not be tested in those courts.

Various expedients were introduced to mitigate the king's immunity from process in his own court. A citizen who had made a contract with a government official and alleged that its terms had been broken could sue by a special procedure known as petition of right. The claim would be decided according to the ordinary rules of contract and any damages would as a matter of grace be paid by the relevant government department. That procedure was not available to one who complained that a particular official had committed a wrongful act against him. In England, unlike France, the executive and its officers have, in general, no powers over the individual unless they have been expressly conferred on them by the legislature. Anyone aggrieved by the act of an official could sue him personally and his liability was determined according to the rules applicable to a claim against an ordinary citizen. The official could not defend himself on the ground that what he was doing was in the interest of the state. Before the Revolution of 1688, the royal prerogative, what the king and his officers can do in the name of the Crown, was potentially wide. However, certainly since the eighteenth century, no public official has been allowed to plead the public interest or to hide behind the Crown's immunity. Normally in cases in which an employer of a private citizen would have been liable for his acts, the government department to which the official belonged would pay any damages awarded against him.

The United States took over the doctrine of sovereign immunity from process as part of the English common law. After the Second World War, changes were made in both Britain and the USA. In 1946 the US Government was made liable to pay compensation for the wrongful acts of its officials 'in like manner and to the same extent as a private individual under like circumstances' (Federal Tort Claims Act). The following year, by the Crown Proceedings Act 1947, a British government department was made liable to ordinary actions in contract and in tort 'as if it were a private person of full age and capacity'. In both the USA and Britain this general liability of the government for the acts of its officials has been qualified by many exceptions introduced by statutes which allow government departments to do what it would be unlawful for a private individual to do.

Where the complaint was that a public official had exceeded his powers or had failed to carry out some duty laid upon him, the ordinary remedies would be of little use. Instead the main common law court, the King's Bench, adapted certain remedies, originally called prerogative writs, and now prerogative orders, which had been designed to control the activities of lower courts. They were extended to cover the administrative action of public bodies, local authorities and their officers, by compelling them to appear before the court and account for their use, misuse or failure to use their powers. These remedies are *prohibition*, which restrains an inferior court or public body from exceeding its powers; *mandamus*, which commands such a court or public body to do something that it ought to do; and *certiorari*, which reviews what has been done to discover whether the court or public body has exceeded or abused its powers, and if so, invalidates any order made as a result of such excess or abuse. Since 1977 a complainant applies generally for judicial review of administrative action by whichever of these orders is most appropriate in the circumstances.[8] Finally a public body which is said to be detaining a person unlawfully is subject to the writ of *habeas corpus*, which became the traditional safeguard of the Englishman's liberty. The writ provides for the court to review the reason for the detention of any person by any other person, and, unless good cause for such detention is shown, the court will order his release.

It has been well said that 'the absence in the common law systems of a distinct body of public law, whereby proceedings against public authorities are instituted only before special administrative courts and are governed by a special body of rules, is directly traceable to the extensive use of prerogative writs by the Court of King's Bench'.[9]

At the end of the nineteenth century, English legal scholars, particularly A. V. Dicey, rejoiced that the common law subjected public bodies to the same rules as private individuals and that English law recognised nothing comparable to the alien French administrative law. But this attitude has had curious consequences. Just because the ordinary courts were hostile to arguments based on the public interest, Parliament was persuaded to confer on public bodies greater powers than they needed to carry out their functions, so as to minimise the possibility that their actions will be challenged in the courts.

The coming of the Welfare State impelled Parliament to confer on government departments unprecedented powers to enable them to

8. RSC Ord 53; cf Supreme Court Act 1981, s 31.
9. S. A. de Smith *Judicial Review of Administrative Action* (3rd edn, 1973) p 513.

administer the various services that were now provided. To avoid the danger that effective administration might be impeded by applications for prerogative orders, the relevant statute often provided expressly that any objection to the use of the powers should be made not to the regular courts but to a special court, an administrative tribunal. At first such tribunals were regarded almost as appendages of the department concerned and their impartiality was doubted, but as they proliferated, their position had to be regularised. The Tribunals and Inquiries Act of 1958[10] required that they have independent chairmen and that their decisions should be supported by reasons. As a result, the relevant prerogative order became available to correct procedural errors by administrative tribunals, and so the ordinary courts acquired some degree of control over them.

Judicial review ensures that public bodies keep within the powers granted to them by Parliament, but Parliament is sometimes persuaded to make those powers very wide precisely to avoid such control. Furthermore it is not always easy for the victim to obtain compensation for loss inflicted on him by a public body. A public body which exceeds its statutory powers is liable to pay damages if it has done something which would make a private person liable. This will not, however, help a person injured if the powers granted to the public body allow it to do things which would not be allowed to a private individual, such as to commit acts which would be a nuisance if done by a private individual. And even if the public body has exceeded its powers, what it has done may not necessarily constitute a recognised actionable wrong.[11]

For example, if what is complained of is the way the public body exercised a discretionary power to choose among different possible courses of action, it is difficult to show that it has been at fault when it chose one course rather than another. In recent cases the courts have made a distinction between planning decisions and operational decisions.[12] A planning decision is concerned with how a type of problem is to be tackled. It will typically involve the adoption of one way of tackling it and the rejection of another, which would cause less inconvenience to the public, on the ground that resources are scarce and the second way would be much more expensive than the first. The courts will not review such planning decisions at all, since they feel unable to assess the policy considerations involved. An operational decision, on the other hand, is concerned with the way a planning decision is applied. Here courts are prepared to award

10. Now Tribunals and Enquiries Act 1971.
11. *Dunlop v Woollahra Municipal Council* [1982] AC 158 (Privy Council).
12. P. P. Craig 'Negligence in the exercise of a power' (1978) 94 LQR 428.

damages if, in carrying out the policy adopted, the public body has shown a lack of reasonable care, from which foreseeable damage has resulted. The reluctance of the courts to look at decisions of policy and the difficulty of proving that a public body has been at fault mean that 'the existing remedies available to a private individual who has suffered loss as a result of governmental action are limited'.[13] Thus the underlying assumption that the same principles apply to actions against public bodies as apply to actions against private individuals may paradoxically work in favour of public bodies.

So also in the case of contracts with British government departments, in principle the same set of rules applies as is applied to contracts between private individuals. In practice, however, such contracts have acquired 'a special administrative character'.[14] Partly this is the result of standard conditions which government departments require their officers to incorporate into the contracts they make for the supply of goods and services. These conditions normally give the government officers involved more control over the performance of the contract than an employer or customer would have in the private sector. As a result, although an ordinary action for damages for breach of contract may be brought against a government department, just as against a private individual, the occasions for such action are rare. Litigation is infrequent, and disputes are settled by negotiation, in which the government officer is guided by a series of departmental instructions and Treasury minutes which have no legal force, but which ensure uniformity of practice in the making of ex gratia payments by way of settlement of claims. 'Thus while in theory government contracts are subject to the ordinary rules of contract law, such rules have in practice only a residuary or contingent applicability to the relations established by the contract.'[15] It should be emphasised that the special situation of British government departments in such matters does not extend to local authorities whose powers are strictly controlled by statute and who may be sued in the same way as private individuals.

The English approach to disputes between the citizen and the government illustrates the cautious piecemeal manner in which the common law has traditionally faced new problems, by contrast with the more decisive, or as the French themselves would have it, more logical approach of French law. However, an English public law, distinct from private law, has now arrived[16] and a litigant may even

13. P. P. Craig 'Compensation in Public Law' (1980) 96 LQR 434.
14. C. C. Turpin, IECL VII.4.33.
15. Ibid, 44.
16. Cf C. C. Harlow ' "Public" and "Private" Law: definition without distinction' (1980) 43 MLR 241 and G. Samuel 'Public and Private: a private lawyer's response' (1983) 46 MLR 558.

be penalised if he tries to use an ordinary action against a public body instead of seeking the remedy of judicial review. In a recent case,[17] Lord Diplock, recognising that the distinction between public and private law was 'a latecomer to the English legal system', held that it was an abuse of the process of the court for a person seeking to establish that a decision of a public body had infringed rights, 'to which he was entitled to protection under public law', to proceed by an ordinary action instead of by application for judicial review. For in an ordinary action he could evade the provisions laid down by public law for the protection of such bodies.

We have so far been considering the remedies available to an individual who claims to have been personally prejudiced by the acts of a public body. In some situations the acts of a public body affect the public as a whole rather than a particular individual and the question arises as to what remedies are available to challenge such acts.[18] For example, where a crime has been committed, there is a public official whose duty it is to initiate a prosecution in the criminal courts, the Chief Officer of a Police Authority, but he also has a discretion to decide whether or not to prosecute a particular person against whom there may be evidence of criminal acts. He is not obliged to proceed against every possible offender. This discretion, however, does not extend to the adoption of a deliberate policy of not prosecuting in certain types of criminal behaviour, since in such a situation the police would be substituting their will for that of Parliament. Any member of the public who believes that the police have adopted such a policy may challenge its legality by way of procedings for judicial review.[19]

A member of the public can only use the procedure for judicial review against a public body if he shows 'a sufficient interest in the matter to which the application relates'. In deciding whether the applicant has such an interest, the court will take into account the seriousness of the allegations which he is making. Everyone has an interest in the prosecution of crimes. In *Inland Revenue Commissioners v Federation of Self-employed*,[20] a federation of tax-payers challenged the legality of a practice adopted by the Inland Revenue in relation to another group of tax-payers, who, they alleged, were being given preferential treatment. Lord Diplock said that it would 'be a grave lacuna in our system of public law if a pressure group, like the federation, or even a single public-spirited tax-payer, were

---

17. *O'Reilly v Mackman* [1983] 2 AC 267 at 277 and 285; cf J. A. Jolowicz, [1983] CLJ 15.
18. J. A. Jolowicz 'Civil Proceedings in the Public Interest' (1982) 13 Cambrian LR 32.
19. *R v Metropolitan Police Commr, ex p Blackburn* [1968] 2 QB 118.
20. [1982] AC 617.

prevented [by procedural rules] from bringing the matter to the attention of the court to . . . get the unlawful conduct stopped,'[1], but his colleagues denied that it had a sufficient interest.

The procedure for judicial review is limited to public bodies and is therefore not available against private individuals. When we use that expression we normally think of ordinary citizens, but large companies and trade unions, since they are not public bodies, also come into the category of 'private individuals'. As such they are liable to the ordinary civil actions of private law, and such actions can only be brought by other private individuals whose interests have been harmed. The problem is that large bodies, such as companies and unions, sometimes engage in acts which are of great public concern but where no criminal offence has yet been committed. An ordinary citizen, threatened by the acts of another, which will harm him if they continue, can apply to the court for an injunction to prevent their continuance. Does he have sufficient interest to bring an action against a person whose acts threaten the public as a whole?

In *Gouriet v Union of Post Office Workers*,[2] an attempt was made to bring proceedings in the civil courts against a trade union, to prevent the members from carrying out their declared intention of interrupting communications with South Africa because of their opposition to the policy of apartheid. Such interruption would almost certainly have involved the commission of criminal offences by Post Office employees. However no offence had yet been committed and so no prosecution could be brought. The plaintiff, as a member of the public, brought a civil action for a declaration and an injunction ordering the union to desist from what was proposed. The House of Lords disallowed the action on the ground that such proceedings could only be brought by those having a private right over and above the right that all members of the public have in seeing that the law is obeyed. Lord Wilberforce explained that 'the rights of the public are vested in the Crown, and the Attorney-General enforces them as an officer of the Crown. And just as the Attorney-General has in general no power to interfere with the assertion of private rights, so in general no private person has the right of representing the public in the assertion of public rights'.[3]

Any member of the public can in fact apply to the Attorney-General for leave to proceed in his name on a matter of public interest. In theory the action is that of the Attorney-General but in practice it is the 'relator' who is responsible for the proceedings, and

1. At 644.
2. [1978] AC 435.
3. Ibid, at 477.

in particular for the costs involved. (In *Gouriet's* case the Attorney-General had refused to give such leave.) But except as a relator, no private citizen can sue another citizen in a private law action in respect of a public wrong. As a result an ordinary member of the public may be able to bring an action on a matter of public interest against a public body, in circumstances in which he could not bring an action against another member of the public. This limitation is justifiable to protect private individuals. The problem is that, by treating large corporations and unions as private individuals, the law may fail to reflect the realities of modern industrial society.

Conclusion

Notwithstanding these recent developments, which recognise the distinction between public law and private law, that distinction is still not felt in English practice to the degree that it is in continental countries. There are no separate courts, no special body of practitioners and no distinctive atmosphere which distinguishes public law cases from private law cases. Lord Mackenzie Stuart has given an apt example of the way a lawyer who has not grown up with the distinction will categorise cases quite differently from lawyers for whom it is fundamental. He was discussing with a German lawyer the case of an importer who had paid, under protest, a certain sum demanded by the customs authorities and wanted to claim it back:

> 'Said I, without thinking, "His claim to restitution, of course, rests on a quasi-contract". His reaction was most indignant. "Not in *public* law. The question must always be the legality of the act of the state agency. If it is declared illegal, then it automatically follows that the state must then repair the consequences".'[4]

It is good that in England public officials are not privileged to act in ways that would not be open to private individuals. On the other hand, as has been well said, 'the citizen has no greater right to compensation from the state than from his fellow citizen; yet the state can now cause him harm much more easily than his fellow citizen can, especially with regard to those interests of his (the exercise of trade or profession and the development of property) which are barely protected at all by the rules of private law'.[5] The failure to make a distinction between public and private law for fear of giving an undue advantage to the state may have delayed the

4.   *The European Communities and the Rule of Law* (1977) p 47.
5.   T. Weir, IECL I. 2.130.

proper development of public law, since the judges did not have to face the need to elaborate the principles applicable only to public law situations.

In countries which implement the distinction, the very existence of public law, with its avowed aim of reconciling the public interest with the interests of private individuals, has repercussions on the way private lawyers see their law. They tend to emphasise private property and individual freedom of contract without taking account of public matters. Yet today many private law disputes have a public aspect. The sale of a house involves planning considerations, with limitations on the use to which the house may be put or the possibility that the property will be affected by public works, such as a new road in the back garden. The financial settlement on a divorce has a social security aspect. There is a taxation dimension to most problems of property and contract. What may appear to be a purely private matter may turn out to have consequences for the public which cannot be ignored, for example, if a bank closes, or if a private transport company is forced by its creditors to suspend operations, and rural areas are deprived of their bus service.[6]

Such considerations make it increasingly difficult to find a theoretical justification for making too rigid a distinction between public law and private law. Whereas England rejected it because all law was thought to be private, socialist countries have rejected it on the ground that all law is public, in the sense that all aspects of the citizen's relations with others must be subject to the control of the state if the communist society is to be established. The collectivisation of the means of production and the setting up of state enterprises to manage the commerce of the country mean that private property is confined to a small range of goods and that most contracts are likely to have a state agency as one of the parties, so that the scope for pure private law is much reduced. Nevertheless although the distinction is rejected, there are in socialist countries, as in England, different rules applicable in cases where a state agency is a party and in cases where the parties are both private citizens.

If public considerations now intrude on most private disputes in every modern state, whatever its political form, it may be asked whether any dispute should be treated by the courts as affecting only the parties to it. Socialist legal systems impose a duty on the courts to put the general interest of the community before purely private interests even in cases in which both parties are private citizens. Thus judges in socialist systems are not bound to consider only the parties' claims and to look only at the evidence they have adduced. They can take account of matters which neither party has

6. David *French Law* pp 106–107.

raised and can make awards which neither party has asked for. 'The principles of community life' override the parties' interests, and the judge, as the representative of the community, must take an active part in the proceedings to ensure that factors relevant to such principles are brought to his notice.[7]

In Western countries the general principle has been that it is for the parties to determine the issue before the court and that the judge should not go beyond it. His duty is to decide whether the plaintiff is or is not entitled to the remedy that he seeks. Yet Western systems differ in the powers they accord to the judge to intervene actively, for example, by asking for extra evidence with a view to getting at the truth rather than confining himself to the questions raised by the pleadings. There is more opportunity for the judge to do this in the professional procedure of continental countries than in the English procedure.

7.   On 'socialist legality', I Szabó, IECL II.1.99.

9 The institutional system of private law

Private law regulates disputes between one citizen and another. Typically an action in private law is directed to make the defendant deliver something or pay money; it is concerned primarily with the property assets of the parties. In modern English law, private law is not seen as a system. Its various branches, such as land law, contract, tort, family law and so on are presented in discrete boxes with little indication of how the boxes, when fitted together, form a coherent pattern. Modern continental laws, on the other hand, see private law as a whole composed of particular categories. Legal theorists, even in England, have tended to use the categories of continental law as the starting point of their analysis of legal institutions, and they are valuable as providing a bird's eye view of the ground covered by private law in any modern society. These institutions are arranged in the 'institutional system'. This system was developed in Roman law but provided a model for the presentation of private law not only in countries whose law was based on Roman law but also in England.[1] The most important medieval treatise on the laws and customs of England, that of Bracton in the thirteenth century, and the foundation of modern English law, Blackstone's *Commentaries on the Laws of England* in the eighteenth century, were both based on the institutional system.

After outlining the origin and development of this system we shall consider its various parts, first in Roman law and in the two main systems derived from it, French and German law, and shall also indicate some of the main features of the equivalent English law.

Most of the institutions of modern private law were developed in Roman law, and it is to the Roman Republic that we must look for the beginnings of systematic thinking about private law.[2] The early first century BC was the period when the ideas of Greek popular philosophy came to have a general influence on Roman ways of thinking. In particular the methods of Greek dialectic were used to organise various branches of knowledge in an orderly way by

1. Examples in A. Watson *The Making of the Civil Law* (1981) pp 62ff; cf H. F. Jolowicz *Roman Foundations of Modern Law* (1957) pp 61ff.
2. P. Stein 'The development of the Institutional System' in P. Stein and A. Lewis (eds) *Studies in Justinian's Institutes in memory of J. A. C. Thomas* (1983) pp 151ff.

classification. The Greeks themselves had used these methods in certain fields but had paid little attention to legal phenomena. For them, as we have seen (p 17), law was not a subject for professionals, and they preferred lay courts to professional. They were fascinated with rhetoric, with different modes of discourse, and they were interested in how to present an argument to a court of lay judges in the most effective way and in speculation about the role of law in society. But they produced no class of professional lawyers and appear to have given little attention to the analysis of legal rules. In Rome, on the other hand, as we have noted, there were specialist jurists from the late third century BC and it is understandable that they should want to present their craft as a science, worthy of comparison with grammar, rhetoric, architecture and the other sciences which were being presented in a systematic way.

Two techniques in particular were used in the classification process. The first, *diairesis* in Greek, or *divisio* in Latin, starts with the disparate mass of material to be classified and divides it into categories or *genera*. The second, *merismos* or *partitio*, starts with the whole which is formed by the sum of those categories and identifies the essential elements or parts of that whole.

The earliest work which attempted to classify the Roman civil law into *genera* is a treatise on the civil law by Q. Mucius Scaevola around 100 BC. It begins with wills, legacies and intestate succession. Problems arising out of the succession to the estate of someone who has died produced more legal disputes than any other kind of case. The traditional social order was based on the family, and the main purpose of a will was to designate the heirs who would continue the family into the next generation. They would take his place in the eyes of the law. Apart from instituting his heirs, a testator could by a will confer legacies of various types, appoint tutors to his children under puberty and free slaves. It will be seen that, especially in a society in which property had been concentrated in the family rather than in individual members, succession on death was a matter of concern to all families, and the subject occupied about a quarter of Mucius' treatise. The remaining topics do not fall into any recognisable order, although methods of acquiring ownership and possession appear to be grouped together. The scheme seems primitive, but it represents the first groping moves towards establishing the categories that were thought to be present in the law.

A century after Mucius, another jurist, Masurius Sabinus moved a stage further in the process of systematisation. His scheme is obviously based on that of Mucius but he has made some rearrangement to bring together topics whose relationship with each other had become recognised. He also begins with succession on death and follows it with some other matters concerned with the family, such as the power of the family head and the adoption of children into the family. Whereas theft of property and damage to property were separated in Mucius, they are now brought together, and certain other forms of wrongdoing are added to them, so that the category of delict, or wrongdoing, which gave the victim an action for a penalty, has emerged. There is however no category of contract and individual forms of creating a binding obligation are still separated from each other.

The great leap forward in the systematic presentation of private law was taken by a relatively obscure law teacher, Gaius, in the mid-second century AD. Gaius published a students' manual in four books, known as the Institutes, and it is his institutional scheme of arrangement which is the ancestor of modern civil codes. Gaius dealt with approximately the same topics as did Mucius and Sabinus before him, but he made one major addition – the law of actions treated separately from their subject matter. He then superimposed on this material a scheme for which there were no known precedents in legal literature. He divided the whole of private law into three parts, concerned with persons, things and actions. The largest of the three parts is things and that is further divided into three sub-categories, physical things, inheritances and obligations. Mucius and Sabinus would have regarded the designation 'things' as concerning only physical things, so that Gaius' classification of things involves the acceptance of at least three new conceptual notions: first, the recognition of incorporeal things as things alongside physical things; secondly, the classification of inheritances and of obligations as incorporeal things; and thirdly, the recognition of contract and delict as sources of obligations. In Gaius' scheme the category of things thus has to bear most of private law.

Why did Gaius adopt this scheme? The most likely answer is that he was trying to move from the stage of *divisio*, grouping isolated phenomena into categories, to that of *partitio*, identifying the parts of the law as a whole. By his time he could regard the contents of the civil law as more or less fixed and could identify its essential component elements. Such categorisation, especially one intended for students' use, had to be brief and concise, and it had to use large umbrella categories that would each cover a variety of topics which had not previously been brought together.

Gaius' Institutes was the model for Justinian's Institutes and through that work the institutional scheme was transmitted to later ages. There were, however, differences of emphasis between Gaius and Justinian. For Gaius the civil law was still, as it had been for his predecessors, a series of established legal institutions waiting to be described and classified, with an account of how they arise and how they cease. Under 'persons' Gaius gives an account of how slaves become free, how non-citizens become citizens, how the family head acquires power over his children. Under 'things', we are told how ownership is acquired and lost, how obligations arise and so on. Under 'actions' we are told not about the procedure for bringing or defending an action but about different kinds of action, such as the difference between actions that can be brought against anyone and those that can be brought only against particular individuals.

At the time of Gaius, the notion of 'a right' belonging to an individual had not been separated from the notion of the 'legal position' of an individual in a particular situation. In English we use different words for 'the law' and 'a right' conferred on an individual by the law. The objective sense of the word right is in English confined to morality, as when we speak of right and wrong. In Latin, and in modern European languages other than English, the same word (*ius, droit, Recht, diritto*) is used both for the law and for a right, and so it is not always clear which meaning is intended, or indeed whether one meaning rather than the other is intended. Between the time of Gaius and the time of Justinian, considerable progress had been made in developing the notion of the individual right, and consequently there was a movement towards looking at the whole law as a set of rights conferred in certain circumstances on persons capable of holding them.

The lawyers of Justinian's time were also beginning to recognise a distinction between substantive and adjective law, that is, between that part of the law which is concerned with rights and duties, and that part which is concerned with the enforcement of such rights through the procedures established for that purpose. Before lawyers thought in terms of rights, they put the remedy in the forefront of their minds. The question they asked themselves in a particular case was, 'has this man an action and if so, what action?' or 'is there a defence recognised by the law that is applicable in this case?' The law of actions was not distinguished from the rest of the law. The conditions in which a person could litigate could hardly be separated from the circumstances which were his justification for litigating.

Once they began to think in terms of rights, the means whereby those rights were vindicated became separated from the rights themselves. The procedure itself was a secondary matter, and non-procedural matters which had been treated under the heading of actions, such as whether, if a plaintiff or defendant died, the action could continue by or against his heir, now came to be regarded as matters of substantive law, qualifying the extent of the rights. It was now seen that the law could be regarded as conferring two kinds of right, first a primary right, for example, the right of the owner of property to use it as he wished, and then a supporting secondary right to an action against anyone who interfered with the primary right. In the case of rights concerning physical things, it was not difficult to distinguish the right of the owner to use them from his right to an action, which would only arise when someone interfered with the primary right. In the case of obligations, however, it was difficult to see what right the obligation conferred on the holder except to bring an action in certain circumstances. A creditor under a contract or the victim of a private wrong had a right to sue the debtor or the wrongdoer and that was all. So there was a tendency already in Justinian's law for obligations to be separated from the rest of the law of things and to be joined with what was left of the law of actions.

Thus the law of persons came to be seen as dealing with those who could be the subject of legal rights and duties, the law of things as dealing with the substance of those rights and duties and the law of obligations and actions as concerned with the conditions in which a person could sue and be sued.

We now turn to the parts of the system.

10 Persons

Roman law

In Rome the law of persons was organised around three factors: liberty, citizenship and family position. The fundamental distinction among human beings was between freemen and slaves. Only freemen were properly persons: slaves were things. A slave was the object of ownership by a freeman. He became a slave on birth if his mother was a slave or on capture in war. But slaves were different from all other things in that they were capable of becoming persons if their owner gave them freedom. Furthermore their activities could have a considerable effect on their owner's legal position, and an owner could use slaves as a modern man would use his employees. A slave could acquire property for his owner, and in an age when communication was not so easy as today and when transactions, which today would be carried out by correspondence or by telecommunication, had to be conducted personally, this was very useful to a man of property. Not only could the slave represent his owner in acquiring physical things; if a person promised to deliver something to Julius's slave, the promise could be enforced by Julius.

At first, although a slave-owner's position could be made better by his slave's activities, it could not be made worse, so that although the slave could receive a benefit for his owner he could not impose any obligation on him. The slave himself could not have enforceable rights or duties. The praetor helped to make him more effective in commerce, by introducing certain actions by which a third party who had dealt with the slave could in certain circumstances sue the slave's owner. If the owner had expressly represented the slave to the third party as acting on his behalf, then the owner would be liable on any contract the slave made with the third party. The practice grew up whereby, if a slave showed an aptitude for trade, his owner would give him a fund to trade with. The fund, known as *peculium*, belonged in law to the slave's owner. But by allowing the slave to trade with it, the latter was impliedly saying, to those who might deal with the slave, that he was authorising any transactions that the slave might engage in with the *peculium*, and that he, the owner, would be liable on those transactions. The advantage to the owner was that, apart from avoiding the social stigma that in certain periods attached to those who soiled their hands by engaging in trade, he was only liable to those with whom the slave dealt up to the limit of the *peculium*. This use of the slave and the parallel use of the services of the children in the power of their family head meant that there was no need for Roman law to develop two institutions which have become of crucial importance in modern commercial society, agency and limited liability. The slave fulfilled the role of the modern commercial agent and the fact that the damages obtainable in actions by the slave's creditors against his owner were limited to the amount of the *peculium* meant that the owner could vicariously engage in trade without risking all his assets. If the slave committed a wrong against someone outside the family, his owner had the choice of either paying damages to the victim or surrendering him to the latter (pp 26–7).

Assuming that a human being is either freeborn or has been freed, the next question is whether he is a citizen or not. In many early societies there is a substantial difference between the legal position of the insider, the member of the community, and the outsider who has not yet been admitted to the privileges of membership. The law is personal rather than territorial. It applies only to those who are regarded as members, who accept its mysteries and special traditions, but it has no application to foreigners who are not of the nation, even though they may be resident in the state. In the early Republic Roman law was no exception; the civil law was law for *cives*, citizens, and by definition did not apply to foreigners. When the number of foreigners was small, this did not matter much and it was possible to assume, for the purposes of litigation, that a foreigner was by a fiction a citizen. When the numbers increased, as we have seen, the Romans made special arrangements for cases involving foreigners to be dealt with by a specialist praetor, applying not the civil law but the law considered to be common to all civilised people. Eventually these rules of the *ius gentium* were fused with the traditional civil law. The effect was to bring the non-citizen into the ambit of Roman law for certain purposes, commercial transactions for example, while still excluding him from the more traditional parts of the law concerned with family and succession on death. A foreigner could not contract a Roman marriage, so that his children, although regarded as legitimate, were not in the same legal relationship to him as were Roman children to their fathers. Since he could not participate in the relevant ritual, which was part of the civil law, he could not own certain kinds of property. These differences gradually became less important. By the third century AD, practically all the inhabitants of the Empire were citizens, and so the distinction between citizen and non-citizen ceased to be significant and the elaborate rules governing the ways in which citizenship could be acquired became a dead letter.

If a person was free and a citizen, the next question was his position in the family. In early Roman society, the unit with which the law dealt was the family. Property was largely agricultural and was thought of as the family's. But it is difficult for a family to sue or be sued in a law court and already by the time recorded law begins, family property was ascribed to the family head, the *paterfamilias*, as owner. Socially he was considered the manager of the family farm and all that went with it, but legally he was sole owner and could dispose of it, for example, without the need to obtain the consent of other members of the family. It was legally and commercially convenient that he should have this power but it was only tolerable in a society in which the pressures of good faith and family solidarity controlled the way it was exercised.

As long as the *paterfamilias* lived, all his descendants through the male line (so-called agnatic relations) were subject to his power, unless he emancipated them from it and made them independent. He alone was *sui iuris*, subject to no-one's power. They did not gain legal independence from his power merely by becoming adults. From a modern standpoint the power of the *paterfamilias* seems tyrannical and primitive. He was said to have absolute authority, 'the power of life and death' over his sons and daughters and over his sons' children (his daughters' children were in the power of their father or his *paterfamilias*). In practice this meant that he could control who was admitted to membership of the family and could, for example, require the exposure of a baby who appeared to him to be handicapped and therefore a prospective burden on the family which it could not tolerate. He could also control whom his children married since that would affect who continued the family into the next generation.

Those subject to the power of the family head could have no property of their own and any acquisitions they made went to him. Unless he formally emancipated them, his descendants remained in his power until he died. Indeed their services to the family were more important when they became adults. Thus in law the position of a son in power was not so different from that of a slave. Like the slave he could be surrendered to someone he had wronged, if his family head would not pay damages. Like a slave he could be given a *peculium* which he could treat *de facto* as his own, but in the Empire this idea was extended so that anything the son acquired on military service, and later from any other outside source, was treated as if it were part of his *peculium*. In effect he was owner of such property in all but name, and could enjoy a high degree of economic independence, but the basic principle that only the *paterfamilias* was *sui iuris* independent was preserved.

Other institutions of the law of persons, marriage, adoption and guardianship, were considered as they affected paternal power. Roman marriage was a means of giving the paterfamilias that power. The Romans treated marriage in an enlightened way. They realised that most aspects of the relationship are of too intimate a character to be properly regulated by legal rules and that the law should restrict its application to the requirements for constituting and dissolving a marriage, and to the property consequences.

The earliest form of marriage was constituted by a religious ceremony or by the sale of the bride from her father's family group into that of her husband. If she was in power, her marriage merely transferred her from that of her own father or grandfather to that of her husband. If she was independent because her male ancestors had died, she lost her independence and her property and became her husband's (or his family head's if he was himself in power). This property would be her share of her father's estate. However, for those who were capable of contracting a Roman marriage, in that they had reached the age of puberty (which came to be fixed at 14 years for boys and 12 years for girls), and either had Roman citizenship or belonged to some specially privileged group of non-citizens and were not prohibited from marrying each other, for example, on grounds of close blood relationship or affinity (relationship through marriage), a formless type of marriage came to be recognised. This required only the consent of the parties and their family heads and evidence of their intention to constitute marriage rather than a lesser relationship. The advantage of this new type of marriage was that it left the wife's status unchanged and any property belonging to her remained hers.

Since the consent that provided the foundation of this marriage was necessary also for its continuance, the marriage could be dissolved by the withdrawal of consent by either party, that is by unilateral repudiation. This freedom for either party to divorce the other at will was restricted after the Empire became officially Christian in the fourth century. Repudiation without good cause was still valid in ending the marriage but the offending party was penalised. Normally when a marriage took place a wife or her family provided a dowry, which, as long as the marriage lasted, was the property of the husband, who could use it for the expenses of the household. At the conclusion of the marriage by death of the husband or by divorce, the wife was entitled to recover it, but the husband was allowed to retain certain fractions in respect of children of the marriage who remained in his care, the wife's misconduct and on other grounds (p 156).

Apart from his children by a Roman marriage the *paterfamilias* had paternal power over those who had been adopted into the family. There were two forms of adoption, according to whether the person adopted was subject to power or independent. If he was subject to power the matter was treated as a private transaction between the existing *paterfamilias* and the adopting *paterfamilias*. The motive for such a transaction would often be economic. If the adopting family lacked young males, because of death or a surplus of daughters, its head would seek to remedy the gap in the family team by adoption from a family with sons to spare, rather in the way that football players are transferred from one club to another today (except that the latter have some choice about being transferred!). If, on the other hand, the person being adopted was himself independent, his adoption would involve the extinction of his family, even if that family only consisted of himself. The public, and in particular the religious authorities, thus had an interest in the proposed transaction, known as adrogation, which had therefore to be approved by a popular assembly in the Republic and by the imperial chancery in the Empire. Such approval would only be given on certain conditions.

Those who were independent, because their male ancestors had died, might still not have full legal capacity. They might be under the age of puberty, and in that case, although they would have inherited their share of the family property, it would be managed on their behalf by guardians, called tutors. Originally this function went to the adult male agnate or agnates nearest in relationship to him, found by counting the steps up to the common ancestor and then down. They would succeed to that property if the child, known as the pupil, died before he reached puberty and so attained the power to dispose of it. Thus the tutor's concern was to preserve the property for the family, but he not only had an interest in the safety of his pupil's property; he also had an interest in his death. Already the Twelve Tables provided that if the father had nominated a tutor for his children under puberty, he was to have precedence over the nearest agnate. Later the institution came to be regarded as wholly for the benefit of the pupil, and safeguards were introduced to ensure that the tutor administered the property carefully. When the pupil was able to understand what was happening, the function of the tutor was to authorise the transaction which was carried out by the child himself. Any transaction that might prejudice the pupil, which was carried out without such authorisation, could not be enforced against the pupil.

Originally a child *sui iuris* attained full legal capacity on reaching puberty. His tutor ceased to function, but in a relatively simple society a youth of 14 could usually cope with life. As society became more complex and the forms of gaining and losing property became more difficult to grasp, a statute was passed to protect young adults who lacked experience in the ways of the world. If such a youth had been prejudiced in his dealings with an outsider, the obligation he had undertaken could not be enforced against him, and the transaction could even be set aside completely. To avoid these consequences, those dealing with young adults would insist on the transaction in question being approved on the youth's behalf by an independent person. Since the latter's role was similar to that of the curator, who looked after the affairs of one who through insanity could not look after his property for himself, he was also called curator. Any young man under 25 years could have a curator.

Women who were *sui iuris* were not considered to have full legal capacity even on becoming adults and retained a tutor. It was recognised in practice that women were capable of looking after their property and the tutor's powers were gradually reduced until his authority for any transaction desired by the woman could be compelled. It would have been more logical to have abolished tutors for adult women, but as in the case of the *peculium* of the adult son in power, the Romans disliked making drastic legal changes, especially where such a pivotal social institution as the family was concerned. So they preserved the institution but denuded it of its practical inconveniences.

Modern law

The law of persons in the modern civil law and in the modern common law can be treated together because it displays many common features in both kinds of law. There are two reasons for this. First, in all European countries, and in England as much as anywhere else, the Church in the early middle ages took over the supervision of matters concerned with personal status, the family and with succession to movable or (as it was called in England) 'personal' property (p 181). The Church courts, applying canon law, had exclusive jurisdiction in any matter concerning clerics (and many people performing what would today be regarded as secular functions were then in holy orders). The Church courts decided all questions relating to marriage, because marriage was a sacrament, and since such questions as the legitimacy of children and the powers of parents over children depended on the validity of the marriage, these matters too were regulated by canon law. That law was itself heavily influenced by Roman law, and tended to follow the Roman rules unless Christian doctrine or morality dictated otherwise. Its procedure was based on that of the late Roman Empire. When jurisdiction in personal matters was transferred to the ordinary secular courts (with an intermediate stage, in the case of Protestant countries, when they were dealt with by Protestant

Church courts), the established principles of the old law were retained, so that the basis of the law of persons everywhere was Roman law filtered through canon law.

The second reason for the similarity of the law of persons in most systems today is simply that, for the last century or more, all industrial countries have undergone similar social changes which have altered people's attitudes to the relationships between members of society generally and particularly to those within the family. As a result the law has been subjected to a sustained critique with a view to eliminating unequal treatment of those who should be treated alike. Much of the old law has been superseded and, although they have been greater in some countries than others, the changes have been everywhere motivated by the same ideas.

1. Legal persons

The first point to note about the modern law of persons is that it is not only concerned with natural persons, that is human beings, but also with legal or juristic persons. These are collections of persons which are treated as having separate personalities from those of their members. In continental countries they are sometimes strangely called moral persons, although all moral decisions made in their name must be taken by natural persons. When the Romans spoke about persons they had in mind only human beings. They did recognise that in a few cases, such as a municipality, or a guild of craftsmen, a group of persons could be legal subjects, in that they could sue and be sued separately from their members. But they did not speak of them as persons and in general they were reluctant to allow such groups to be regarded as having a similar position before the law as a family head. The medieval canonists, on the other hand, in their desire to clarify the legal position of ecclesiastical groups, such as an abbey or a cathedral chapter, prepared the way for the recognition of a group as itself a person.

Modern legal systems recognise many such legal persons, most commonly commercial companies. Their property is distinct from that of their members, who own transferable shares in the company, but do not own the company property (that belongs to the company itself). A company which has a legal personality may or may not have limited liability in the sense that its creditors can recover what is owed to them only up the amount of the company's property; they cannot proceed against the shareholders in respect of *their* property. The civil law developed the commercial company out of the institution of partnership. In Roman law, as in English law, a partnership was not a separate legal person from the partners, and partnership property was jointly owned by all the partners. But the developed civil law attributed personality to partnerships and by the early nineteenth century had recognised the possibility of companies created by the will of the members (subject only to requirements of registration). As a means of encouraging investment in industry and commerce by those who were not prepared to risk the whole of their property, such companies were allowed to have limited liability.

English law, on the other hand, was much slower to recognise commercial companies.[1] A corporate body, known as a corporation, could exist, but only if created by a special charter from the Crown or by special Act of Parliament. The procedure was costly and such creations were rare, and some well-known associations, such as Lloyds of London, the Stock Exchange and the Inns of Court were not incorporated. The difficulties about keeping the property of the association distinct from that of the members was overcome by the device of the trust, which will be described later. When traders began to form companies, in which a number of individuals had transferable shares in a common fund, they were regarded as legally permissible. The problem was how they should be classified. Since the only persons whose existence the common law acknowledged, apart from individual human beings, were corporations, such companies could not have a separate personality from their members. So they were regarded as partnerships. After the wave of company promotions in the early eighteenth century, culminating in the failure of the South Sea Company, Parliament intervened to stop what the so-called Bubble Act[2] of 1720 called the 'growth of dangerous and mischievous undertakings and projects wherein the undertakers and subscribers have presumed to make their shares transferable', and declared them illegal. The Act was repealed after a hundred years, and companies again became legal. Twenty years later it became possible for people to form themselves into a joint stock company merely by satisfying certain formal requirements of registration. Although a joint stock company could sue and be sued separately from its members, the latter were still liable in full for its debts. Such a company was still regarded as a special sort of partnership rather than a special sort of corporation and so was not classified as a person. Even after limited liability was allowed in 1855, the leading authority classified companies as partnerships and so did not consider them to be persons like corporations.

By the end of the century, however, and under the influence of continental theories, English lawyers were clear that a limited company was as much a person in England as on the continent. They

---

1. P. Stein 'Nineteenth century English company law and theories of legal personality' (1982–3) 11–12 Quaderni Fiorentini 503.
2. 6 George I, c. 18.

were more concerned about the status of trade unions, which had been banned but were receiving increasing legal recognition. By then continental law had moved one stage further in the development of legal personality. For nineteenth-century German legal theorists applied the notion not only to associations of natural persons but also to funds of property, the income of which was set aside for carrying out specified purposes. Such foundations, or *Stiftungen*, could continue indefinitely and the problem for the civil law was to find an owner for them. Once again English law dealt with the problem by means of the trust, but that was not available on the continent. The French Civil Code of 1804 did not recognise foundations. The Austrian Code of 1811 recognised 'property destined for a purpose', but did not attribute personality to it (ABGB 646, 849). By 1900, however, when the German Civil Code appeared, foundations had emerged as full legal persons (BGB 80–88).

2. Natural persons

Most of the law of persons deals with natural persons. It traditionally included three kinds of rules:[3] first, those laying down the conditions under which persons belonging to different classes of people may be the subjects of rights and duties, that is, rules of status and capacity; secondly, those dealing with the rights exercised by persons over other persons rather than over things, such as a father's right over his child or a guardian's right over his ward in regard to their education and manner of life; and thirdly, those dealing with rights which cannot be quantified in money terms, such as a man's right to personal liberty and reputation. These rights cannot belong to the law of things and therefore fall more appropriately under the law of persons.

In the nineteenth century, however, a distinction was introduced between those rights which affect a person as an individual member of the community and those which affect him as a member of a family. The law of persons was then divided into the law of persons proper and family law. In the French Code Civil of 1804, family law is still treated under the heading of persons in Book I, but in the German BGB of 1900, persons are dealt with in the general part in Book I and family law appears quite separately in Book IV.

In the modern law of persons proper, the rules controlling the legal capacity of people in different classes have been much simplified since the Roman law of antiquity. Slavery has disappeared, but until the eighteenth century many legal systems ascribed a different legal status to different social groups. England eliminated most of these survivals, but in some continental countries

---

3.   H. F. Jolowicz *Roman Foundations of Modern Law* (1957) p 69.

members of the nobility, serfs, peasants, city merchants, and others had differing legal capacity, the most elaborate examples being found in the final manifesto of the ancien régime, the Prussian ALR of 1794. In the nineteenth century, however, these distinctions were swept away, and although some rules, especially in relations between employers and workers, favoured one party rather than the other, social distinctions were no longer reinforced by legal differences. So in a famous aphorism Sir Henry Maine was able to say in 1859 that 'the movement of progressive societies has hitherto been a movement *from Status to Contract*'.[4] The slave had been replaced by the free servant, the female no longer needed a tutor, a son of full age was no longer subject to his father's power. Many perons whose legal position had previously been fixed by their birth, sex or other circumstances outside their control could now fix their legal position for themselves by agreement with others. The only legal differences that remained were those based on lack of one of the attributes of a normal person, such as adulthood or sanity.

In England citizenship, although important in relation to such matters as immigration into the country, is less relevant in private law, since English law is applied to all who are domiciled in England, in the sense of having an intention permanently to reside there. In civil law countries, on the other hand, citizenship is still important in private law, because a person's capacity in matters of family and succession on death is determined by the law of the country of which he is a citizen rather than that of the country in which he lives. A person's capacity to enter into a valid marriage is fixed by his national law; after his death succession to his estate is governed by the law of the state of which he was a citizen when he died.

In most matters of daily life, however, all residents are now treated as equals before the law, and efforts are made to give more substance to the personal rights that the law attributes to them. In some countries which have a written constitution, the rights of individuals are not only stated but are expressed in such a way as to enable an individual to bring a private law action against anyone who interferes with them. The German Federal Constitution or Basic Law guarantees the individual protection not only of his personal freedom but also of his 'personality'. In a famous decision in 1954, the Federal Constitutional Court enabled the writer of a letter to a periodical, which published it in a doctored and misleading form, to sue for damages in a private law action based on the invasion of 'the private sphere of the author as protected by the right of personality'.[5]

4. *Ancient Law* ch 5 (Everyman edn, p 100).
5. Horn, Kötz, Leser, p 167.

In recent years, efforts have been made through legislation to promote the equal treatment of individuals by penalising certain forms of discrimination. For example, in Britain the Sex Discrimination Act 1975 forbids giving some people less favourable treatment than others, on grounds of sex, in employment, education (with the exception of exclusively single sex establishments) and the supply of goods and services to the public. The Act set up the Equal Opportunities Commission which investigates abuses and may provide financial support for actions by individuals who allege discrimination against themselves. The Race Relations Act 1976 makes similar provisions against discrimination on grounds of 'colour, race, nationality or national origins', and established the Commission for Racial Equality to provide for its enforcement. Previously, although all were formally equal in the eyes of the law, people could use their bargaining power to discriminate against particular groups. This kind of legislation introduces a new notion of equality which overrides their freedom to deal with others in any way they please.

3. *Family law*

Family law is normally subdivided into the law of husband and wife, of parent and child and of guardian and ward.

The law of marriage was developed by the canonists on the basis of Roman law and the essential requirements of a marriage in modern systems are the same as in Roman law. The parties must have reached a certain age; they must not be within the prohibited degrees of relationship in kindred and affinity; they must give their consent freely to the marriage; and, in the case of a party who has not yet reached full age and therefore is not of full capacity, the parents' consent is also needed. The main difference between modern law and Roman law is the requirement of a formal public celebration. It was far more important for the canon law to require a clear cut formality than for Roman law to do so, since in principle Roman law considered that a marriage lasted only as long as consent continued, whereas the Church regarded marriage as a binding commitment for life and did not recognise any divorce which allowed remarriage. Yet until the end of the middle ages the canon law retained the Roman rule that allowed the parties to express their consent informally. Even an informal agreement by the parties that they would marry in the future, followed by sexual intercourse between the parties, was sufficient for a marriage to be presumed in the absence of any ceremony. The law offered much scope for arguing that an apparent marriage was not a marriage at all. As F. W. Maitland put it:

> 'Of all people in the world lovers are the least likely to distinguish precisely between the present and future tenses. In

the middle ages, marriages or what looked like marriages, were exceedingly insecure. The union which had existed for many years between man and woman might with fatal ease be proved adulterous.'[6]

The canonists alleviated some of the hardships by the rule that if at least one party believed that a valid marriage existed, the children would be legitimate. Finally in 1563 the Council of Trent required that marriages of Catholics should be constituted before a priest and at least two witnesses, but England retained the medieval rule until 1753. In Scotland 'irregular' marriages, either by the informal expression of the parties' present will to be married or by the expression of a future intention to be married, followed by intercourse, were possible until 1940 and even today marriages may be constituted by cohabitation 'with habit and repute', where the parties live together with the repute of being man and wife. Today the celebration of marriage in England may be either by a religious ceremony or by a secular ceremony before a state official. In both France and Germany marriage must be celebrated before a state official. The parties may add a religious ceremony if they wish, but it has no legal force.

The effect of marriage until relatively recently was to subject the wife to her husband's control while at the same time making him liable to maintain her and the children of the marriage. Both the French and German codes expressed this authoritarian idea of the family by identifying the husband squarely as its head. All decisions affecting the family were taken by him, and in such matters as place of residence, the wife was bound to defer to his wishes. His permission was required for her to accept a job outside the home and if he decided that she should stay at home to look after the household, he could require her to give up a job that she had.

So far as property relations of husband and wife were concerned, continental law offered a bewildering variety of marital property schemes, ranging from complete separation of the property of husband and wife to a general community which included all their property whether brought to the marriage or acquired during it. Most of them were derived from regional customs which the makers of the codes did not feel able to unify. The parties could at the time of the marriage choose which scheme they wished to apply to their property relations and, in the absence of such agreement, the law provided that one of the schemes should apply. Normally, whatever the rights of ownership, the husband actually administered the property.

6. F. Pollock and F. W. Maitland *History of English Law* (2nd edn, 1899) II. pp 368–9.

As part of the general movement to put husband and wife on an equal footing, the old rules have been drastically amended. In Germany the main changes were made by the Law of Equal Rights of Man and Woman of 18 June 1957 and in France by the law of 13 July 1965. These statutes eliminated the formal traces of the subjection of wife to husband by providing that such questions as the management of the household and work outside the home should be decided by agreement between the spouses. Both laws also introduced a new property scheme which applies in the absence of agreement to the contrary (which is normally to maintain separate property). It is essentially a community of acquisitions and applies only to property acquired by either spouse during the marriage. The aim is to help the wife who has remained at home looking after the household and has not had the chance of earning money for herself by giving her a share of any increase in the family property.

Under the English common law the effect of a marriage was to make a husband and wife one person. She could have no property of her own and could make no contract on her own behalf. By the end of the nineteenth century the principle of separate property had been introduced, but although this was suitable for the rare case in which both spouses had substantial assets of their own, it does not fit the usual situation where neither spouse has much capital and the main income is that of the husband. Proposals for the introduction of some scheme of community of property on the continental model have so far not found favour in England although a series of statutes have given the wife rights in particular kinds of property, such as in the matrimonial home.

Normally the rules are of little interest to the spouses while the marriage lasts but they become of great practical importance when it ends, whether by death or divorce. The wife's claims on her husband's death belong to the law of succession. For a long time, even in Protestant countries which accepted the notion, divorces were difficult to obtain. When social pressures compelled the general availability of divorce, it was based on the principle of fault, that is, it was only allowed when one spouse had committed a 'matrimonial offence' against the other, such as adultery, desertion or cruelty. The character of the legal process, therefore, inevitably required one spouse to be found guilty and the other innocent. In recent years, most countries have replaced the principle of fault by that of the breakdown of the marriage as the basis of divorce. The new principle was introduced in England by the Divorce Reform Act 1969 (now consolidated in the Matrimonial Causes Act 1973), in France by the law of 11 July 1975, and in Germany by the law of 14 June 1976. Some details vary, as in regard to the period during which the spouses must have lived apart where one of them does not agree to the divorce. But the general effect is now that divorce can be obtained on demand if both parties agree that the marriage has broken down, and even if only one of them so desires, it can be obtained after a period of living apart. Thus modern law has almost returned to the classical Roman notion of marriage based on consent and dissoluble at will.

After a divorce, the property of the spouses is divided in France and Germany on the basis of the community regime to which it was subject. In England, the court that grants the divorce has a wide discretion to transfer the property of one spouse to another after taking account of all the circumstances of the case. A rule of thumb which has been commonly followed is that a wife should receive half of the proceeds of the matrimonial home, and in respect of income should get one third of the joint resources.

The father's control over his children has now become a parental control, exercised by both parents. It is no longer thought of as power over the child but rather as control over the child's mode of life and education exercised for the child's benefit. The change of attitude was symbolised by the German law of 18 July 1979 which substituted the term 'parental care' for that of 'parental power'. The control ceases when the child reaches full age, which has now generally been fixed at the age of 18 years. Adoption of children has to be approved by a court (in England the magistrates' court has jurisdiction in such matters), which must be satisfied that it is in the interests of the child, and, if the child is old enough, his wishes are consulted. The child's parents or guardian must also agree to the adoption. Adoption orders may be made in favour of married couples or of single unmarried persons. In France a married couple must have been married five years before they can seek to adopt and, except in the case of the adoption of a relative, the unmarried adopter has to be at least 30 years of age.

A guardian of a child may be one of the parents or a person appointed by the will of a deceased parent or by a court to control the upbringing of the child and look after his property on his behalf. In England the court may itself assume the responsibilities of a guardian by making the child a 'ward of court'.

11 Property

Roman law

The law of property grew out of the law of physical things and it is with the relations between persons and physical things that we are now concerned. In simple societies, these relations are looked at more in regard to the social position that they confer than in regard to their economic function. In a society based on agriculture, land has a different significance than it has in a society based on commerce, in which money is the basis of status. Ownership of land does not merely give control of the most important means of production; it confers a particular position in society, which may impose on the owner duties to others as well as power over others and which may pass from one generation to another in a family. Movables, on the other hand, lack this symbolic significance and pass more readily from one individual to another.

The law of property fixes the circumstances in which particular things belong to particular persons, when they can say that the things are theirs rather than someone else's. At this stage it is not necessary to specify the precise character of the right of the person entitled. Even in a relatively simple society, however, it may happen that B has in his possession things that belong to A, and it becomes necessary to define B's legal position and distinguish it from that of A. At a certain stage A may want to allow other people to do certain things in relation to his things, without himself giving up enjoyment of them, for example, by giving his neighbour a right of way over his land; or he may want to split up the entitlement to his property after his death by, say, allowing his widow to enjoy it during her lifetime only, after which it should pass to his children. When society demands these developments, it becomes necessary to define the relationship between a person and his things in a more abstract way by saying that he has ownership and the others have rights less than ownership.

The Romans recognised the natural distinction between movable things and immovable things. Land and the buildings on it are in all societies of great economic and social importance. The fact that land is permanent and cannot be moved cannot be ignored by the law. The Romans, however, did not structure their law of property

144

around the distinction. For them, things were classified rather into *res mancipi*, a category which included land, slaves and the animals used for farm work, such as oxen, horses and mules, on the one hand, and all other things (*res nec mancipi*), on the other. The importance of the distinction in early times was that *res mancipi* could only be transferred by a formal method of conveyance requiring considerable publicity, whereas other things could be transferred by informal delivery.

1. Ownership and possession

The Romans distinguished between ownership (*dominium*) and possession. Normally, of course, a man owns what he possesses, and there is no need to distinguish what he possesses from the things to which he is entitled. But he may own things that are possessed by someone else and the notions are distinct. Ownership is a matter of entitlement.

Whoever was entitled to a thing, of whatever kind, could claim it from anyone who had it in his control by an action called *vindicatio*, in which he offered to prove that the thing was legally his. The formula for this action did not even name the defendant. His identity was irrelevant, for if the plaintiff proved that the thing was his, the defendant would lose the action unless he had a specific recognised defence. The owner, then, is the man who can claim a thing by bringing the *vindicatio*. Possession is essentially a matter of fact; the possessor has the thing in his control. The distinction becomes important in law for two reasons. First, certain persons who have things in their control are given legal protection as possessors, irrespective of entitlement, while others are not. Secondly, through possession one can in certain circumstances acquire ownership.

Certain possessors were given remedies, possessory interdicts, by which they could prevent others from disturbing their possession or recover possession from those who had dispossessed them. The aim of these interdicts was to maintain the peace by discouraging those who believed they were entitled to property from resorting to self-help. Even an owner should not physically dispossess a possessor; he should assert his ownership by *vindicatio*, and a possessor should be able to sit tight by virtue of his possession alone until someone else proved in a *vindicatio* that he was entitled as owner. There was, however, a limit to Roman powers of self-restraint. One who had taken the thing by force, or secretly, or by permission from another was not protected as against him, although he might be protected against others.

In general those possessors who had the benefit of the possessory interdicts also claimed to be entitled to the thing; they held the thing in the manner of an owner. This category included the owner-possessor, the *bona fide possessor*, who had acquired the thing from one whom he believed to be owner but who was in fact not so, and also the *mala fide possessor*, the thief who knew he was not owner but was pretending to be.

The great advantage of the possessory interdicts to those to whom the praetor granted them was that they did not have the bother of proving that they were entitled to the thing as owners. They just had to prove that they were in control, and that was largely a question of fact. The owner-possessor would find it simpler to rely on his possession to recover his property than to prove his ownership in the *vindicatio*. The possessor who was not owner could ensure that he stayed in possession until the owner successfully vindicated from him. Where rival claims are put forward, it is always an advantage to be the defendant, since it is the plaintiff who has to prove that the thing is his.

Those who held the thing by virtue of a contract did not generally have possessory protection. For example, a tenant under a lease held the thing in the name of the lessor and it was the latter who could bring the possessory interdict if the control of the tenant was disturbed by a third party. This rule meant that entitlement to the possessory interdicts might be separated from actual physical control, but it was justified on the ground that to lend or grant a lease of something should not interrupt the possession of the lessor, particularly since uninterrupted possession was a means of acquiring ownership. In a few exceptional cases those holding under contract *were* given the possessory interdicts, the main case being the pledgee who held the thing as security for a debt owed to him by the owner. If the pledgee were not a protected possessor, the owner could have just taken his pledge back. As it was, he had to fall back on *vindicatio* and if he tried to bring that, he would be met by a defence based on the contract of pledge. In legal language only those protected by the interdicts were said to have 'possession', as opposed to physical control, and so possession became a technical legal notion.

Possession was related to the acquisition of ownership in two ways. The transfer of possession was an integral part of the main method by which an owner conveyed his rights to another; and if one received the thing from a non-owner one could through possession sometimes acquire ownership.

The main method of conveying ownership was by physical delivery of the thing (*traditio*). By the time of Justinian, when the distinction between *res mancipi* and other things had been abolished, this was the only method of conveying physical things. The act of handing something over is itself neutral. Its legal effect will depend on a prior arrangement between the parties. If A delivers his chariot to B, it may be because he has agreed to lend to to B, or it may be because he has sold it to B or wants to make a gift of it to B. In the first case A will remain owner, even though he has handed it over. (He will also remain technically in possession.) In the other two cases B will become owner. But he will only become owner if A has been the owner, since delivery of the thing cannot make him more entitled to it than A was. Delivery thus constitutes a method of acquisition if the transferor is entitled to deliver and if the delivery is accompanied by an appropriate 'cause', a transaction as a consequence of which ownership would normally pass. Sale and gift are such causes, for the seller or donor retains no entitlement to the thing, but loan is not since the lender retains his entitlement.

The classical jurists made a sharp distinction between contracts, which had no effect on ownership, and conveyances, which did transfer ownership. The arrangement for sale of a thing was a contract, but the seller remained the owner until he conveyed the thing to the buyer. If, after he had sold the thing to B, A got a better offer from C, he could sell to C, and if he delivered the thing to C, he would make C the owner. The only remedy that B would have was an action against A on the first contract for whatever loss he had suffered in not having the thing. The contract would give him no claim to the thing itself, since it had never been conveyed to him and so he had never become owner.

The arrangement that explained the purpose of the physical delivery was thus as essential a part of *traditio* as the delivery itself. The two parts could, however, be separated. If the transferee of ownership had already received physical delivery, then an appropriate contract would supply the necessary indication of intention to transfer ownership to him and there would be a valid *traditio*. For example, if B borrowed a chariot from A, A would retain both ownership and possession. But if B later agreed to buy it from him, all that was required for the transfer of ownership was proper evidence of the sale. Before the sale, B held the chariot on behalf of A; afterwards he held it for himself. This was known as 'delivery with the short hand' (*traditio brevi manu*).

The classical lawyers had more hesitation in admitting the opposite situation in which the transferor having agreed to sell or make a gift, nevertheless keeps control of the thing as a borrower or tenant. That was too obviously an evasion of the requirement that the transfer of ownership required physical delivery as well as manifestation of intention. It became accepted, however, at least in the case of land, that where the sale or gift was evidenced by a written document, it could contain a clause allowing the seller or donor to keep control for a limited period (*constitutum possessorium*). So long as this clause referred to a specific transaction under which the holder made no claim to ownership, such as loan or lease, the ownership was transferred immediately without physical delivery. It was but a short step to recognising that ownership could be transferred by delivery of title deeds to the thing rather than delivery of the thing itself.

We have noted that *traditio* was only effective to transfer ownership when the transferor was owner, since he could not convey a better right to the thing than he had himself. If the person receiving the thing believed that the transferor was owner when he was not, the recipient became *bona fide possessor*. From early times Roman law recognised that such a possessor could become owner if he continued to possess for a period of time. It was undesirable that entitlement to property should be subject to doubt for too long. Those entitled to things they did not possess should assert their claims quickly or lose them. Anyone who acquired possession in good faith from a non-owner as a result of a transaction which would normally have provided a cause for the transfer of ownership, such as sale, would become owner if he kept possession without interruption for one year in the case of movables and two years in the case of land (*usucapio*). There was, however, an important proviso which limited the scope of this rule. It did not apply if the thing had at any time been stolen. *Usucapio* also operated to make a person owner if he received a *res mancipi*, which he had bought from the owner, by mere informal delivery instead of by the appropriate formal ceremony.

Usucapio is a form of what is today called acquisitive prescription, whereby a non-owner acquires ownership through lapse of time. The alternative way of approaching the matter is extinctive prescription, whereby the owner's right of action to recover his thing is cancelled after a certain period. It was only because of the short periods needed for *usucapio* that classical Roman law was able to require the claimant in *vindicatio* to prove an absolute title to the thing, valid against everyone, instead of merely a better right than the defendant. Anyone whose title was defective could usually rectify it by possessing the thing, so long as it had not been stolen, for one or two years. Roman law also had rules of extinctive prescription (*longi temporis praescriptio*), which were fused with those of *usucapio* by Justinian. Thereafter in the case of land, 10 or 20 years' possession was required, depending on whether the owner and the possessor lived in the same or in different provinces; in the case of movables 3 years' possession was needed. However the possessor could now add to his own possession the period of possession accumulated by the person from whom he had acquired the thing. If those entitled failed to take action to recover their property within the requisite periods, they lost their rights. Even where the property was stolen and the owner was unable to assert his rights because he was unaware of where it was, his rights were barred after 30 years.

The methods of acquiring ownership that we have considered were the most important in practice. The jurists also gave much attention to so-called original methods, whereby the person acquiring the thing becomes owner without regard to whether the person from whom he acquires was owner or not. The situations to which these methods apply do not occur frequently in everyday life, but they do arise occasionally, and the Romans considered that they should be settled by natural and universal rules, which were discoverable by careful and logical analysis. The institutions which they worked out in discussion of hypothetical cases in school have a more academic flavour than those of *traditio* or *usucapio* but they are worthy of notice as illustrations of the thoroughness with which the jurists analysed fact-situations. Whenever such situations arise today, it is the Roman analysis that is followed.

By occupation, a person acquires ownership in things that have no present owner, by taking possession of them. Examples are wild animals, birds or fish, which are only capable of being owned when they are captured and continue to be owned only as long as they are kept in captivity. If they escape, they cease to be owned (tame creatures, on the other hand, continue to be owned, even if they evade their owner's control).

Situations in which one thing is joined to another attracted much discussion. If the two things can be separated, as when A's wheel has been attached to B's cart, they retain their distinct identities, and the joining does not affect the change of ownership. If the two things are inseparable, but the union has been made by agreement between the two owners, no problem will arise because either they will have agreed about the ownership of the resulting whole or it will be presumed that they intended to own it jointly in proportion to the value of the respective components.

It was when things were joined inseparably without any prior agreement that problems arose. In this situation everything depended on the relationship between the components and the whole created by the joining of those components. If the whole could be identified as still the same kind of thing as both components, but there was just more of it, there was joint ownership of the whole (*confusio*). This would be the case if A's wine got mixed with B's wine or if A's lump of metal was melted and fused with B's lump of metal. Where, however, one thing retained its previous identity, but the identity of the other was merged in it, the owner of the principal thing became owner of the whole by *accessio*. Thus if A's patch was sewn into B's coat, the coat was still recognisably B's, but A's patch was no longer identifiable as a distinct thing and so ownership in it passed from A to B. Where a movable acceded to land, whether by planting or by building, the land was always the principal thing, and so the tree, crop or building passed to the owner of the land. In some cases it was possible to identify the building materials even after the building had been completed. However an old rule, found already in the Twelve Tables, provided that no-one could require the demolition of a building to recover his materials. If, when the house was pulled down for other reasons, the materials became separated from the land, their previous owner could then claim them, as his ownership was held to revive, once the materials had recovered their identity as separate things.

Finally there was the case when a thing belonging to A, or things belonging to A and B, were changed by the work of C so that they became a new thing different from what had been there before (*specificatio*). C makes a pie out of A's apples and B's flour, or C makes a statue out of A's silver or of B's wood. In the absence of agreement, who owns the pie or the statue? Is it the owner, or owners, of the materials or is it the maker? A good case could be argued in favour of either view, and the matter was vigorously debated by the Sabinian and Proculian schools of jurists. The Proculians were sticklers for exact description and in their view the owner of the materials could not vindicate the new thing. If he 'described the thing as he owned it, he would be describing what no longer existed and if he described it as it actually was, he would be describing something he had not previously owned'.[1] Since the thing in its present form had not belonged to anyone before, they ascribed it, perhaps on the basis of occupation, to the maker. The Sabinians, holding the original thing to be still the same thing notwithstanding the changes, thought the Proculian view too legalistic, and they appealed to common sense to justify their ascribing the new thing to the owner of the materials. Justinian adopted a third view. If the thing could not be reduced to the original materials it belonged to the maker. If the materials could be restored to their former state, there was no change of ownership, unless the maker had contributed some of his own materials, in which case he owned the new thing. Although presented as a compromise between the two views of classical law, there was a sound economic basis for Justinian's view. In most cases where the materials were of greater value than the labour, for example, where something was made out of precious metal, the rule would give the new thing to the owner of the materials, because it could be reduced back into its former state. In the cases where the materials could not be so reduced, for example, where something was made out of wood or of marble, the value of the labour in relation to that of the materials would be higher, and so the maker's claims would be stronger.

---

1. J. A. C. Thomas 'Form and substance in Roman Law' [1966] Current Legal Problems 154.

A somewhat similar debate revolved around the problems of who was entitled to treasure, valuables found in the ground, whose owner could no longer be traced. In this situation there are three competitors for the thing, the finder, the owner of the ground on which the find is made and the community as a whole, represented by the head of state. The rule eventually adopted was that if the finding was by chance on private land, the finder and the owner of the land shared it equally.

In the cases considered, the question of entitlement to the thing, to whom did it belong, was treated as quite distinct from the question of compensation of the loser by the gainer. That would depend on other considerations, such as whether the materials had been stolen. If so there would be actions against the thief, even though the thing stolen no longer existed. The rules about acquisition were concerned with who could claim the thing by *vindicatio*.

2. Rights less than ownership

We have seen that to be owner of a thing does not necessarily imply that one is actually enjoying the use of it. Ownership was the ultimate right to a thing which might for the moment be in other hands. It might be possessed by a thief who had let it out to a tenant who himself had actual physical control. Both the thief and his tenant would lose the thing if the owner traced it and claimed it. Once he had the thing in his possession, the owner could enjoy the use of it. These rights of enjoyment could themselves be severed from the ownership, through the creation of rights in things owned by another (*iura in re aliena*). Such rights fall into three main categories: praedial servitudes, personal servitudes and rights of real security.

The earliest to be recognised were *praedial servitudes*. They could be created where two adjoining pieces of land were in separate ownership and they enabled the owner of one piece (the dominant land) either to do something on the other (the servient land), which he would otherwise not be allowed to do, or else to prevent the owner of the servient land from doing something which he would otherwise be entitled to do. For example, the owner of land A might have the right to walk or drive cattle over a path on land B. Or the owner of land A might have the right to stop the owner of land B from building on his land in such a way as to interrupt the flow of light to the windows of A's house. In each case the exercise of B's ownership of his land was in some way limited. The right had in some way to be for the benefit of the dominant land and was a restriction on the ownership of the servient land, but the owner of the latter could not normally be required to do anything; he merely had to put up with the limitations on his ownership (and in many cases he would have received payment for it). Indeed the range of possible praedial servitudes was limited precisely so that there should not be too great a reduction of the servient owner's enjoyment of his ownership.

Such a right could, of course, always be created by a contract between the two owners, but in that case it would be enforceable only so long as they both owned their respective pieces of land. A praedial servitude, by contrast, was attached to the land, and the benefit and burden of it 'ran with' the two pieces of land, so that it was enforceable by or against anyone who owned the relevant land, whether they were aware of it when they acquired the land or not. It thus conferred a right which, like ownership itself, was enforceable against anyone.

Personal servitudes can also be regarded as parts of ownership, but whereas praedial servitudes are fractions of the content of ownership, the main personal servitude, usufruct, divides ownership in time by giving the enjoyment for a limited period to one person and then letting it revert permanently to another. A personal servitude is a right held by a person to enjoy the property of another in some way for a limited period. Like a praedial servitude, it is a right in the servient property itself and can be claimed against all persons who may come to own or possess that property, whether they know about it or not, but it is limited to the life of the holder or a lesser period.

Usufruct is the right to use a thing belonging to another, whether land or movable, and to acquire ownership of whatever it produces, 'the fruits', but without substantially altering its character. The other personal servitudes were more limited rights, such as to use without taking the fruits. The main purpose of usufruct, for which it was probably invented, was to enable a man making his last will to provide for his widow during her lifetime, while not depriving his children of their inheritance. He could leave his property to them subject to a usufruct to her for life. They became owners as soon as the will took effect, but their enjoyment was deferred during the life of the usufructuary. The latter could not dispose of the usufruct but could let out the enjoyment of it. For example, a widow who had a usufruct of land could put in a tenant under lease and receive the agreed rent in money from him, while he cultivated the land and gathered produce for himself. He could not, of course, have any greater right than she did, so that he could not change the type of farming, since that would be to alter the character of the property, and if her usufruct ended, as it would by her death, his rights would automatically cease.

A usufruct over things consumed by use was theoretically impossible. However, consumables, sometimes called fungibles, of which the main example is money, are normally readily replaceable by equivalent items of the same kind. Where a testator left a usufruct of such things in his will, the difficulty was overcome by letting the usufructuary become the owner of the consumable things and imposing a duty to restore an equivalent amount. This 'quasi-usufruct' meant that a person could be given control of a capital sum, with the right to administer it and take the income, but with a duty to maintain the capital.

Both the owner of the land to which a praedial servitude is attached and the person entitled to a personal servitude have species of property rights. They do not have ownership but each has a right to part of the ownership of things belonging to another. Their position may be contrasted with that of a tenant of land or hirer of a movable under a contract of lease or hire (since Roman law did not distinguish between land and movables in this respect, the contract was the same in both cases). The tenant has no right in the thing which he has rented; he has merely a personal right under the contract against the lessor. If a third party disturbs him, all he can do is to complain to his lessor and let him take proceedings to recover the thing, for example, by possessory interdict or *vindicatio* against the third party. If the lessor has agreed that the tenant shall enjoy the thing for a certain period, the tenant will have an action on the contract for damages if his enjoyment is interrupted before the period ends, but that is all. His action is a personal action (*in personam*) whereas his lessor's action is a real action (*in rem: res* = thing). A person entitled to a servitude also had a real action against anyone who challenged it.

Where the contract between lessor and tenant was for a lease of land for a long period, such as a hundred years or even in perpetuity, on payment of fixed rent, it was inappropriate to regard the tenant's right as only contractual. So long as the tenant paid the rent regularly all the owner was entitled to was the rent. The person with the main interest was the tenant. So a new institution called *emphyteusis* was recognised in such a case. This gave the holder the right to the possessory interdicts and the right not to the *vindicatio* proper (only the owner had that) but to a concessionary *utilis vindicatio*. The grant of these remedies meant that the *emphyteuta* had a property right, which he could convey to another by delivery or by will. Being of late origin, *emphyteusis* was never called a personal servitude but it was similar in that it was also a right to a portion, in this case a very substantial portion, of the contents of another's ownership.

The third kind of right in a thing owned by another does not entitle the holder to enjoy any part of that ownership; it is rather a right to restrict that ownership in a way that will guarantee payment of a debt owed by the owner. A creditor wants to ensure that when a debt becomes due it will be paid; he wants security. There are two ways of achieving this. One is by finding a person other than the debtor who will guarantee the debt by binding himself to pay the creditor if the principal debtor defaults. This is personal security and belongs to the law of obligations. The other way is to secure the debt on some particular property, belonging to the debtor or another, in such a way that the creditor can keep that property until the debt is paid, or, at least can readily get hold of it. This is *real security*. It is arranged by contract but creates a right over the property which, like servitudes, can be enforced against anyone whether they are aware of the existence of the right or not.

The form of real security is normally dictated by the creditor, since if he is not satisfied he can prevent the debt arising. From his point of view the best security is to have ownership of the relevant things. The earliest form of security to be recognised in Roman law was a formal conveyance of a *res mancipi* by the debtor to the creditor, but with an agreement attached to it (*fiducia*) that the creditor would not dispose of it before the debt was due and would convey it back to the debtor when the debt had been paid. Since, however, the creditor became owner, he could validly transfer that ownership to a third party, even in breach of the *fiducia*. The debtor would then have a claim for damages against him but would have no claim to his former property.

The next form of real security was a transfer of possession to the creditor with the debtor retaining ownership (*pignus*). Since he was not owner the creditor could not dispose of the thing unless he was specifically authorised to do so by the debtor. But the latter was deprived of the enjoyment of his property as long as the security lasted. This was tolerable if the thing was a luxury, but frequently the only things that debtors can offer by way of real security are the things they need in order to earn the money to pay the debt, such as their equipment or stock in trade. To overcome this difficulty what was needed was to devise a right over the thing which could be enforced against anyone into whose hands it came, but which left both ownership and possession with the debtor. This was achieved when the praetor came to the aid of landlords who had accepted a *pignus* of their tenant's property to secure payment of the rent, but had allowed the tenant to go on using the property. The praetor gave the landlord not only an interdict to gain possession from the debtor, and thus implement the *pignus*, but also an action to recover the property from anyone to whom it had passed. When these remedies became generally applicable to all arrangements for real security, the creditor had a charge, known as a hypothec, which enabled him to get hold of the property to secure the debt whenever it was required.

Since the property was merely charged without the creditor having possession, it was now possible for different creditors to have hypothecs over the same property. As long as the total amount of their debts did not exceed the value of the property, they would all be secured. If there was a shortfall, an earlier hypothec took precedence over a later. However the debtor might not reveal the existence of prior hypothecs to his creditor, and although this was condemned as 'lizard-like' conduct on the part of the debtor, it would not help a creditor who suddenly found that his own rights of security were subordinated to others of which he had been unaware. Quite apart from hypothecs created by the debtor in favour of ordinary creditors, certain 'tacit hypothecs' were implied by the law to benefit certain parties who were considered to have a greater claim on the debtor's assets, for example, in favour of the public treasury to secure payment of taxes, in favour of a pupil over his tutor's property to secure satisfaction of claims for maladministration, in favour of a wife over her husband's property to secure restoration of her dowry. An attempt to deal with the problem of discovering existing servitudes was made in the late Empire when a system of public registration of hypothecs was introduced. Thereafter priority was determined not by the date of creation of the hypothec but by the date of their registration. Tacit hypothecs however did not have to be registered and the problem of a plurality of hypothecs remained.

3. Equity

The more technical and rigid rules of law become, the more litigants yearn for justice. They make a distinction between justice and law to the disparagement of the law. At this point some legal systems introduce equity, defined by Sir Henry Maine as a set of 'principles entitled by their intrinsic superiority to supersede the older law'.[2] Developing legal systems thus mitigate the contrast between law and justice by recognising some mechanism for the introduction of these principles into the application of the law.

In Roman law the formulary procedure allowed the praetor considerable discretion to grant remedies whenever as a matter of policy he thought it right to do so. In his hands it became the instrument for the introduction of equitable principles into the traditional law.

For example, the praetor applied the principle that those who

2. *Ancient Law* ch 3 (Everyman edn, p 26); P. Stein 'Equitable principles in Roman Law' in R. A. Newman (ed) *Equity in the World's Legal Systems* (1973) pp 75ff.

seriously enter transactions should have their intentions fulfilled even though they fail to comply with particular forms prescribed by the law. We have noted that in early law ownership in important items of property, such as land (*res mancipi*), could be transferred only by particular formalities. What then was the effect of a sale of land, followed merely by delivery of possession to the buyer? In strict law ownership remained in the seller. Normally a Roman owner could assert his ownership by bringing a *vindicatio* and this action would be successful against any non-owner. In two years' time the buyer would become owner himself by operation of *usucapio*, but until then he was vulnerable to the seller's *vindicatio*. However the praetor was persuaded that it would be inequitable to allow the seller to recover his property by *vindicatio* when he had not only sold it but also handed over possession. The praetor therefore allowed the buyer, the defendant in the *vindicatio*, a defence to the action, so long as he could show that he had bought the property from the plaintiff and received delivery of it. This remedy enabled the buyer to retain possession of the property long enough to become full owner by operation of *usucapio*. If he lost possession before the two-year period elapsed, he could not recover the property by *vindicatio*, since he was not yet owner. But the praetor granted him a specially devised action, the *actio Publiciana*, to achieve the same result. This action was based on the fiction, which all parties were bound to accept, that the period necessary for *usucapio* had already elapsed. These two remedies, one a defence and the other an action, constituted a complete protection to a buyer who had received a *res mancipi* informally, giving him a kind of temporary ownership until he became legal owner by *usucapio*. He was not the owner according to law, but he had the legal protection normally afforded to the owner, whereas the person with the title of owner did not have that protection.

A similar separation of the legal ownership and a protected beneficial or 'equitable' ownership is found in regard to property forming part of a dowry provided for a wife at marriage. The husband was the owner of such property for the duration of the marriage but after its end the wife was entitled to sue for its return. In classical law she only had a personal action against the husband or his heir, with the disadvantage that the defendant might have no money to satisfy the judgment. So restrictions were placed on the husband's ownership during the marriage. He was prohibited from alienating land without his wife's consent and from creating charges, such as hypothecs, over it even with her consent. Finally, the wife was allowed a special *vindicatio utilis*, like that of the *emphyteuta*, against the husband and against third parties who had acquired the dotal property knowing it was dotal or without paying for it. Once she acquired such an action *in rem,* Justinian could speak of the wife as having an ownership of her own under natural law. In both these cases the person intended to have the benefit of property was put into the position of an owner, although the strict law attributed ownership to another.

Modern law

Modern legal systems, whether of the civil law or the common law tradition, base their law of property on the distinction between rights *in rem* and rights *in personam.* The first are rights in the thing itself, protected against everyone, whereas the second only exist between particular persons and can be enforced only between them. Since rights *in personam* can be created by agreement, the persons involved are in general free to create new forms of right as they please, or as the ingenuity of their legal advisers suggests. On the other hand, the number and scope of rights *in rem* are normally fixed by the law and persons involved are not at liberty to modify their character.

Modern systems, like Roman law, recognise the distinction between ownership, the entitlement to a thing, and possession, the factual control of it. English law, like Roman law, has no authoritative definition of ownership, but the French and German codes offer similar definitions. In the French code it is 'the right to enjoy and dispose of things in the most absolute way, provided that no use is made of them forbidden by law or regulations' (CC 544). The German code allows the owner of a thing to do what he likes with it and to exclude others from it 'subject to the limits of the law and the rights of third parties' (BGB 903). Both these definitions express an individualistic idea of ownership that ignores community interests. In German law, ownership of private property is expressly protected by the Basic Law as being essential for the free development of the individual. It avails even against the state itself, so that expropriation for public purposes is allowed only within narrow limits and subject to the payment of compensation.

In civil law systems the owner can demand the return of his thing from the person in possession of it unless the latter has a right to hold on to it derived from the owner himself. His action is an action *in rem* based on the Roman *vindicatio* and requires the claimant to prove an absolute title to the thing. This was not difficult in classical Roman law because anyone who had possessed in good faith for the short periods required for *usucapio* would have acquired absolute title. In modern civil law the periods of acquisitive prescription vary according to the circumstances but are never less than ten years, so that it is difficult for a claimant to prove his entitlement absolutely. Normally he will prove a derivative title based on that of the person from whom he acquired the thing. Such a proof will raise a presumption of ownership in his favour and the defendant must then either rebut that presumption or else give up the thing. The defendant can rebut the presumption by showing that he himself has a better right to the thing than the claimant or that a third party has a better right than the claimant. A possessor need only give up the thing to an owner, and a possessor with a weaker title than the claimant can still defeat him in a *vindicatio*-type action by showing that someone else has a better right than the claimant. For if that is so, the claimant cannot be the owner.

English law, although traditionally recognising the distinction between the owner and the possessor, did not require the owner to prove ownership in order to recover his thing. Rather a person claiming to be owner would succeed in recovering it from a possessor if he merely proved that he had a better right to possess. Entitlement was thus relative rather than absolute, and success in an action by A against B did not prevent C from recovering the thing later. However this idea has been modified in modern English law. Registration of title to land provides a species of absolute ownership and in the case of movables, the Torts (Interference with Goods) Act 1977 provides that in an action between two parties each claiming that the thing is his, the defendant will 'be entitled to show' that a third party has a better right than the plaintiff, thus ensuring that all competing claims can be settled in one action.

1. Movable things

In Roman law the differences between the treatment of land and movables were not so marked that they required separate treatment, but modern laws accentuate the differences. We will first consider the law of movables, known in English terminology as *chattels*, from cattle, the typical movable in an agricultural society. In Roman law transfer of ownership was based on two principles. First, a mere agreement was in principle insufficient to transfer ownership; it had to be followed by physical delivery. Secondly, one could not acquire ownership except from someone who was himself owner or was authorised by the owner. Both these principles have been modified in modern laws.

In German law, as in Roman law, transfer of ownership in a movable requires an agreement between the parties followed by physical delivery. The Code recognises that if the transferee already has the thing, it is enough if the parties agree that ownership should pass to him (*traditio brevi manu*; BGB 929). If the transferor keeps the thing after agreement has been reached, delivery can be replaced by an agreement setting up a relationship, such as deposit, loan or hire between the parties (*constitutum possessorium*; BGB 930 and 936). A person holding a thing by virtue of such an arrangement with another is under German law the actual possessor, and the person from whom he holds it is considered the indirect possessor, and both forms of possession are legally protected (BGB 868). Thus the effect of a sale, followed by an agreement for the seller to keep the thing on loan, is to give the buyer ownership and indirect possession. The other Roman principle governing transfer of movables has not been followed in modern German law. Instead, a rule of old Germanic law has been preferred whereby one who acquires a movable in good faith from a non-owner immediately acquires ownership of it, so long as it has not been stolen from the true owner.

French law, on the other hand, rejected the Roman requirement of delivery in transfer of ownership and followed the doctrine of the eighteenth-century natural lawyers that agreement between the parties is sufficient to transfer ownership in movables. So the code provides that ownership is transferred by virtue of a contract alone and that is constituted by the consent of the parties. In the case of sale, the buyer becomes owner as soon as agreement has been reached on the thing sold and on the price, even though the thing has not been delivered nor the price paid (CC 1583). A gift which has been accepted is also completed by mere agreement without the need for delivery (CC 938). Where a transferee receives from a non-owner in good faith he immediately becomes owner, so long as the true owner has voluntarily dispossessed himself of it (ie, there is no acquisition of a stolen thing or of a thing that has been lost). This principle is expressed in the code (CC 2279) by the statement that, so far as movables are concerned, 'possession is equivalent to title'. That being so, in the case of movables, French law does not distinguish actions to protect ownership and actions to protect possession. A possessor in good faith can usually vindicate, since he is presumed to have title.

English law has preferred to deal with transfer of movables by having separate rules for each type of situation. Ownership in movables can be transferred by physical delivery, except that in the case of particular things like ships and motor cars, registration of title is provided to prove ownership. But in the case of a transfer of ownership as a result of a sale, the rule is that unless the parties have made a special agreement about the time when the buyer is to acquire ownership, he acquires it at the time when the contract is made, even though payment of the price or delivery of the goods, or both, may be postponed. So in the case of sale of goods there is no distinction between contract and conveyance. In the case of a gift, however, a promise by the donor is not effective to transfer owner-ship – indeed a mere promise to make a gift is not even enforceable – and delivery must be made for ownership to pass to the donee.

As in Roman law, so in English law, the principle is that no-one can transfer a better title to a thing than he has himself. However, in English law, many exceptions to this principle have been intro-duced. In the middle ages markets and fairs were of great com-mercial importance and profit to those who held them. To encourage people to use them the rule was that a buyer of goods in 'market overt' received ownership whether he bought from an owner or not. Again, by statute, if a buyer leaves the goods with the seller after buying them and the seller resells them, the new buyer will acquire ownership, even though the seller was no longer owner when he sold to him. Similarly, if a buyer gets possession of goods which he has agreed to buy but of which he has not yet acquired ownership, he can convey ownership to one who buys from him in good faith. By a further statutory exception, although a person acquiring a car on hire-purchase is not its owner, a private citizen, not in the trade, who innocently buys from him, will become owner.

As in German law, English law protects possession of movables, independently of title, not only in those who hold the thing in the manner of an owner but also in the case of other possessors, known as bailees. Bailment exists when a physical movable is delivered by one person to another for a particular purpose, usually fixed by contract, then to be returned. It includes loan, hiring or pledge of the thing, but it excludes the situation where an employee has con-trol of his employer's property and is under his directions.

German, French and English law thus adopt quite different approaches to the transfer of movables, but the practical results are often the same.[3] If A agrees to sell a thing to B, but does not deliver it, and later sells it and delivers it to C, in all three laws C becomes owner but for different reasons. In German law, as in Roman law, it is because the contract between A and B did not transfer ownership to B, so that A was still owner when he delivered to C. In French law it is because of the rule that possession is equivalent to title. Since A retains possession with the consent of the new owner B, he can pass a good title to a subsequent transferee in good faith (CC 1141). In English law the result follows from the statutory exception (in the Sale of Goods Act) to the general principle that one cannot acquire ownership from a non-owner.

The Roman rules applicable when things are joined together are

3.   K. W. Ryan *An Introduction to the Civil Law* (1962) p 172.

expressly repeated in the German code (BGB 947–950) and are often applied in English law without an express reference. In the case of treasure found by accident, both the French and German codes repeat the Roman rules giving half to the finder and half to the owner of the ground (CC 716; BGB 984). English law, on the other hand, ascribes all treasure to the Crown on behalf of the community as a whole, although the finder is normally given a substantial ex gratia payment.

The main difference between the modern law of property and the Roman law of property is probably that many of the most important items today are non-physical movables, rights exercisable against others which are in such a form as to be marketable and so have become assets.[4]

Stocks and shares are typical examples. Stocks are issued by public bodies and are transferable acknowledgments of loans to those bodies at fixed rates of interest. Shares in a company give no right to any part of the assets of the company but are rather transferable rights to such dividends as the directors, elected by the shareholders, may declare and to part of the capital of the company if it is wound up. Stocks and shares are registered in the name of the person entitled and are transferred by a simple document authorising the substitution of the transferee's name for that of the transferor in the relevant register.

The rights known as intellectual property are exemplified by trade marks, patents and copyrights. They are transferable monopolies to exploit new ideas for a limited period. In Britain, the patent of an invention confers the right to use, manufacture and sell it for 20 years. Copyright in original writings or compositions normally lasts for the life time of the author and 50 years after his death.

In commercial life, negotiable instruments, such as bills of exchange, play an important part. These are essentially promises to pay money, evidenced by the bill, which have been made transferable by being put in a particular form. Their special feature is that anyone receiving them in good faith and for value becomes entitled to demand payment of the sum promised, even if the person who transferred it to him was a thief. The present value of such a document will normally be less than the sum named in it and will depend on the time that has to elapse before payment is due and also on the likelihood of the person liable to pay being able to meet his obligation.

Such non-physical movables are known in English law as *choses in action* since the owner cannot assert his ownership by taking possession but only by bringing an action.

4.   F. H. Lawson and B. Rudden *The Law of Property* (2nd edn, 1982) pp 26ff.

Physical and non-physical things are often combined in a fund, a collection of things which has an identity separate from its contents. The advantage of this is that the fund as a whole preserves its identity although the individual components may change.[5] The income can be divided among several persons in a predetermined proportion or successive interests can be created in it, for example, by granting the income to one or more persons for their lives and then giving the capital to others.

In civil law countries, such a function is achieved by usufruct. Roman law recognised a usufruct of a collection of changing components in the case of a flock of sheep or herd of cattle. The usufruct was in the flock rather than in the several beasts, so that the usufructuary could deal with them and dispose of them when he thought fit, subject only to his duty to maintain the flock as a whole. This idea combined with that of the quasi-usufruct of consumable things, of which the usufructuary became owner subject to an obligation to return equivalents at the end of the period of the usufruct. Today the ownership of the fund is in the people to whom the capital will eventually pass while the income goes to the usufructuary, but the control of the fund, in the sense of deciding when certain investments should be bought and sold, may be given to the usufructuary or to a third party such as a bank.

In England, funds are usually put under a characteristic institution of the common law, not found in the civil law, – the trust. The origin will be considered later, but in modern law a trust exists whenever things are transferred to certain persons, known as trustees, who hold them either for the benefit of other persons, the beneficiaries, who may include the trustees themselves, or to carry out certain specified purposes. The trustees are the legal owners of the trust fund, which is separated from the rest of their property. They may derive no benefit from being trustees (although they may receive what is due to them as beneficiaries), and are only allowed to charge for work they do if the document setting up the trust (often the will of a deceased person) expressly allows it. So their ownership has a custodial or managerial rather than enjoyment function. The beneficiaries have personal rights against the trustees to compel them to carry out their duties but they are also regarded as having a form of lesser ownership ('equitable ownership') in the trust fund itself. The trust enables the enjoyment of property to be split up in various ways, and is more flexible than the usufruct. Trusts for charitable purposes, for example, perform the same function as the civil law institution of the foundation (p 138).

---

5.   Lawson and Rudden, op cit, p 38.

Old Germanic law recognised a pledge type of security similar to the *pignus* of Roman law, and so all modern systems, whether of the common law or of the civil law tradition, recognise an institution whereby the creditor has possession of a movable, while the debtor retains ownership. In the case of non-physical things, the relevant documents of title, such as the share certificates, are deposited with the creditor. The debtor cannot dispose of the thing until he redeems the pledge by paying the debt, and if he does not pay the debt when due, the creditor has a right to sell the thing and pay himself from the proceeds.

Another form of possessory security is known in civil law as a right of retention and in English law as a *lien*. This arises typically when, as a result of a contract between the owner and another, the other has possession and is owed money by the owner. He can refuse to restore the thing until the debt has been paid. In the modern French and German law such a right is restricted to specified categories of people, the most important being those who are out of pocket as a result of work done on the thing, such as a garage owner who has repaired a car.

The inconvenience of possessory security, that the debtor is unable to use his property as long as the security lasts, has led to a revival of so-called proprietory security, in which the debtor transfers ownership to the creditor but retains control. When this 'security title' became common in Germany, it was argued that in effect it was a pledge and so the practice constituted an evasion of the legal rules requiring the transfer of possession for the creation of a pledge, but the courts rejected the argument. The difficulty about such transfers of ownership purely for purposes of security is that an outsider cannot know whether movables, apparently belonging to a debtor, are really his or not. This difficulty is avoided by the English 'bill of sale' in which a debtor executes a document of transfer of ownership which must then be recorded in a register, so that those considering dealing with the debtor can discover whether his apparent ownership is real.

In French law the code not only allows hypothecs to exist over movables but enables them to be created over a class of unspecified things, such as a manufacturer's equipment or a trader's stock. Thus the debtor can continue to trade with his assets, and the hypothec applies to whatever falls within the class of things at any time. English law allows a company to create such a 'floating charge' over its assets for the time being, but it is not possible for a partnership or sole trader, for then it would be a bill of sale transaction, requiring the registration of specified things. German law demands specificity in all security transactions and so does not recognise the floating charge at all.

2. *Immovable things in the civil law*

In all modern systems immovable property, essentially land, is governed by a separate set of rules from those applicable to movables. The reason is mainly historical. In the middle ages feudal law attributed to land-holding a significance far wider than mere entitlement to the benefits of ownership, and a whole range of legal notions was developed which applied only to land. Although most of these notions have been much modified in modern laws, a separate regime for land is generally observed.

Except in Scandinavia, where land was *allodial* (ie the landholder had ownership, as in Roman law), most land in medieval Europe was feudal. When the machinery of central government was limited in scope, its functions were devolved on local leaders through the holding of land. In feudal theory all land is owned by the Crown, and is assigned to 'tenants in chief' who hold it from the Crown as vassals in return for the performance of services of various kinds, including military service. The tenants in chief put themselves into a position to provide these services by granting parts of their land in turn to lesser vassals who hold from them in a similar way, thus creating a pyramid of land-holding. The set of terms on which the land is held is called tenure, and there were two basic types, free and unfree. Free tenants held freehold land in return for services which did not demean them. Unfree tenants were the successors of the serfs or villeins of a manor who were bound to the land and compelled to do its menial work. Eventually this was converted into free tenure.

The medieval commentators attempted to harmonise the realities of feudal land-holding with the institutions of Roman law.[6] They saw some similarity between the position of a feudal tenant and a Roman *emphyteuta* (p 153) and noted that the latter had a *vindicatio utilis*, while the owner had a *vindicatio directa* (for example, to recover the land if the *emphyteuta* failed to pay the rent). They inferred that these actions corresponded with two forms of ownership, a *dominium utile* in the feudal tenant and a *dominium directum* in the feudal lord. Eventually full *dominium* was attributed to the tenant, and the lord was said to have merely a *ius in re aliena,* similar to a hypothec, over the tenant's land. Modern codes have retained this absolute notion of ownership in land; the main limited interests are in the form of usufructs and leases, and the Roman rules of praedial servitudes have survived in essentials. Hypothecs are the main form of security. The main innovation in the modern civil law of land is the intro-duction of forms of registration, both of the documents evidencing title and of the title itself..

French law applies to immovables the rule, already mentioned in

6.　Ryan, op cit, pp 160ff.

regard to movables, that ownership is transferred as a result of a contract between the parties. This rule is tolerable in regard to movables because of the existence of the other rule that possession is equivalent to title. But the latter rule does not apply to immovables, and the transferor of land cannot convey a better title than he has himself. It is, therefore, important that publicity should accompany the transfer. For although it is the parties' agreement that transfers ownership, it is priority of registration of the transfer that governs priority of rights. The French system is one of registration of the relevant documents rather than of title. A buyer of land who fails to register the deed of transfer from the owner still becomes owner (by virtue of CC 1138), but if another buyer receives another deed of transfer from the (former) owner and registers it first, then the earlier buyer will lose his ownership to the later. Other interests in the land such as usufructs, leases for more than twelve years and hypothecs are similarly registrable.

German law requires for the transfer of ownership in land both a formal agreement, fully authenticated by a notary, and entry on the register (*Grundbuch*). The register is built on an elaborate survey of all pieces of land, called the *cadaster*. It is a register of title, not merely of documents, so that ownership is not acquired until the transfer has been registered and the new owner's name appears in the register. This 'constitutive effect' of registration applies equally to other interests in the land, such as usufructs and praedial servitudes. Anyone who acquires the land is entitled to rely on the accuracy of the register and on registration will become owner with a good title, even if there was a mistake in the previous registration. In France the register has a publicity function only, and so will not provide such a guarantee to one whose title is defective.

Where hypothecs are created, registration is essential in both countries to warn those dealing in the land that it is charged as security. Foreclosure is not allowed, but a forced sale of the land to pay what is owed to the creditor is permitted under strict conditions. Where there are several hypothecs over the same land, priority is governed by the time when each was registered.

3. English land law

English land law is still permeated by the notions of feudal law. Land is known as realty since originally only those entitled to land had actions *in rem*. In regard to movables they had merely personal actions for damages against those who detained them and so movables, or chattels, were also known as personalty.

(a) COMMON LAW The temporal extent of the English feudal tenant's interest in the land is indicated by his estate. Since no-one except the king can own the land itself, all a subject can own is an estate in land. It can be for his life only or for as long as the original holder or any of his heirs survive. The latter estate is the nearest thing to ownership and is called a fee simple, fee being derived from the latin *feudum* (other variants being *fief*, and in Scotland *feu*). At first it could not be alienated and had to descend to the heirs, but in the thirteenth century the holder was allowed to alienate it in his lifetime but still could not dispose of it by will. When it became alienable the existence of the estate no longer depended on the survival of heirs of the original grantee.

Two forms of alienation of an estate between living persons were possible. The lord could accept a new holder of the estate in place of the old by substitution or the holder could 'subinfeudate' by granting an estate in the land to someone who would hold of him as lord and he would continue to hold it from his lord. In 1290, the statute *Quia Emptores* prohibited the alienation of land by creating new sub-fees in this way, and the holders of freehold estates were allowed to alienate their land by substitution without the lord's consent.[7] The effect was to prevent the creation of any new mesne or intermediate tenancies, and thereafter no-one except the Crown could create any new tenures. It was possible for the holder of a fee simple to create a life estate out of his interest but any conveyance of his whole estate had to be a complete transfer without the exaction of any services. No service could be demanded by an intermediate lord unless he could show that the duty to render it existed before 1290. Thus a fee simple estate in freehold land came to be substantial ownership. The importance of the statute can be seen by comparing the situation in Scotland, which had a very similar system of feudal land holding, but where there was no such legislation and subinfeudation continued. Feu duties commuted to money payments, payable by the holders of freehold land (known as vassals) to their lords, remained common in this century.

Although the fee simple itself could not be subinfeudated, it was possible to grant a more limited estate out of it. Land could be granted by X 'to A for life', or 'to A during the life of B'. In such cases A had an estate for life, and while A's estate lasted X had the fee simple 'in reversion', since in due course it would revert to him. If X had granted the land to A for life and after A's death to B in fee simple, B would during A's life have had the fee simple in remainder, since after A's death the land would remain away from X. B's estate was said to be 'vested' in him even during A's life, since A was bound to die some time and the fee simple would necessarily come to B or his heirs. If B's estate had been made conditional on

7. Baker, p 208.

some event that might not happen, for example, when A m
was said to be not vested but 'contingent'. The aim o
arrangements was to control what happened to the land in the fu
and to try to keep it in X's family as long as possible.[8]

In addition to such 'freehold estates', medieval land law
recognised a 'term of years'. Its aim was essentially commercial: to
provide the freeholder with an income from the rents of his estate.
Like the tenant under an ordinary Roman lease, the tenant under a
term of years did not originally have an action *in rem* to recover his
land, but only a personal action for damages against his landlord.
Later he was allowed an action for damages for ejectment against
anyone who had dispossessed him, and finally, in 1500, it was
decided that the tenant could demand from the ejector not only
damages but also recovery of the land itself. This gave the tenant a
right *in rem*.

Originally the only method of conveying an estate in land, was by
'feoffment with livery of seisin', a ceremony held on the land in
which the transferor transferred the fee by symbolic delivery of
physical possession with recitation of the words appropriate to the
estate. The act would not only be remembered by the participants
and witnesses but would also come to the notice of the mesne lord
who stood above the transferor in the feudal pyramid. Later this
ceremony was replaced, as in Roman law, by the transfer of a deed.
Seisin was essentially quiet possession by someone who was bound to
perform the feudal duties, and so the lessee under a term of years,
whose duty was to pay rent to his landlord under the lease, did not
technically have seisin, although he was in physical occupation.

The history of real actions for land is one of great complexity, with
litigants continually seeking more satisfactory remedies than those
currently offered by the courts. There was a *writ of right* by which
one who was out of possession of a freehold estate could claim it from
a possessor by proving his title to it. However the mode of trial was
battle, and although the defendant was allowed to opt instead for
investigation by an 'assise' of neighbours, his opponent could never
be sure that he would not insist on his right to battle. There were
also possessory actions, 'petty assises', in which neighbours were
asked to decide particular questions of fact, such as whether the
person seised of the land had recently been forcibly disseised, with a
view to the recovery of seisin by the claimant (*novel disseisin*). Since it
came to be held that anyone with a right of entry could at any time

---

8. Another form of freehold estate was that 'in fee tail', which was limited to the
grantee and the heirs of his body, so that on failure of such issue the land
reverted to the grantor or his heirs. Much legal ingenuity was expended in
devising means of barring an estate tail and converting it into a fee simple.

exercise that right by force, these actions were extended from being limited to matters of possession to a concern with matters of title. By the sixteenth century they had become so complex and technical that they were themselves superseded just as they had superseded the writ of right. The action of ejectment had been extended to give a leaseholder a real remedy to recover his lease. By a series of fictions involving the assertion of leases that had never existed, a freeholder seeking recovery of land was able to arrange that the issue left to the jury necessarily involved a decision on whether he had a better title than the defendant.

English law recognised no acquisitive prescription of land but limited a claimant's right of action to a period of years after which his claim, however well founded it may have been, could not be enforced. Thus the possessor of land was entitled to stay by virtue of his possession. Since 1833 lapse of time extinguishes not only a claimant's right of action but also his title. This was important because, although in the action of ejectment the courts were at first only concerned with which of the two parties to the action had the better right to possess, they came to be more concerned in some cases with who had the best title. Where the action is brought to enable a possessor who has been dispossessed to recover his possession, third party rights are irrelevant. But where someone claims the land from a possessor by virtue of having a better title to it, it is sometimes open to the possessor to defend the action by showing that a third party has an even better title, even though the possessor does not claim the land through him. The period after which a claim can no longer be enforced is therefore important. For land it is now twelve years from the time when the cause of action first arose.

(b) EQUITY   The common law of the royal courts recognised freehold estates, such as fee simple and life estate, and terms of years, but it had become extremely technical and there were many grants that holders of land in fee simple wanted to make but which were not possible at law. So they resorted to the device of the use, that is, of conveying land 'to A to the use of B'.[9] The word 'use' has nothing to do with using the land but is derived from the Latin *opus* through Old French; 'to the use of' meant 'on behalf of'. The use was the ancestor of the modern trust. Many of the grants which could not be made in law could be achieved by the use if a man was prepared to convey his estate to his friends and trust them to carry out his wishes. For example, the rule prohibiting alienation of land by will could be avoided by conveying it in his lifetime to friends to

9.   Baker, pp 210ff.

the uses expressed in his last will. After the grantor's death the friends would convey it to the persons named in his will. The common law courts refused to enforce uses, so their performance was left to the conscience of the so-called 'feoffees to uses'. In the fifteenth century, however, the Chancellor began to compel them to perform uses, even though they were means of avoiding the law. It was against conscience that a man should accept land on conditions and then not carry them out.

In offering remedies that the common law courts did not provide, the Chancellor's court, the Court of Chancery, was consciously applying the principles of equity. Law and equity became parallel systems, each with its own rules, enforced by different courts. Those who had no rights which could be enforced at law but who were given relief by the Chancellor were said to have equitable rights. Equitable rights were inferior to legal rights, since legal rights were enforceable against everyone, whereas equitable rights were only enforceable against someone who, in the Chancellor's view, had as a matter of conscience to acknowledge them. The rule was eventually established that equitable rights are enforceable against everyone except a bona fide purchaser of the legal estate for value without notice of the equitable rights. Thus the Court of Chancery would enforce the rights of a beneficiary under a trust not only against the trustees who held the legal estate but also against others to whom the trustees had transferred the legal estate, so long as they did not fall into that category. One who received the legal estate with notice of the trust was bound by it; so also was one who received it without notice of the trust but as a gift. But one who paid for it and had no knowledge that those he bought from were trustees on behalf of others was just as much entitled to the court's protection as the beneficiaries under the trust. Their equitable claims were equal but, since he had the legal estate, his claim to the land was preferred to that of the beneficiaries. In that case, they could sue the trustees personally for damages. Despite this exception, however, a beneficiary's interest was protected against nearly everyone and could be regarded as an interest *in rem*, protected against the world at large, and not merely a personal right against the trustees.

In 1540 the Statute of Wills allowed the holder of a freehold estate in land to dispose of it by will without resorting to equity. Later the common law reacted to the challenge of equity by allowing a wider range of legal rights than had been possible before. But equitable rights continued and the possible existence of elaborate series of both legal and equitable rights over the same piece of land made the law of property in land in the eighteenth century a matter of enormous complexity.

Simplification came at last with the great property legislation of

1925. This series of statutes tried to reduce to a minimum the differences between the law of land and the law of movables and to make transfers of land as simple as possible. The situation today is that the only possible legal estates that can exist are the fee simple absolute (ie unconditional) in possession and the terms of years absolute. The first is the equivalent of ownership in freehold land; the second the equivalent to ownership in leasehold land, where the interest is limited to a term of years. All other major interests in land, such as a life interest or a fee simple in remainder, subject to a life interest, can only exist as equitable interests behind a trust. A strict settlement of land is still possible by which the legal estate (whether fee simple or terms of years) is conveyed by a 'vesting deed' to the tenant for life subject to trusts which are set out in another deed, the trust deed. The trustees of the settlement are mentioned in the vesting deed so that if the tenant for life exercises the estate owner's powers of sale, the buyer will see only the vesting deed and not know the nature of the trusts. Yet he will receive the legal estate free of trusts, so long as he pays the price to the trustees. They will then invest the money and apply the income according to the same trusts that were applicable to the land. Thus the desire of land owners to tie up family property for generations is reconciled with the need to make land alienable at the discretion of the tenant for life, and the family capital, now represented by the proceeds of the sale, will remain intact.

Such settlements are, however, rare, and normally when it is desired to create, say, a life interest followed by a series of limited interests it is done by a trust for sale. Land is conveyed to trustees under a trust that they must sell it and apply the proceeds in a certain way, for example, to give the income to A for life, then to B for life and then to B's children. If it is hoped that the land will be retained, it seems odd to impose a trust to sell it. However by the doctrine of conversion (based on the principle that Equity considers as already done what ought to be done), the land is treated as if the sale had been made from the moment of the conveyance to the trustees for sale. Whether they hold the land or the proceeds of sale, the trusts on which they hold are the same. They can normally postpone the sale indefinitely and their power of sale can be made exercisable only with the agreement of a particular person, such as the holder of a life interest.

The beneficiaries' proprietary interest in the trust property (under a strict settlement or a trust for sale) is unaffected by dispositions made by the trustees. Whether the property subject to the trust happens to be land or the proceeds of sale of land or other things bought with those proceeds, it will be 'traced' into its new form and the beneficiaries' interests in it maintained.

(c) RIGHTS IN ANOTHER'S LAND   English law recognises two classes of what in Roman law would be praedial servitudes, *easements* and *profits à prendre*. An easement is a right to do something on another's land, such as exercise a right of way, or to prevent him from doing what he would otherwise be entitled to do, such as prevent him from building on his own land in such a way as to obstruct the light to one's window. A profit is a right to take something from another's land, such as to fish, pasture cattle or cut turf from it. The rules for easements are similar to the rules for praedial servitudes and require a dominant and a servient land, but profits can be enjoyed by a person who had no land, and can be enjoyed in common with others. In both cases the rights can be acquired positively by prescription, 20 years of continuous use immediately before the action being required for an easement and 30 years for a profit.

It is also possible to impose *restrictive covenants* which limit the use that can be made of one piece of land in order to benefit another piece of land, such as to retain it free of buildings. Unlike ordinary contractual obligations these covenants can be made to run with the land so that they can be enforced by and against owners other than those between whom they were created.

Real security began in English law, as in Roman law, with the debtor conveying his land to the creditor with a contractual undertaking by the latter to reconvey if the debt was not paid by a certain date. If it was not paid, the creditor could keep the land which became a dead pledge (*mortgage*) in his hands. At first the mortgagee (creditor) could 'foreclose', if the debt were not paid when due, and so keep the land even though it was worth much more than the outstanding debt. But the Court of Chancery intervened to control him and made him account so strictly for his actions especially regarding the sale of land, that he became almost a trustee of the land in respect of the 'equity', ie the difference between the value of the land and what was owed to him. As a result the mortgagor had an equitable estate in the land to that extent. Nowadays mortgage is usually created through a charge by deed expressed to be by way of legal mortgage, which is essentially similar to the hypothec of civil law.

Today there are two forms of conveyance depending on whether the land in question has been registered or not. Since 1862 a system of public registration of title to land has been gradually extended to different parts of England and Wales. Once compulsory registration has been extended to an area, the person acquiring at the next transfer of land in that area has the duty to have his title registered by proving it to the Land Registrar by the method for unregistered land.

Unregistered conveyancing depends on the existence of a 'good root of title'. Unless the parties have agreed otherwise, the seller of land must prove that he derives his right to his estate from some deed, such as another conveyance on sale, which transferred it to a particular person and that deed must be at least 15 years old. If he is not the person named in the deed, then he has to trace all dealings which connect him to that person. Often a buyer's problem is not with the seller's title but with the existence of possible charges on the land in favour of third parties. Certain interests such as easements and leases for 21 years or less are said to be overriding. They always bind a transferee, and so he must make inquiry about them and inspect the land and the deeds to find if there is a lessee in occupation of if a mortgagee has the deeds. Other interests are registrable as Land Charges, even in the case of land whose title is not registered, and they must be registered if they are to bind a buyer of the land. Restrictive covenants are registrable and, although they are equitable rights and so do not bind a buyer without notice of them, registration constitutes notice to everyone. Mortgages created without deposit of deeds, as would be the case with a second mortgage, and a spouse's right to the matrimonial home, are similarly registrable as Land Charges and so a buyer must always search the Land Charges Register to see if any exist.

In the case of land whose *title* is registered, the position is simpler. Each holding is given a number and entered on three registers: the Property Register which describes the holding by reference to a plan and, if it is leasehold, gives details of the lease; the Proprietorship Register, which gives the name and address of the owner; and the Charges Register which gives those rights of others in the land, such as morgages and restrictive covenants, which have to be registered. The title of the registered proprietor is guaranteed by the state and he is given a Land Certificate as evidence. When he conveys the land he completes a simple deed of transfer, similar to that for the transfer of shares in a limited company, and the registry staff substitute the name of the transferee for his name in the Proprietorship Register. The register is not open to public inspection without the written permission of the proprietor.

12 Succession

Roman law

The aim of the rules of succession in Roman law was to ensure the continuance of the family into the next generation after the death of a family head. His place was taken by his heirs, who were responsible for looking after the family property, paying debts and as far as possible maintaining the family as a going concern, not only in its economic aspects but also more generally. Thus it was the heirs of a deceased family head who were charged with the support of the religious cult of the family, on which its prosperity was thought to depend. So the first object of succession was to identify the heirs, and this could be done either by the law (rules of intestacy) or by the deceased himself through nomination in a will.

In the classical period it was usual for a Roman man of property to make a will. Testamentary succession became the norm, and the rules of intestacy came to be seen as subsidiary, providing what a reasonable family head would have done, if he had made a will. But the idea that a property owner should be able to dispose of his property not only in his lifetime but also after his death is itself the product of an advanced stage in the movement from family property to individual property. It is, as Adam Smith pointed out, 'one of the greatest extensions of property we can conceive',[1] and indicated a highly developed notion of individual property. Historically, therefore, intestate succession preceded the introduction of wills, and apart from identifying the heirs, it was designed to keep in the family the property which the deceased had owned but which his descendants expected to inherit.

1. Intestate succession

In Rome at the time of the Twelve Tables, when a family head died without leaving a will, his heirs were all those who were freed from paternal power by his death, ie his sons and daughters and his grandchildren by any son who had pre-deceased him (his grandchildren by his daughters would, of course, be in the power of their

---

1. *Lectures on Jurisprudence* (ed R. L. Meek, D. D. Raphael and P. G. Stein, 1978) p 38.

father or of his family head). The heirs were responsible for gathering the assets of the deceased, for recovering any debts owed to him and for paying any debts by him, and generally were regarded as stepping into his shoes legally. They were 'the same legal persons as the deceased'. Each of them had an individual share of the whole complex of things, claims and debts that had been his. Originally these descendant-heirs were not thought of as acquiring what had been another's but rather as taking over what had already been in some sense their property even in their father's lifetime. They became heirs automatically on the death of the family head, so that the continuation of the family was not interrupted. Brothers and sisters shared equally without any preference for males over females or for the elder over the younger. Grandchildren by a deceased son together shared their father's share. This is known as representation *per stirpes*, by stems, by contrast with equal shares for all members of the class, *per capita*. Thus if the family head had had two sons and a daughter, and one of the sons had died leaving two children of his own, the surviving son and daughter would each be heirs as to a third share and the two grandchildren each heirs as to a sixth.

If an heir was under the age of puberty his share would be looked after by his tutors, who would, in the absence of a will, be the male agnates nearest in degree of relationship to him, who were qualified (p 134). If the child-heir himself died before reaching puberty, he could not have contracted a valid marriage, and so could not leave any legitimate descendants in his power, who could be his heirs. In the absence of persons made independent by the death of the deceased, his heirs were his nearest agnates, who would usually be his brothers and sisters or, if he had none, his father's brothers (females more remote than sisters were excluded) and brothers' sons. There was no representation *per stirpes* at this stage.

This class of heirs, who were not made independent by the death of the deceased, did not succeed automatically but could choose whether to accept or not. The choice was important because the merging of the deceased's legal position with that of his heirs meant that they were liable for his debts. If his assets exceeded his liabilities there was no problem, but in the reverse situation, when the deceased had been insolvent, the inheritance was *damnosa* and the heirs had to use their own money to satisfy the claims of his creditors. The praetor intervened to protect the automatic heirs by allowing them to abstain from the inheritance, although remaining nominally heirs. The creditors of the deceased then arranged for the sale of his property and divided the proceeds among themselves. If the deceased had been a man of property but an heir was in debt, the deceased's creditors could ask the praetor to separate the property of the deceased from that of the heir, so that their claims did not compete with those of the heir's own creditors.

It will be seen that the aim of these rules was to keep the property within the agnate family and to keep it together as a whole. However whatever the economic advantages of keeping the family property as a unit, several heirs could not be forced to co-operate indefinitely and they were allowed to divide up the property. This required the bringing of a legal action, significantly called action for splitting the family (*actio familiae erciscundae*), which resulted in a judicial apportionment of the property.

The original system of intestate succession was modified during the course of Roman law with an increasing recognition of cognatic (blood relationship on both sides) in place of agnatic kin. Justinian's final scheme was to pass the inheritance first to the deceased's descendants, with representation *per stirpes*; if there were none, then to ascendants and brothers and sisters together. Children, but not remoter descendants, or deceased brothers and sisters took *per stirpes*, so long as there was at least one brother or sister alive to allow the inheritance to go to that class. Failing anyone in that class, the heirs were the nearest other collaterals *per capita* with no representation.

From a modern point of view the most surprising aspect of the Roman law of intestate succession was the absence of provision for a surviving spouse, particularly the widow. The praetor and, later, Justinian did allow her to claim her husband's property but only in the absence of any blood relations of the deceased. The Romans expected a wife to receive a share of her own family property on the death of her family head and the dowry, to which she became entitled on her husband's death, would usually be an advance payment towards that share.

2. Testamentary succession

Already at the time of the Twelve Tables a family head was given the power to make a will by which he could nominate heirs, appoint tutors for his under-age children and free his slaves. Later he could also grant legacies either of money or of other things; they were gifts out of his inheritance which, unlike an heir's share, carried no duties with them. The nomination of heirs was the most important function of the will and was crucial to its success. As in intestate succession those heirs who were released from paternal power by the death of the deceased became heirs automatically, whereas others could decide whether to accept or not. If none of those who were nominated accepted, the will failed.

This freedom of testation given to a Roman family head is remarkable and can be explained only on two assumptions. First, the traditional rules of succession, with their even-handed treatment of all children and ignoring of the widow, must have aroused dissatisfaction when the heirs began to use their powers to divide up the family property and so create uneconomic units. Secondly, Roman social pressures must have been strong enough to ensure that a family head who used his testamentary powers to divert the family property from his intestate heirs did so in a responsible way which would not prejudice the family as a whole. Thus he might choose one of his sons to be his principal heir and the family manager and make provision for his other children by giving them smaller shares of the inheritance or by legacies. Later he might make provision for his widow by granting her a legacy of a usufruct of part of his estate.

The earliest wills were made publicly in front of the same popular assembly, based on kinship groups, which supervised adrogations, an institution similarly concerned with providing an heir and maintaining the family (p 134). Later this open declaration of intention was replaced by a secret will written down and formally authenticated by the testator as his last will. It was sealed by seven witnesses and the seals were broken only after his death so that until then it was secret. It 'spoke from death', in that it applied to property owned by the testator at the time when he died, and indications of beneficiaries were understood as at the date of death. Up to that time the testator could revoke it whenever he wanted. To show that he had not overlooked his intestate heirs, the testator was required to disinherit them expressly or the will was void.

Towards the end of the Republic, as a result of the breakdown of family solidarity, testators could no longer be relied on to make wills which satisfied their families, and new regulation was required. Testators were inclined to overestimate the property that they were likely to have at the time of their death and granted such large legacies of money or things that there was not enough for the heirs, who took what was left, to make it worth their while undertaking the burden of administering the inheritance. A statute, the *lex Falcidia*, guaranteed to the heirs a minimum of a quarter of the net estate, after deduction of funeral expenses, debts, the value of freed slaves, etc. If the legacies as granted by the testator did not leave a quarter in the 'residuary estate' for the heirs they were reduced accordingly. The calculations involved were quite elaborate since legacies of periodical payments and usufructs had to be given a capital value. In the case of usufruct this required some estimate of the usufructuary's life expectancy.

If the family's objection to the will was more serious, namely that the testator had excluded his immediate intestate heirs without sufficient cause, there was originally no remedy. So long as the will was formally valid and was made by a testator with legal capacity, it could not be challenged. The jurists, pressed to find a means of overturning the will, concentrated on the latter point. If it could be shown that the testator was not in his right mind when he made the will, it would be void. Could it not be argued that a will that for no good reason overlooked the claims of his immediate family was itself evidence of insanity? This was the basis of a remedy, the *querela inofficiosi testamenti*, or 'complaint of an unduteous will', which became available in the late Republic. No-one could bring the *querela*, if he had received under the will at least a quarter of what he would have received on intestacy (his *legitima portio*). If he brought it successfully the will failed and there was an intestacy. The inconveniences of this were mitigated by Justinian who introduced an action to make up the claimant's share to the *legitima portio*. Justinian also recognised an unsealed will made without witnesses, if it was written wholly in the testator's own hand ('holograph') and was in favour of his children.

Since legacies could not be left to certain classes of persons, such as those not yet born when the testator died, testators took to leaving property to an heir or legatee with a request that he pass it on in due course to those whom they wished to benefit. As with the original English 'uses' (p 168), these requests were not, at first, legally binding but were merely 'committed to the faith', *fideicommissa*, of the 'fiduciary' so requested. However, the early emperors enforced them and thereafter they became an important institution, with much of the flexibility of the English trust. In particular, testators used them to tie up property and pass it from one beneficiary to another. The heir would be charged with a *fideicommissum* to pass on the inheritance or part of it to someone else on a certain date or on the happening of some event and on certain conditions. For example, a testator could leave property to his son with a *fideicommissum* to keep it and bequeath it in turn at his death to his own son on similar terms. Roman law before Justinian was undecided on the question of how long it was desirable to allow property to be tied up in this way but Justinian allowed it to remain inalienable for four generations. *Fideicommissa*, unlike the English trust, could only be made by a will or by codicil, a less formal addition to a will.

Modern law

Modern systems, both of the civil law and of the common law tradition, accept the principle of universal succession whereby the whole of the deceased's assets and liabilities pass as a single unit without having to be transferred individually. They differ, however, as to the persons to whom this unit, the deceased's 'estate', passes. In French and German law, it passes to heirs immediately on the death of the deceased, and this applies whether the heirs are descendants of the deceased or others. The heirs are identified either by the rules of intestacy or by will and have the duty to administer the estate and a right to a share in it. They may disclaim the inheritance within a limited period, and any heir who so disclaims is treated as if he had never been heir. In England, on the other hand, the deceased's estate passes to the personal representatives, who may or may not derive some benefit from it. It is their duty to administer the estate, pay debts and taxes, and distribute what is left to the beneficiaries under will or intestacy.

1. *Civil law*

In both French and German law the rules of intestate succession are designed to protect the deceased's family as he would presumably have wished. In this aim they appear to have been successful since men of property have often been satisfied to allow their property to pass to their heirs by operation of law rather than make a will. Both laws give preference to the children of the deceased, with representation of deceased children *per stirpes*, as in Roman law. If there are no descendant heirs, the law turns to the parents and *their* descendants. French law gives a quarter to each surviving parent and the remainder to the brothers and sisters (or their descendants, if they are dead). If there are no brothers or sisters (or their representatives), the estate is split into a paternal half and a maternal half. A surviving parent takes half, and the remainder goes to the nearest surviving relatives on the other side of the family (CC 731–755). In German law surviving parents take the whole estate to the exclusion of brothers and sisters, who only become heirs if at least one parent is dead (BGB 1924–5). The system in Germany is based on *parentelae*. A person's *parentela* consists of all his living descendants, the nearer excluding the more remote, but with representation *per stirpes*. The first *parentela* comprises the deceased's own descendants, the second his parents and their descendants, the third his grandparents and their descendants.

All these claims are, however, subject to the right of a surviving spouse, and that differs in France and Germany. Traditionally French law protected a widow more through the rules of matrimonial property and by succession in her own family than in that of her husband. But the rules of the code have been modified and the surviving spouse now has a usufruct over an increasing share in the estate, depending on how close the heirs are to the deceased. Where there are children of the marriage, the spouse has only a usufruct in one quarter of the estate; where there are brothers and sisters, a usufruct in one half. Where there are neither children nor brothers and sisters and ascendants in one line only, the spouse takes the share that would otherwise have gone to the collaterals in the other line absolutely. In German law the surviving spouse is treated more generously, being entitled to one quarter of the estate absolutely if there are heirs in the first *parentela* (ie descendants of the deceased), to one half if there are none in the first but at least one in the second and to the whole estate if there are heirs in neither the of the first two *parentelae*. Indeed the spouse's share may be increased if the married couple were subject to the regime of community of acquisitions (p 142). Instead of calculating the actual amount of acquisitions during the marriage, a surviving spouse who is so entitled may claim an extra quarter of the estate, whether or not there were any such acquisitions.

Although both French and German law provide for the making of wills – either formally authenticated by a notary or unwitnessed holograph wills, written and signed by the testator's own hand – they restrict what the testator can freely dispose of to a part of his estate. In this they have been influenced by the *legitima portio* of late Roman law, which guaranteed to the heirs who would succeed on intestacy a quarter of their intestate shares, unless they had disqualified themselves by bad behaviour.

The compilers of the French code found two forms of testamentary restriction in operation in the existing law.[2] The customs of southern France recognised the Roman 'legitim', applicable to all forms of property, while in northern France there were customary rules of Germanic origin aimed at keeping land within the family. Under the *retrait lignager*, the relatives of an owner of inherited land, even collaterals, could require a conveyance by him of such land to be cancelled within a year, and his powers to dispose of it by will were restricted by the *réserve coutumière*, or forced heirship, which ensured that a substantial part, usually four-fifths, went to the heirs. The code produced a combined form of restriction. Where the deceased leaves descendants or ascendants, the heirs have a *réserve* over both land and movables. The amount available for the testator to dispose of freely varies according to the number of heirs and is never less than a quarter of the whole estate, but any gift which he ever made that decreased the heirs' entitlement can be retrospectively recalled (CC 913ff). If there are neither descendants nor ascendants, the testator has complete freedom to dispose of his property as he wishes (CC 916). The surviving spouse has no *réserve*.

German law gives the children, the parents and the surviving spouse rights to 'legitim'. They are not heirs but have claims against

2.   J. P. Dawson *Gifts and Promises* (1980) pp 29ff.

the heirs for half of what they would have received on intestacy, less anything that they have received under the will (BGB 2303ff). Past gifts can be recalled, as in France, but only if made in the previous ten years. The Code contains elaborate rules detailing the circumstances in which a testator is entitled to deprive an unworthy claimant of his 'legitim' (BGB 2333–5).

It is the existence of such limitations on the testator's powers of disposition which explains, at least in part, why modern civil law systems have not developed complex family settlements of property, such as developed in England. A grant of land or movables to C, subject to usufructs first in favour of A and then in favour of B, is always valid in the civil law as a way of creating limited interests. The property will be enjoyed first by A, then by B and finally by C (or his heirs) who alone will be able to dispose of it. But such an arrangement is only possible if all the parties are in existence at the time when the grant is made. Owners of property often want to ensure that after their death it passes to persons who are not yet born.

An institution devised to answer this need is the fideicommissary substitution,[3] a post-Roman combination of the *fideicommissum* with the practice of Roman testators of substituting an alternative heir if the inheritance was rejected by the heir whom they had first instituted (not being an automatic descendant heir). It became popular, particularly in France, and enabled property to pass from one heir to another in a prescribed order of succession, so that although each heir could enjoy the property during his life, none could alienate it. Thus it would remain in the family from one generation to another. So much land was in this way taken out of circulation that in the sixteenth century Justinian's limit of four generations for *fideicommissa* was reduced to two generations. The Code Civil restricted the power to make fideicommissary substitutions drastically. A parent may grant property (subject to the *réserves* in favour of members of his family) to his child subject to an obligation on him to transfer it to *all* his children, born or to be born, equally and a person who dies without descendants of his own may do the same for his brothers and sisters on the same terms (CC 1048–9). The grantee may look like a usufructuary but in law he is actually owner of the property. Although his ownership is subject to the limitation that it must be transmitted to his children, his powers are greater than those of usufructuary, and if he does not have any children his ownership becomes unlimited.

German law is more tolerant of substitutions. It allows a testator to appoint a series of heirs (without limitation of number) to take the

---

3. K. W. Ryan *An Introduction to the Civil Law* (1962) pp 206ff.

whole or part of his estate in succession, so long as it vests finally in the last heir either within 30 years, that being regarded as the period of a generation, or within a life in being (BGB 2109). By the last provision the estate may pass to a 'provisional heir' on the testator's death and the appointment of the final heir may be delayed until his death. The testator may if he wishes free the provisional heir from many of his duties to preserve the property for the final heir. For example, instead of making his widow a usufructuary, with limited rights over his property, he may make her provisional heir with powers to dispose of it, subject only to a *fideicommissum* to transfer what is left at her death to a named relative (BGB 2137).

2. English law

English law formerly had separate rules of succession for land and for movables. The rules for land (realty) were feudal in origin and were based on the need of the landed gentry to keep the family land intact from one generation to another. Heirs were identified according to *parentelae*, starting with that of the deceased himself, ie his descendants, then that of his father, and so on. Males were preferred to females of the same degree and the eldest son was preferred to the younger sons. Primogeniture only applied to males, and if the heirs were females (because there were no males but there were females in a certain degree), they shared as 'co-parceners'. The land passed directly to the heir or heirs. The holder of an estate in land could dispose of it by will but was often restricted by family settlements.

In the case of movables (personalty), English customs originally recognised the rights of the widow and the children to certain fractions or 'parts' of the estate. The deceased himself had a part, and of that part alone could he dispose freely. He often bequeathed it to the Church to pay for masses for the repose of his soul, and the family rights ensured that he did not divert too great a part of his wealth for that selfish end. The Church supervised the administration of movable estates in its own courts, and it was the Church courts which, to facilitate such administration, encouraged testators to appoint 'executors' in their wills and, in the absence of executors, the courts themselves appointed 'administrators'. They thus introduced the system of personal representatives of the deceased. After the Reformation the Church courts gradually allowed the testator to dispose of the whole of his movables, although complete freedom of testation was not allowed over the whole of England and Wales until the eighteenth century.

The system of personal representatives was extended to succession to land in 1897, and the Administration of Estates Act 1925 introduced a uniform succession for both land and movables. When a person dies intestate, his estate passes to 'administrators', appointed by the court from his relatives in a given order of priority. They hold all his property on trust for sale (p 170) and then to pay expenses and to distribute. The English system of distribution on an intestacy today is designed primarily to safeguard the interests of the surviving spouse and offset the absence of a system of community property during the marriage (p 142). The surviving spouse is entitled to the deceased's personal belongings, such as the car, household furniture and so on, and to a sum of money, 'the statutory legacy', the amount of which is periodically varied by statutory order. In 1981 it was fixed at £40,000, where the intestate leaves descendants, and £85,000, where there are no descendants. The home may form part or all of the legacy according to valuation. As a result, in the case of small estates the surviving spouse takes everything. Where the estate is larger, the surviving spouse takes the statutory legacy and a life interest in half the rest of the estate. The children (with representation *per stirpes*) take the other half immediately and the first half on the death of the surviving spouse. Subject to the surviving spouse's rights, first parents, then brothers and sisters and then remoter relations succeed in the absence of descendants.

In English law a person has in principle freedom to dispose of his property, both land and movables, as he wishes, and if he makes a will, no one else, however closely related, has a right to any part of his estate when he dies. Nevertheless the modern law gives relief to the surviving spouse, children and other dependants of the deceased by giving the court a discretion, on their application, to make such provision for them as it considers appropriate. The idea of giving the court such discretion was introduced by the New Zealand Family Protection Act of 1908, and was extended to England in 1938. It is now regulated by the Inheritance (Provision for Family and Dependants) Act 1975, which allows application to be made not only to alter the dispositions of a will but also to alter those provided by the rules of intestacy. The court must take into account such factors as the applicant's own resources, the applicant's conduct and the amount of the estate, and may make an order for periodical or lump sum payments. The very existence of the court's power is a powerful incentive to the executors and beneficiaries under a will to make concessions to dependants who have received inadequate provisions in order to avoid the costs of a court action.

A will must be in writing signed by the testator and witnessed by two witnesses who are present together either when the testator signs or when he acknowledges his signature. To prevent frauds, a witness is debarred from receiving any benefit under the will. The executors named in the will have a duty to obtain from the court a grant of probate, which is an official recognition that the will is authentic. Having paid debts and expenses and the applicable capital transfer tax, the executors must pay specific and pecuniary legacies, and distribute the residuary estate to those mentioned in the will. They are allowed a year from the death to wind up the estate, before they can be challenged by a beneficiary for delay.

In the case of substantial estates, the testator may use his will to create a series of limited interests. He must ensure that any future interest – one which arises at some time in the future, such as on the conclusion of a life interest – vests in the beneficiary within the period of a life in being and 21 years afterwards. The effect of this rule, known as the Rule against Perpetuities, is that the property may be bequeathed to a child of the testator for life and then to that child's child when he reaches the age of 21 years even though the testator's child may have no children of his own when the testator dies. (A period of gestation may be added, for example, if the grandchild is born posthumously.)[4]

Care has to be taken in such cases to minimise the incidence of capital transfer tax. Transfers between spouses or to a charity do not normally attract tax, but any other disposition is usually taxable, and the passing of property from the holder of a life interest to the remainderman is treated as such a disposition. Under the Finance Act 1978, s 68, the beneficiaries under a will can, if they all agree within a limited period, vary the arrangements laid down in the will so as to lessen the tax burden, for example, by allowing property left to A for life and then to B to jump a generation and pass directly to the remainderman B, or, in the case of a legatee to whom the testator has bequeathed an absolute gift, to pass it directly to the legatee's child without passing through the legatee's hand. As a result CTT is payable only once instead of twice.

4. The rule applies to all future interests, whether created while the grantor is alive or in his will.

13   Obligations

An obligation is a non-physical thing. In so far as it is an asset, it is a right enforceable only against a particular person or persons on whom certain duties are imposed. It is thus a legal relationship between two parties, the creditor, who is entitled to the performance of those duties, and the debtor, who is bound to perform them, and essentially it is of concern only to them. (In bilateral obligations each party is both creditor and debtor.) By contrast a property right denotes mainly a relationship between the person entitled and a thing. The advantage of a property right is that it is enforceable by action *in rem*. This means that it is normally possible to assert the right against anyone who has the thing or interferes with it. If the man who was detaining it has it no longer, the person entitled follows the thing and sues the person in whose hands it is now to make him hand it over. An obligation, on the other hand, is enforceable only by action *in personam* against the debtor, and the usual remedy is the payment of money damages by the defendant to the successful plaintiff. But if the defendant has no money, the plaintiff's success is a hollow victory; actual satisfaction depends on the defendant's ability to pay. The financial position of the person bound by an obligation is therefore all important to the question of the value of the obligation as an asset.

Roman law

In Roman law an obligation was envisaged as a legal bond or fetter constraining the debtor to some specified behaviour. In earlier classical law it was held that all obligations were derived from two sources, contracts and delicts. Later it was realised that there was a small number of obligations which could be traced neither to an agreement between the parties nor to a wrong committed by one against the other, and they were said to arise as if from contract (*quasi ex contractu*) or from the law itself.

1. Contractual obligations
Roman law did not regard agreements as being necessarily binding on the parties. Many kinds of agreement are made in circumstances

184

in which the parties have no expectation that what they are undertaking to do should be enforceable in the courts. They may be purely social arrangements or provisional understandings to which neither side wishes to be bound. Commercial contracts are different. When they make agreements in the course of business transactions, people must be assumed to understand that they are legally bound. But in early societies commerce is little developed. Sales are in the form of barter or cash transactions with the simultaneous transfer of the goods and price and no need for credit.

In Roman law parties who wished to be legally bound were expected to indicate that they appreciated the seriousness of what they were doing in particular ways. In the developed law an agreement became binding either if it was 'clothed' in a certain form or if its object fell within certain recognised types of agreement which commonly occurred in everyday life.[1]

In early law the only agreements creating binding contracts were formal and the usual form was the *stipulation*. This was an oral exchange of question and answer in which the promisor unequivocally accepted the proposal put to him by the stipulator. It was therefore unilateral in that only one party, the promisor, was bound by it, but it was possible to link two stipulations, the promisor in one being the stipulator in the other. The need for the party to be bound to accept what was proposed without reservation was a useful way of marking the moment at which bargaining ended and agreement was reached. Sometimes, when parties have been vigorously negotiating, they may think that they have ironed out all their differences, whereas in fact there are still unresolved points which they have overlooked. The requirement that the contract be set out in a set of proposals put by one side and accepted by the other made them pause and consider whether agreement had actually been reached. Stipulation was very simple. The only formality required was that the promisor's answer should be an unequivocal acceptance of the proposal and this originally had to be shown by the use of the same verb in the answer as that in the question, for example, 'Do you promise . . .?' 'I promise' or 'Will you give . . .?' 'I will give'. Naturally the parties would normally ensure that the stipulation was evidenced either by witnesses who were present at the oral exchange or more usually by a written document, but how they proved the stipulation was up to them; all the law required was the oral exchange. In principle there was no limit to the content of the agreement which could be turned into a binding obligation by being 'clothed' in the stipulatory form.

The main disadvantage of stipulation, apart from a certain rigidity

---

1. Lawson *Common Lawyer* pp 113ff.

imposed by its unilateral character, was that it required the presence of both parties; it could not be concluded by exchange of letters or through messengers. An agreement may, however, be reached even though the parties are not physically present, and mere agreement was recognised as creating a contract in certain typical situations. The four particular contracts which could be created in this way were binding from the moment that agreement was reached and were known as the consensual contracts. They were all of commercial importance: sale (*emptio venditio*), hire (*locatio conductio*), partnership (*societas*) and mandate (*mandatum*). They were all bilateral in that they imposed duties on both parties, which allowed for more flexibility than the unilateral stipulation. Since the duties of the parties were inter-dependent, a great deal more discretion had to be given to the *iudex*, who decided any disputes arising from them, than was the case in disputes arising from stipulations.

Stipulation was originally for payment of a fixed sum of money or delivery of a specified thing and in the action to enforce it the creditor had to prove that the exact sum or thing that he claimed was owing. If he proved that a lesser sum was owing, he lost his action. Originally the civil law looked only at the form. If that had been complied with, the obligation was enforceable according to the letter. The fact that the promisor might have been induced to enter into the stipulation by the fraud or threats of the other party was irrelevant if the form had been carried out. Towards the end of the Republic the praetor allowed a debtor who was sued on a formal contract to plead such factors in the formula by way of defence to the creditor's claim. If the debtor had to admit that the obligation was validly created in form, but could nevertheless convince the *iudex* that it was in fact tainted by fraud or duress, the *iudex* had to give judgment in his favour. But since the powers of the *iudex* were derived from the formula, he could only take account of matters that were pleaded in it.

When the consensual contracts came to be recognised the praetor instructed the *iudex* in the formula of the relevant action that if he found that one of the recognised contracts had been made, he should condemn the defendant in whatever sum he ought to pay the plaintiff 'in good faith'. The three words *ex fide bona* allowed the *iudex* to take into account such allegations as fraud or duress, as he thought fit, without the need for them to be expressly pleaded in advance of the trial. Furthermore they enabled the *iudex* to set off the claim of one party against the counter-claim of the other and give judgment for the balance. The *bonae fidei* character of the actions given in the case of the consensual contracts, by contrast with the *stricti iuris* character of the actions on stipulation, allowed successive generations of *iudices* to elaborate in detail the duties which good faith demanded of the parties.

Individual consideration of the four consensual contracts will indicate the wide range of transactions that they covered. The most important particular contract in any legal system is *sale*.[2] The Romans looked at it neutrally and called it 'buying and selling'. Its essential elements were an identifiable thing, a fixed price in money and agreement. An agreement in regard to goods identified only by description, which were to be supplied by one party to the other, such as 'twenty pounds of best Cox's apples', was not a sale. Such an agreement had to be made by two stipulations, one for the delivery of the goods and the other for the payment of the price. There was dispute as to whether the price could be in goods or had to be in money. The Proculian argument that if it were not in money it would be impossible to distinguish the buyer from the seller prevailed. The respective duties of the two parties were defined with increasing precision. The buyer had merely to take delivery and pay the agreed price at the agreed time or after reasonable notice, but the seller's duties were more onerous.

The making of a contract of sale had no effect on the ownership of the thing sold. That passed to the buyer when it was conveyed (p 147) but the risk of accidental loss or damage passed to the buyer once there was an unconditional contract, unless the parties agreed otherwise. It was felt that once the buyer had contracted to buy the thing he should accept the responsibility for it. The seller had to look after the thing with due care until after delivery, he had to deliver vacant possession of the thing and he had to compensate the buyer if, after receiving the thing, he was evicted from it by someone with a better title.

The Romans were much preoccupied with the problem of liability in respect of defects in the thing sold. Originally the seller was not liable for any defects if the thing he had sold turned out to be defective, unless he had expressly promised by stipulation that it was free of such defect. As the idea grew that the duties imposed by the contract were determined by good faith, the seller came to be liable for any defects of which he knew at the time of the sale. The problem was that it was difficult for the buyer to prove that the seller did know about something that was not discoverable on inspection – and if it was so discoverable then the buyer was expected to have noticed it himself. Liability was imposed specifically by the magistrates in charge of markets, on sellers of slaves and animals. They had something of the same reputation in the ancient world that used car dealers have in the modern, and they were made liable for failing to reveal certain specified defects, both physical and moral, such as the tendency of a slave to run away from his owner, whether they

2.   F. de Zulueta *The Roman Law of Sale* (1945).

knew about the defects or not. By the time of Justinian this rule had been generalised into a seller's liability for serious latent defects in all sales. The original rule of 'let the buyer beware' (*caveat emptor*) had been completely reversed through the increasing requirements of good faith.

Because of the exclusion of sales of goods by description, Roman sale was somewhat narrower in scope than its modern equivalent, but that is certainly not true of the second consensual contract, 'letting and hiring' which covered a breathtaking range of transactions that seem to us to have little in common with each other. It included all arrangements whereby one party placed something temporarily in the hands of another party and payment was to be made. The thing that was 'placed' might be physical, such as a house or field or horse or plough. The Romans saw little difference between the relationship of landlord and tenant of land under a lease and that of the lessor and hirer of a movable. In each case a thing was placed by the owner for a limited period in the hands of another who agreed to pay rent for it. Alternatively the thing 'placed' might be something to be worked on by the recipient, such as cloth to be turned into a cloak by a tailor or goods to be carried from one place to another. In that situation later civil lawyers saw the thing 'placed' as the job to be done rather than the thing to be worked on. Yet again the thing 'placed' could be the whole services of a worker who offered them to an employer. The work involved had to be of a menial kind, and performance of 'liberal services' was not included. The Romans had scruples about allowing a freeman to hire *himself* to another (since a freeman's person was not a thing) but they recognised that he could offer his services. Payment would be made *to* 'the placer' of things let out on hire and of services given to an employer, but in the case of a job to be done, payment was made *by* 'the placer' to the person carrying out the job. The Romans saw no difficulty about the apparent discrepancy, since the circumstances would always make it clear which party was entitled to payment from the other.

The Roman contract of hire thus covered all English bailments (p 160), where payment was made either by bailor or bailee. However it was purely a contractual arrangement between the parties and created no rights to the thing which was the object of the contract. A tenant or hirer had no right *in rem* and was not a protected possessor. If his control of the thing was disturbed by an outsider, all he could do was to complain to the lessor, who had agreed that he should enjoy the thing. If an owner, who had let out a thing on hire, then sold and conveyed it to another person, who decided to vindicate his newly acquired ownership against the hirer, the latter could not defend the action by relying on the contract of hire. For that contract was made not with the present owner but with the former owner. The hirer had to give up the thing to the new owner and sue the former owner (if he could find him) for damages.

The third consensual contract, mandate, was the result of an agreement whereby one party, the mandatory, undertook to perform a service for another (the mandator). It differed from the hiring contract just considered in two respects. First, it was gratuitous so that although the mandatory was entitled to be indemnified for any expense he had incurred in carrying out the task that he had undertaken, he was not able to sue for any payment for the work. Secondly, it included the liberal services, such as those of an advocate, which could not be the subject of hiring. The gratuitous character of the contract is surprising in modern English eyes, because we are accustomed to the idea of a contract as a bargain from which both parties gain some benefit. We would normally assume that an arrangement whereby someone agreed to do something on behalf of another for nothing was not intended to create a legal liability. The social milieu in which mandates arose was that of upper-class Roman friends, who were accustomed to make onerous demands on each other in the knowledge that on another occasion they could themselves be called on to render similar help. They regarded such undertakings as serious, and expected them to be legally binding. Sometimes a separate arrangement for the payment of a so-called *honorarium* was made by the parties, although it could not be enforced by the contractual action.

Mandate had many functions. It was a substitute for agency where a person wanted to have something done for him by someone other than one of his own slaves or sons in power. A contract made by A and C could in principle only create legal relations between them even though A acted in the interests of and at the request of B. So if B gave A a mandate to buy a horse for him and A bought one from C and the price was not paid, C would have to sue A on the contract of sale and A would then sue B for reimbursement of what he had paid to C. There was no legal relationship between C and B, although the horse was bought for him. The inconveniences of this situation were tolerable where the mandatary undertook a single transaction only. But where he was the regular manager of a business (*institor*), or the master of ship, and in that capacity undertook a series of transactions for the owner, legal policy required that those with whom the manager or shipmaster contracted should be able to sue the owner directly. Since it was his resources which had financed the undertaking and he who took the profits from it, the praetor made him liable in full on contracts made in the course of the undertaking by his manager or shipmaster, whether the latter was his slave or son in power or a free mandatary. This was an exception to the principle that no-one except the parties to a contract could either benefit or be bound by it, but its advantages were so clear that it was eventually extended to cover even the case where the mandatary only undertook a single transaction.

Although Roman law recognised various forms of real security (p 154), the Romans had a preference for personal security, whereby the payment of a debt is secured by the promise of a guarantor or surety to pay it. Their strong sense of the duties owed to each other by friends meant that Romans expected that their debts would be secured in this way. The main way of creating an obligation of suretyship was by stipulation, the surety promising the creditor that he too would be liable for the debtor's debt. But mandate provided an alternative. If B requested A to lend money to C and A did so, but C failed to repay the loan, A could say that it was money spent in carrying out B's mandate and claim reimbursement from B.

Mandate could also be used to produce an assignment of a contractual right from one person to another. In principle the personal character of contract precluded substituting one party for another. If, however, the creditor–assignor gave the assignee a mandate to sue the debtor as representative of the creditor, but relieved him from the normal duty of a mandatary to account to the mandator for anything that he had received on his behalf, the mandatary was in effect given the benefit of the right.

The last consensual contract was partnership, which was multilateral in that there could be more than two parties. The agreement had to involve co-operation for a common purpose but it did not need to be for profit. The purpose might be limited to a single thing, such as the purchase of a field by two neighbours to prevent it being acquired by a third party, or it might extend to the complete merging of all the partners' assets, so that they were left with no individual property at all. All partners had to contribute something, whether it be money or labour or technical expertise, and if there was a profit, all had to have a share in it, although the shares might well vary from one partner to another. Like mandate, partnership was strictly personal and if one partner dealt with a third party in the course of the partnership business, he in no way bound his fellow partners to the outsider. However, if the partnership agreement could be interpreted as including also a mandate to one of them to be the manager of a particular section of the partnership business, then an outsider with whom that partner contracted could sue the others, by virtue not of the partnership but of the mandate they had given.

The four consensual contracts covered many of the agreements of everyday life and the standard of good faith which was applied to all of them by laymen acting as *iudices* ensured that the duties which the law required of the parties reflected current social expectations. However an agreement which did not fall under any of the four categories was not legally binding on the parties. It was a bare pact, and from a bare pact no action arose. The parties could always make it binding by simply making it a stipulation, but if they failed to do so, it created no obligation, and either party could withdraw with impunity. If neither party had actually done anything to carry out the agreement, no great harm would be done by withdrawal, but what if one party had performed his side of the agreement? If A informally agrees to lend B a sum of money and goes back on his agreement, he is not penalised since he is not bound; it may be said that B should have insisted on a stipulation. But if A actually lends B the money without taking a stipulatory promise from B to return an equivalent amount, a different situation arises. By receiving the money B becomes indebted to A, and if he were allowed to keep it, the law would be condoning the unjust enrichment of B at the expense of A. So A had an action to recover the money from B, and it came to be seen that, although an agreement to make a loan was no contract, an actual loan was a contract since, like a stipulation, it created a unilateral obligation in the borrower to make restitution.

The same principle was applied in other transactions where something was handed over, the obligation arising only when delivery took place. One such case was loan of a specific thing. The Romans logically distinguished between loan of fungibles, such as money, in which the obligation is to return an equivalent (*mutuum*) and loan of a specific thing, such as a horse, in which the obligation is to return the thing lent (*commodatum*). In the first case, since what is handed over is consumed by the recipient, he receives ownership of it; in the second case, ownership remains in the lender and the borrower has merely physical control.

Protection of the lender was not so essential in the case of the loan of a specific thing as in the case of loan of fungibles since he remained owner and possessor and could therefore either vindicate it or bring a possessory interdict (p 145). But there might be other claims arising from the agreement both by the lender if, for example, the borrower had used the thing in a manner contrary to the agreement, and by the borrower if, say, he had incurred some exceptional expense beyond ordinary maintenance of the thing. Loan was essentially gratuitous. In the case of loan of money, it was possible to make a separate stipulation for the payment of interest but any agreement to 'lend' a specific thing for payment was treated as a contract of hire and not of loan. There was, therefore, a question, as in the case of mandate, whether the law ought, as a matter of policy, to treat such gratuitous arrangements as creating contractual duties. Gradually the praetor increased the duties that could be sued for, and gave the borrower a right of retaining the thing until he had received anything owed to him by the lender. At a certain stage loan of a thing became a fully fledged contract with a formula, couched in terms of good faith, to enforce it. Other contracts in the 'real' category were gratuitous deposit for safekeeping and pledge of a thing by way of real security. Finally the principle was generalised and any agreement in which one party performed his side of it became actionable as a contract from that moment.

Until it was thus executed, however, it remained a mere pact, and from a pact no obligation could arise but only a possible defence. For example an agreement not to enforce an existing debt could be raised as a defence to a subsequent action based on the debt.

Classical law adhered firmly to the principle that it was for the parties to a contract to make the terms of the obligation for themselves, and not for the law to impose duties on them. It was assumed that they were of equivalent bargaining power, that they could exploit their negotiating skills and that any agreement they accepted was freely reached, unless the contrary was proved. They were expected to express themselves clearly and if the words they used were unambiguous, they were bound by them and were not permitted to argue that they had intended something different. At the same time, the jurists had to recognise that where parties trust each other, they do not spell out their respective duties in every conceivable eventuality, so that the law cannot avoid attributing certain intentions to them according to the nature of the contract they have made.

This occurred particularly in regard to the standard of care which the contract was thought to impose on the parties. This might range from liability if a thing in the charge of a contracting party was even accidentally damaged, at one extreme, to liability only if damage was deliberately inflicted on it, at the other extreme, with liability for damage caused by unintentional fault falling between the two. Contracting parties could never exclude liability for dishonesty but otherwise the standard of care to be applied in any contract was the result of agreement. In the absence of agreement the jurists tended to apply the principle that if a party benefited from the transaction he was liable both for dishonesty (*dolus*) and for fault (*culpa*), whereas if a party did not benefit, as in some gratuitous contracts, he was liable only for dishonesty. Only in exceptional cases was he held to insure the other party against loss not due to his fault, and some such cases were due to difficulty of proof. A borrower was liable if the thing was stolen while in his charge, even though the lender could not prove that the theft was due to the borrower's fault.

We have seen that although Roman law started from the

assumption that agreements only became binding contracts when they were put into a certain form, this principle was mitigated in the case of certain common agreements having particular objects (*causae*), and then it was accepted that any agreement which was acted upon by one party also became a contract. The total result of these developments was very like a general law of contract. In the Republic the jurists had seen very little similarity between the various kinds of contractual obligation. In the classical period, however, they perceived that behind all the different kinds of contract there lay agreement (*consensus*). The introduction of the defences of fraud and of duress in actions brought to enforce stipulations had shown that, even in the case of contracts which derived their binding force from a form, a genuine underlying agreement was required.

Certain general principles applicable to all forms of contract now came to be recognised. Any agreement having an object that was illegal or immoral was not enforceable, whether it was governed by good faith or was incorporated into a *stricti iuris* form. Any agreement imposing a duty to do something which was either impossible from the beginning or became impossible before the time when performance was due was similarly unenforceable. It was also recognised that there were three factors which typically might vitiate agreement: error as to an essential element in the contract, fraud and physical duress. The rules of error were worked out mainly in relation to sale, and mistake as to the thing sold or the price to be paid prevented agreement from being reached at all. The contract was 'void *ab initio*'. Fraud and duress was investigated more in regard to stipulations and an agreement tainted by either was valid until the party prejudiced pleaded it. Such a contract was therefore 'voidable'.

By the time of Justinian, the form of the stipulation had been modified so that any writing attesting an agreement by stipulation was regarded as proof of a binding contract unless it was shown that it was physically impossible for the oral exchange to have taken place. The principle of privity of contract was, however, retained. A contract only affected the parties to it. So far as imposing duties is concerned, this is understandable. Duties should not be placed on those who have not agreed to accept them. But why should a third party not be able to enforce a contract made for his benefit? The Romans would have pointed out the contract was a personal relationship and so they only recognised the utility of such a notion in very limited exceptions to the rule of privity.

2. *Quasi-contractual obligations*

The realisation that the common feature of all contractual

obligations was agreement drew the attention of jurists to the existence of certain obligations which had been treated as contractual, but in which it was not possible to find an agreement.

In the first place these were cases where the principle of unjust enrichment, as applied originally in loans of fungibles, had operated. A typical case was the payment of money by A to B in the mistaken belief that it was owed, where B received it innocently, so that his acceptance involved no wrongdoing such as would give rise to a delictal obligation. So long as the payment was not meant to be a gift, the law imposed a duty on B to return what he had received. Originally this obligation was considered to be similar to that created by a loan of money and so contractual, but when it was seen that loan necessarily involved prior agreement but payment by mistake did not, the obligation was classified as quasi-contractual. The relevant action (the *condictio*) was extended to cover several situations in which one person has conferred a benefit on another, but the reason for the payment has failed in some way so that the recipient has no justification for keeping it.

Another obligation thus categorised bears a similarity with mandate but also lacks agreement. If a person acts on behalf of a friend who has made no request, in the belief that the friend would wish him to act in that way, the doing of the unauthorised act is not the result of a mandate. Yet it was considered that the parties should be bound to each other by an obligation (*negotiorum gestio*) similar to that created by mandate. The person acting was bound to act with proper care, and if what he did was useful to the absent principal at the time, by being the sort of thing the principal himself would have done had he been present, he could claim to be indemnified by the principal for his reasonable expenses.

3. *Delictal obligations*

Early Roman law treated only certain serious crimes as suitable for prosecution by the state (p 55). Murder and arson, for example, were of such gravity that the sanctioning of them could not be left to the kin of the victim; retaliation by the kin would in any case be calculated to lead to public disorder. But in most other cases of wrongdoing, the state left it to the victim to bring an action against the delinquent. The commission of the wrong created an obligation between the delinquent and his victim which the latter could enforce. There was, however, an important difference between the actions enforcing a contractual or quasi-contractual obligation and those enforcing a delictal obligation. The object of the former was to recover compensation for the economic loss suffered by the plaintiff.

The object of the latter was to punish the wrongdoer, by making him pay the victim a penalty which was usually far greater than the amount of the loss that he had suffered.

The practical consequences of the distinction are considerable. First, if either party to an action based on breach of contract dies, the action can be brought by or against his heir, since it is regarded as restoring the economic position of the parties which has been disturbed by the breach. If a victim of delict dies the action can usually, but not always, be continued by his heir, but if the wrongdoer himself dies the action dies with him, for otherwise his heir would be punished for what he did not do. Secondly, if several people are involved in a contract, either on the creditor or on the debtor side, the benefit or burden of the obligation is normally divided between them. But if several people together commit a delict they are each liable to the same penalty as if they had done it alone, ie penal liability is cumulative. Thirdly, if the wrongdoer is a slave or son in power the family head has the option of either paying the damages that the wrongdoer would have had to pay if free or to surrender the wrongdoer 'noxally' to the victim. The family head was in certain circumstances liable to pay damages in respect of the contractual obligations of his slaves or sons, but had no such option of surrender.

As in the case of contracts the Romans developed the law separately in relation to particular forms of delict rather than applying a general principle of delictal liability. There were three main delicts, two relating to property, theft and damage to property, and one relating to personal injury.[3]

Today thieves are rarely worth suing in a civil action and the normal way of dealing with them is by criminal prosecution. As has been noted (p 55), it was probably the existence of noxal surrender which made civil actions for theft worthwhile in Rome. If a thing was stolen, the victim, if owner, had of course a proprietary action, such as *vindicatio*, to recover the thing once it was traced. Alternatively, he had a *condictio* for its value against the thief, even if the thief no longer had the thing. But the victim had only one such action to recover his thing or its value. In addition, however, he had penal actions against anyone who had stolen the thing.

Theft (*furtum*) was broadly interpreted as any dishonest dealing with a thing, with a view to gain. So one who knowingly accepted money which was paid to him by mistake was a thief. A person might be guilty of theft even though he had a right to the thing. A

---

3. *Justinian: The Digest of Roman Law: theft, rapine, damage and insult* (translated with introduction by C. F. Kolbert, 1979).

borrower was entitled to have the thing but if he used it in an unauthorised way he was guilty of theft 'of its use'. An owner who had pledged a thing by way of security to a creditor could himself be guilty of theft 'of its possession' if he took it back without permission. For it was not only the owner of the stolen thing who could bring the penal action but generally anyone with an interest in its safety, such as a pledge-creditor or usufructuary, or even a borrower, since he was liable to the owner if it was stolen from him. The normal penal action was for twice the value of the stolen thing (which had to be a movable). But if the thief was caught in the act of stealing (manifest theft), his victim was originally not forced to accept a money penalty but was permitted to wreak his vengeance physically on the person of the thief. This was later modified to a fourfold penalty.

The delict of theft was part of the ancient customary law, and the lawyers could therefore modify its details without limitation. Damage to property was regulated by a statute enacted by the popular assembly in the third century BC, the *lex Aquilia*, and the words of the statute limited the range of possible extensions that could be made. The relevant chapters dealing with *damnum iniuria datum* (literally 'loss unlawfully inflicted'), were the first and third. The first dealt with the unlawful killing of a person's slaves or animals and probably repeated existing rules. The third chapter was new and was expressed more generally. In cases not covered by the first chapter, anyone who caused loss to another by 'burning, fracturing or breaking' something of his unlawfully was to be liable to him for the loss caused.

Although the third chapter of the *lex Aquilia* was probably originally restricted in terms of the thing and the kind of injury in respect of which action could be brought, by the classical period it had been extended by interpretation to cover all types of property, movable and immovable, and all kinds of loss resulting from physical injury. Since 'unlawfully' was understood to mean either deliberately or as a result of the defendant's unintentional fault (*culpa*), the ambit of the delict was wide. The plaintiff could succeed if he showed that he had suffered economic loss as a result of a direct physical act of the defendant which was blameworthy. There was no liability for omissions unless they followed a specific assumption of responsibility.

Many cases turned on the question of causation. Was the loss caused by the defendant's fault or was it rather caused by the plaintiff himself or by a third party or by accident? Only in the first case was there any liability under the *lex Aquilia*. The Roman approach was all or nothing, and there was no possibility of apportioning blame for the loss between the defendant and another.

In classical law the damages under chapter III were based on the difference between the highest value of the thing in the month preceding the damage and the value afterwards, and consequential damages (*damnum emergens* and *lucrum cessans*) could be obtained. The stock example was the killing of a horse which was a member of a matched team. The damages included not just the intrinsic value of the horse but also the reduction in the value of the surviving members of the team. A defendant who denied liability, and so put the plaintiff to the trouble of proof, was condemned in double damages if he lost the action. This was the main penal element in an action which was in substance compensatory although having the characteristics of a penal action.

Since the statute laid down that the liability was owed to the owner, no-one other than the owner could bring the statutory action. However the praetor granted special actions based on similar principles to non-owners, as he did also when the plaintiff's loss was caused indirectly, as, for example, when the defendant opened a stable door and the plaintiff's animals escaped and were lost. (If the defendant did it in order that they should be taken by an accomplice, he was liable for theft.) As the *lex Aquilia* was concerned with property, it did not lie in the case of personal injuries suffered by a freeman, for a freeman did not own his body. In late law a freeman had an extension of the Aquilian action to recover his actual quantifiable financial loss in the form of loss of wages and medical expenses, but he could claim nothing for his pain and suffering. Nor did the dependants of a freeman who had been killed have any action for what they had lost through his death.

Although a freeman had no remedy for personal injuries caused negligently, he did have an action for a deliberate injury, based on the separate delict of *iniuria*. At the time of the Twelve Tables *iniuria* was confined to physical assaults, for which a tariff of fixed money penalties was laid down. Later the praetor extended the scope of the delict to cover any kind of insulting or defamatory act or statement, so long as it was made with the intention of hurting the victim. The praetorian action was for damages based on the seriousness of the insult. They were not related to the economic loss suffered by the victim, as in the case of Aquilian damages, but were rather designed to assuage his hurt feelings and at the same time penalise the wrongdoer. In an ordinary case the victim suggested a figure which he considered appropriate and the *iudex* could condemn for any sum up to that limit. Where the circumstances made the *iniuria* aggravated, the praetor fixed the sum and the *iudex*, if he found the facts proved, would condemn for that amount. Since the damages were associated so closely with the reaction of the victim as an individual, he could not sue if he showed no immediate resentment at the hurt done to him, and if he died, his heir could not bring the action against the wrongdoer. So there was no private law remedy where death was caused. One could suffer *iniuria* indirectly through another person, as for example, where a member of one's family was humiliated.

In addition to the regular delicts, Justinian grouped a number of praetorian actions into a category of obligations arising *quasi ex delicto*. They appear to be mainly cases where, as a police measure, persons occupying certain positions were made liable for what happened within the area of their responsibility. The occupier of a house was liable if damage was caused through things thrown or poured down from it or through something fixed dangerously on it. The occupier was similarly liable where death or injury was caused to a freeman. Any member of his family, or in the last resort any member of the public, could bring the action (*actio popularis*). Another quasi-delictal action was that against a *iudex* where it could be shown that he had decided in favour of the wrong party. In these cases it was not necessary to show that the defendant had been personally at fault, but rather that he had accepted a particular rôle and so was answerable when things went wrong.

Modern law

Modern civil law has retained the Roman notion of obligation as an umbrella category covering contract, civil wrongs and unjustified enrichment. Obligations, as in Roman law, arise in various ways but matters of assigning or extinguishing obligations that have been created are dealt with in relation to all obligations together. There has also been a tendency to apply standards of liability to obligations generally rather than to contracts and delicts separately. In both cases the emphasis is on fault, the modern equivalent of the Roman *culpa*, as indicating liability whether it is for breach of contract or for causing loss to another. In English law contracts and torts (civil wrongs) are treated as distinct branches of law. They both give rise to remedies *in personam* but are not considered as falling under one category.

1. Contract

Civil law systems have retained the particular contracts of Roman law, such as sale and partnership, each with its own set of rules. Most of these rules are in effect terms implied in the contract by law if the parties fail to make an express agreement to the contrary. They are based on what normal persons, making that type of contract, would be expected to have decided if they had been asked about the matter. Superimposed on these particular contracts is a general doctrine of contract. Whereas Roman law started from the proposition that an agreement was not binding as a contract unless it had some further element, such as that it was clothed in stipulatory form or had a particular object, modern law reverses the position. It assumes that an agreement is a contract unless there is a particular reason for it not to be binding.[4]

The origins of this general doctrine of the binding force of agreements is to be found in the canon law of the Church. In the middle ages parties to a contract frequently reinforced their promises with religious oaths. This not only gave them greater solemnity, but also, since breaking an oath was a sin, ensured that disputes arising from the contract would fall within the jurisdiction of the Church courts. As the judges in such courts were literate ecclesiastics, the contract was likely to be better understood by them than by the lay judges or juries in the secular courts. The oath was therefore a device for giving jurisdiction to a better qualified court. The canonists developed the doctrine that a promise which had been freely made should be binding on the promisor, whether or not it was supported by an oath, so long as there was a serious purpose or reason for it (*causa*). They also moved towards extending to all contracts the idea of 'good faith', which in Roman law was confined to particular contracts.

By the seventeenth century the natural lawyers had reached the position that any seriously intended agreement created a contract unless the object of the parties was illegal or immoral or contrary to public policy. Most of the rules applicable to contracts generally were taken from the Roman texts on stipulation (without the *stricti iuris* aspects) and on sale. In practice, however, there were still cases in the eighteenth century civil law in which the principle of the innominate real contracts applied and the parties were bound not by their agreement but by the performance by one of them of his side of the bargain; until then either party could withdraw without penalty.

The great civil law codes laid down the general doctrine of contract received from the natural lawyers. It was based on the enlightenment idea that the individual has a freedom which can be restricted only by his own will. The state itself was envisaged as a union of individual wills, and the justification of any legislation by the state which restricted the individual's actions could only be that such restrictions were necessary to protect the freedom of others in the society. When two persons reach an agreement, therefore, what they decide is in effect a private law which they have made for themselves. Thus article 1134 of the French code provides that

4. Lawson *Common Lawyer* pp 148ff.

'agreements legally formed have the character of law for those who have made them'. The underlying assumptions of the doctrine of the autonomy of the individual will are that individuals are the best judges of what is best for them, and that they must be free to enter into an agreement or not and, if they do, to include in it whatever terms they like. If the result is to favour one party unduly at the expense of the other, it is not the function of the law to redress the balance or protect a party from what he has freely accepted. People should not agree to what is not in their interest. Although in the nineteenth century the will theory was dominant, the enforcement of contracts was also justified on other grounds, such as the moral duty to keep one's word, expressed in the natural law principle of *pacta sunt servanda,* and the notion that enforceability was based on the promisee's reliance on the promise which should not be disappointed.

In medieval English law, as in Roman law, agreements as such were not enforceable, but specific forms of agreement were given actions. For example, the writ of covenant covered formal promises made in a deed under seal. As in the Roman stipulation, it was the form in which the promise was clothed which made it binding. The writ of debt was available to a creditor who alleged that the defendant owed him money. Debt situations did not always arise from agreement, but included certain contractual duties, as where the plaintiff had delivered something to the defendant under an agreement and had not received payment for it. The principle of the writ of debt was thus similar to that of the Roman real contracts. The writ from which the modern English contract derives was *assumpsit,* in which the plaintiff alleged that since the defendant had 'undertaken' something, he (the plaintiff) had suffered loss through his reliance on that undertaking. If he had received merely a gratuitous informal promise, he could not say that he had suffered any loss through its non-performance. But if the defendant's promise was part of a bargain, each party's promise being made in return for the other's, the plaintiff's promise was said to constitute consideration for the defendant's promise and so to amount to a sufficient detriment to him to enable him to bring *assumpsit.* One of the forms of the action, *indebitatus assumpsit,* covered the same ground as the action for debt. The plaintiff alleged that the defendant, being indebted to him, (impliedly) undertook to pay but did not do so, to his loss.

Modern English law still enforces covenants under seal, which are binding by virtue of their form. It also has a general doctrine that any agreement which the parties intend to be legally binding is a contract, provided that there is consideration for the promise that is being enforced, unless for some particular reason the agreement is deprived of contractual force. Examples of such reasons are that a party lacks capacity to make a contract because, for example, he is under age or insane; or that the object of the agreement is unlawful. Certain kinds of agreement are required to be evidenced in a particular form, such as agreements for the sale of land, which to be binding must be evidenced in writing. In the nineteenth century English law, like the civil law, was influenced by philosophical ideas of the freedom of the will and the courts were very reluctant to interfere with any agreement that appeared to have been 'freely' reached by the parties. In view of the notion of a contract as a bargain, however, English courts have always looked more at how the parties have declared their will to each other than at what they may have subjectively intended.

In the twentieth century the doctrine of the autonomy of the will has been extensively modified. The role of the state has been extended to include the protection of those whose bargaining power is insufficient to enable them to make contracts providing adequate safeguards for their interests. An obvious example is the series of statutes enacted in most European countries to give tenants under a lease protection against their landlords. The agreement reached between the parties now necessarily incorporates the statutory terms of the tenant's protection, although there is still some scope for negotiation between the parties. In some areas of activity, however, such as the supply of services to consumers, the contract between the supplier and the consumer is not the result of negotiation and agreement between the parties at all, but is rather a standard form, known in France as a 'contrat d'adhésion'. The consumer must either accept it or go without the service. As a result of this trend, certain matters which were formerly regulated by the general law of contract have been made into separate areas of law such as consumer law and labour law (pp 213ff).

Although the fields within which parties may make a contract for themselves are now limited, it is still possible to think of a general doctrine of contract based on the meeting of the parties' will. Emphasis is now put on the practical problems which such a doctrine creates, such as the need to provide adequate evidence of what the parties have actually decided. In all modern systems a contract is analysed into an offer by one party and an acceptance by the other. Since no contract exists until the offer has been accepted, English law allows an offer to be revoked at any time before acceptance, unless the offeror has given a separate undertaking, supported by consideration, to keep it open. Most civil law systems do not allow an offeror to revoke his offer at will. German law expressly binds him to keep the offer open for a reasonable period of time (BGB 145), and although the French code has no express provision on the subject, the courts tend to require the same. The three 'vices of consent' recognised by Roman law, mistake, duress and fraud, invalidate an apparent agreement in all systems, since if any of them is proved, the agreement has not been freely reached. There are, however, variations in detail, particularly regarding the kinds of mistake which have this effect.

If offer and acceptance have produced an agreement, not affected by a defect of will, which is intended to be binding, modern systems vary in how far they control it further. English law requires consideration for any promise, and so will not enforce gratuitous undertakings. It also refuses to recognise certain classes of agreement as binding if their purpose is illegal or if they are against the public interest as being, for example, 'in restraint of trade'. Civil law systems will in principle enforce gratuitous undertakings, but impose restrictions on the making of gifts and promises of gifts, largely to keep property within the family. French law expressly requires as an element in every contract a 'lawful cause'. The nature and value of this element, which derives from the canonist *causa*, is the subject of much debate.[5] The Code Civil states that an obligation 'without a cause, or based on a false cause or on an illegal cause' can have no effect (art 1131) and that a cause is illegal 'when it is prohibited by the law or when it is contrary to good morals or to public order'. Although German law requires nothing more than agreement for a valid contract, a number of rules exclude certain types of agreement from enforceability. BGB 138 makes any transaction void if it is inconsistent with good morals, and the famous 'general clause' of BGB 242 makes any transaction void if it is inconsistent with 'good faith and fair dealing'.[6] These provisions give French and German courts considerable discretion to refuse validity to agreements of whose terms they disapprove.

In recent years legislation in many countries has sought to protect the weaker party to a contract against oppression by the stronger, by invalidating certain kinds of 'exclusion clauses', ie clauses in a contract which exempt one party from liability which the law would normally impose on him. The English Unfair Contract Terms Act 1977 deals *inter alia* with contracts in the area of business and invalidates altogether terms which exclude liability for negligence resulting in death or personal injury and allows such clauses in relation to damage to property only if they are reasonable. The German General Conditions of Business Act, which came into force in the same year, similarly invalidates many kinds of clauses which

---

5. Lawson *Common Lawyer* pp 157ff; J. P. Dawson *Gifts and Promises* (1980) pp 113ff.
6. Horn, Kötz, Leser, pp 135ff.

depart from a 'balanced model' required by the law, while the French law of 10 January 1978 empowers the government, on the recommendations of a *Commission des clauses abusives*, to ban or limit such clauses when they appear in contracts between 'professionals' and 'non-professionals'.

The Roman insistence on privity of contract has been abandoned by all modern systems so far as agency is concerned. English law allows one person, the principal, to authorise another, the agent, to contract on his behalf with a third party. When that contract has been made it can be enforced by and against the principal while the agent can normally neither sue nor be sued. Indeed English law even allows an agent to contract with a third party without disclosing that he is acting as agent, and the 'undisclosed principal' is a party to the contract so made. In civil law systems agency is based on a development of the Roman contract of mandate. The French code defines mandate as an 'act by which one person gives another the power to do something for the principal and in his name' (art 1984). Both French and German law allow an agent to create full contractual relations between his principal and the third party with whom he deals. The contract is made by the will of the agent so that if his will is vitiated, the contract can be avoided by the principal. The third party must know that he is dealing with an agent, although he need not know the principal's identity. The agent must have power to represent; this will normally be conferred on him by mandate. It is, however, possible for an agent to act without prior authorisation. The principal will be bound if he later ratifies the agent's act or if, under the French institution of *gestion d'affaires*, based on the Roman *negotiorum gestio*, the 'agent' intervenes in his affairs in circumstances which made such intervention necessary in the principal's interest.

English law has adhered to the principle of privity of contract so far as conferring a benefit on a third party is concerned. Sometimes the contract can be understood as creating a trust in favour of the third party, which then gives him a right of action against the party who has made himself trustee, but generally the law does not allow a third party to sue on a contract, even though it purported to be made for his benefit.[7] French and German law make it possible for the parties to a contract to confer a benefit on a person who is not himself a party to the contract. The French code lays it down as a general rule that agreements take effect only between the contracting parties (art 1165), but makes an exception to the rule in article 1121. That provides that a person may stipulate for the benefit of a

---

7. For another avoidance of privity of contract in relation to labour contracts, see below, p 217.

third party when that is the condition of a stipulation which he makes for himself or of a gift which he makes to another. The third party does not, however, acquire any right until he has declared that he wishes to take advantage of it and until then the promisor can revoke. German law also allows a person to acquire a right to claim performance of a contract to which he was not a party, but does not require notification of his acceptance, so long as the parties to the contract intended him to acquire it.

In English law a party to a contract is liable for his failure to do what he undertook to do even though that was not due to any fault on his part. He is bound by the terms of the contract. In the civil law it is not enough for a party to show that the other party has failed to carry out his contractual duty; he must also prove that he was at fault. This basic difference in principle is, however, less sharp in its application than might appear at first sight. English law will sometimes imply a term to use due care and the civil law will sometimes make it difficult for a party who has failed to do his part to exculpate himself.

In English law if events unforeseen by the parties make performance of a contract impossible, the contract is said to be 'frustrated' and the parties are excused from futher performance of it. In the civil law a party is in general only liable if he is in some way to blame for the fact that the contract has not been performed as it should have been. If performance is impossible, whether because it was impossible from the beginning or because it has become impossible, a contracting party is excused unless he was himself responsible for the impossibility. In French law, however, although impossibility excuses performance, the debtor must still pay damages for non-performance if he cannot show that his failure to perform was due to an external cause, which cannot be imputed to him. External cause is defined as *force majeure* or *cas fortuit*, ie, the act of a third party or an accident outside the contracting party's control (CC 1147–8). The burden of proof is thus on the party who has failed to perform to show that he has not been at fault. German law also starts by making fault the basis of contractual liability but has recognised a number of special situations in which a contracting party is liable, even though he has not personally been at fault. Where the situation in which the contract was made has changed and the question is whether the contract must still be performed, German law applies the general clause, BGB 242, which requires a debtor to perform according to good faith. If, in the opinion of the court, it would be unfair, having regard to the change in the situation, for the creditor to hold the debtor to his original bargain, the creditor will not be allowed to enforce his original right to performance. In such a case the German courts will modify the original contract and substitute new terms more appropriate to the new situation.

In the civil law, since the duty of a contracting party is to perform what he has undertaken, the law will, in principle, compel him to perform. Only if performance is not practicable, will damages be ordered as a second best. In English law, as in classical Roman law, the primary remedy for breach of contract is money damages. Specific performance may be ordered as an alternative, at the court's discretion, but specific performance will never be ordered where damages provide an adequate remedy.

2. Quasi-contract

Roman law and English law recognised a number of cases in which a person was held to be under a duty to pay money, but where that duty derived neither from an agreement nor from the commission of a wrong. In Roman law these were mainly cases in which for one reason or another a *condictio* was given (p 194); in English law they were forms of *indebitatus assumpsit*. Neither system provided a remedy in all cases in which a person has received money which he ought morally to restore. 'Each system provides a rather haphazard list of cases in which recovery is possible.'[8] In both systems these cases were at first treated as species of contract, even though there was no prior agreement. In Roman law they came to be treated as obligations arising quasi-contractually and in English law they were described as 'implied' or 'contructive' contracts.

As in other areas of law, the commentators of the civil law made great efforts to provide a general doctrine to cover such cases, based on the principle that no-one should be enriched to another's detriment. The French Code Civil recognises only two forms of quasi-contract, 'gestion d'affaires', based on the Roman *negotiorum gestio* (arts 1372ff) and payment of a non-existent debt, based on the Roman *condictio indebiti* (art 1376ff). However the courts have treated these as examples of an unstated general principle of unjust enrichment, which they have then applied in other situations. The German BGB 812, on the other hand, states expressly the general principle that 'a person who through another's performance or in any other manner acquires something at his expense without legal cause is bound to return it to him'. This leaves it to the courts to decide what causes justify the retention of what has been acquired.

An attempt by the great eighteenth-century judge, Lord Mansfield, to generalise the English cases on the basis of an equitable principle imposing a duty to refund was not successful.[9] However, in

---

8. W. W. Buckland and A. D. McNair *Roman Law and Common Law* (2nd edn, 1952) p 336.
9. *Moses v Macferlan* (1760) 2 Bur 1005 at 1012.

the present century, there are signs of a cautious progress in the English courts towards the acceptance and application of such a principle, independent of contract, under the rubric of 'restitution'.

3. Delict and tort

The English law of civil wrongs, or torts, providing remedies for those who have suffered damage as a result of another's wrongful conduct, resembles Roman law in recognising a series of separate situations, each with its own particular rules. The oldest and archetypal tort is trespass, which is a direct and forcible injury either to the victim's person or his land or his goods. Other torts are conversion of another's goods to one's own use (the equivalent of the Roman theft); nuisance, a wrongful activity which interferes with a person's enjoyment of his property; and defamation, the publication of a statement about a person, either in permanent form (libel) or in an oral unrecorded form (slander), which tends to lower him in the eyes of 'right-thinking members of society'. In practice these torts have been eclipsed in importance by the great master tort of negligence, the causing of damage to another's person or property through a failure to take the care required by the circumstances. The liability is defined as a breach of a duty to take care, and so the courts have to settle the circumstances in which such a duty exists and the persons to whom it is owed. In a famous case in 1932, Lord Atkin stated that the duty of care is owed to 'persons who are so closely and directly affected by my act that I ought reasonably to have them in contemplation as being so affected when I am directing my mind to the acts or omissions that are called in question'.[10] Many problems turn on the difficulty of proving that the plaintiff's loss was caused by the defendant's breach of duty.

In the civil law a general principle of liability for civil wrongs has been developed from the Roman *lex Aquilia*. Actions in delict were perceived as aimed at compensation so that the penal elements, which were prominent in Roman law, were discarded. The natural lawyers of the seventeenth century formulated the principle that anyone who, by his blameworthy act, caused damage to another was bound to compensate him. The French code deals with the whole area covered by the English law of torts in five short articles. The most important is article 1382, inspired by natural law: 'any act by which a person causes damage to another obliges the one by whose fault it was caused to make reparation for it', and article 1383 explains that one is liable for damage caused not only by one's deliberate act but also by one's negligence and imprudence. (Deliberate acts constitute delicts and negligent acts constitute

10.   *Donoghue v Stevenson* [1932] AC 562 at 580.

quasi-delicts, but nothing turns on the distinction.) Thus the elements that have to be proved are first, damage, which is interpreted very widely and covers not only physical damage and economic (purely pecuniary) loss but also 'moral damage' to the victim's feelings; secondly, culpable conduct by the defendant; and thirdly, a causal link between the defendant's conduct and the plaintiff's loss.

The German code did not repeat the full French principle of liability. BGB 823, corresponding roughly with Aquilian liability, provides that 'any person who wilfully or negligently injures the life, body, health, freedom, property or other right of another, contrary to law, is bound to compensate him for any damage arising therefrom'. The same obligation arises from an infringement of a statute intended for the protection of others. BGB 826, corresponding with the Roman *iniuria*, obliges a person who wilfully causes damage to another in a manner *contra bonos mores* to compensate him. Thus German law accepts a general liability for all damage caused wilfully, but in the case of damage caused by unintentional fault specifies the interests which are protected. This has made it difficult for German courts to allow compensation for purely economic damage caused negligently, if it is unconnected with personal injury or physical damage to property, unless they have found it possible to exploit the potentialities of the words 'or any other right'.

Where the plaintiff contributed to the loss that he suffered by his own negligence, the common law deprived him of any remedy, since he could not say that the damage was caused by the defendant's act, and this was often the result of applying the strict test of causation in the civil law too. English, French and German law have now all abandoned the all or nothing approach, and apportion the loss according to the relative culpability of the parties. The French courts interpreted article 1382 as allowing them to do so; the German BGB contains an express provision allowing apportionment (BGB 254(1)); and English law was reformed in that sense by statute in 1945.

English law had little difficulty holding employers liable for torts committed by their servants in the course of their employment, and so letting the injured party sue those who control and benefit from the enterprise to which the wrongdoer belongs. Similarly the French code provides, in CC 1384, that a person must pay for damage caused by persons for whom he is responsible. However the German code, faithful to the principle that no-one should be liable unless he has been personally at fault, gives no right against an employer unless he has himself been at fault. However the burden of proof is on the employer to show that he has taken all due care both in choosing his employees and in supervising them, and the courts have been very ready to find fault in both functions. They have also provided a remedy by finding that there is a *contractual* duty of care (*culpa in contrahendo*), even though no contract has been made between the parties, where the plaintiff is injured in a business situation, as for example, where he has entered business with a view to a possible purchase.[11]

Apart from vicarious liability, there are also other cases in which a person has suffered injury but cannot in practice prove fault, yet it is felt that he ought to receive compensation. This is particularly so where the injury is caused through an industrial accident; and social policy requires that those who have created the risk should insure anyone injured thereby. The principle of no liability without fault has therefore been modified.

In all countries the courts have done their best to give suitable remedies by requiring a high degree of care or by presuming fault in situations where the 'thing speaks for itself' (*res ipsa loquitur*), so forcing the defendant to exculpate himself if he can. English courts have recognised particular instances of strict liability, such as in the case of damage caused by the escape of something dangerous which a person has brought on his land. French courts discovered a provision in the code making a person responsible for 'things under his control'. For nearly a century this was thought to apply only to animals and buildings, which were expressly mentioned, but the potentialities of the phrase have since been fully exploited. German law, however, has had to resort to specific statutes to escape the requirement of fault.

Where a person in an industrialised society today suffers an accident, his chances of getting compensation in practice depend very much on whether he or the defendant is insured. In principle the defendant's liability to the plaintiff should not depend on whether or not he is insured but more and more litigation and decisions are affected by this consideration. Insurance is a way of distributing the individual's loss among a broad section of the community, since in a manufacturing process, for example, the cost of the premiums is added to the price of the product. It has been proposed that the whole area of personal injuries would be better removed from the law of tort and subjected to a form of state insurance, and such a scheme has been introduced in New Zealand. In Britain the (Pearson) Royal Commission on Civil Liability in 1978 recommended a no-fault insurance scheme for injuries caused by motor vehicles and strict liability in the case of certain hazardous operations, but proposed that when there was no special reasons for imposing strict liability, tort liability should continue to be based on negligence.

11.   Lawson *Common Lawyer* p 171; Horn, Kötz, Leser, p 108.

14 Variants of contract

In certain transactions of a contractual character, the relationship of the parties, or the special circumstances in which they are situated, require that the ordinary rules of contract are supplemented or even superseded by special bodies of rules. The specialisation has sometimes produced fields of law quite separate from the ordinary law of contract. We shall consider three such fields, commercial law, consumer law and labour law.

Commercial law

In most legal systems the model form of a contract is considered to be an isolated agreement between two private individuals of roughly equal bargaining power who, since they do not make contracts every day, approach the matter with proper caution and deliberation. Merchants, whose work consists in making frequent contracts, have usually looked on the contract rules laid down by the law as straight-jackets that they could readily do without. They have tended to ignore the law and adopt more informal practices of their own, and, since merchants are by nature cosmopolitan, these practices have been recognised internationally.

Progressive legal systems, which are capable of assimilating new ways of doing things and whose courts have not discriminated against foreigners, have been able to incorporate some mercantile customs into the regular law, whereas others have allowed a body of commercial law to grow up independently of the private law system. Roman law not only gave equal access to foreigners and to Roman citizens but also provided a means for settling disputes between parties of different countries. Instead of remitting the case to a single *iudex,* the praetor could send it to be heard by a body of *recuperatores,* chosen from those who were familiar with the milieu in which the dispute had arisen and able to comprehend the different arguments. In certain cases mercantile customs were actually incorporated into Roman contract law, as in the case of the Rhodian law on jettison. This was a custom, which had been adopted by the merchants who congregated on the island of Rhodes in the Eastern Mediterranean, to deal with losses caused by jettisoning things from a ship to save it from wreck. It applied the principle, known today as 'general average', viz, that the ship owner and cargo owners, whose goods have been saved by the jettisoning, should contribute proportionately to compensate those whose goods have been lost. By its very terms the rule would be applied only in a mercantile context but, since carriage of goods by sea was a form of hire, it was incorporated into the cluster of rules regulating the contract of hire.

In England mercantile practice, the law merchant, was originally quite distinct from the common law. Guilds of merchants had their own courts, or perhaps rather 'arbitration services', composed of members familiar with the practices of a particular trade. At the end of the middle ages the Court of Admiralty acquired jurisdiction over many mercantile matters on the pretext that they had a foreign or maritime element.[1] Unlike the common law courts, this court used the procedure of the civil law and had professional judges who were familiar with the collections of international maritime customs and manuals of practice that circulated among the merchant community. The common law courts made great efforts to remove jurisdiction over such cases from the Admiralty, but the merchant community found their procedure and their unwillingness to take account of the special needs of merchants distasteful.

It was not until the third quarter of the eighteenth century that a sustained effort was made to incorporate the customary rules of mercantile practice into the law of contract. It was largely the work of one man, Lord Mansfield CJ. He arranged for commercial cases to be tried by special juries, composed of merchants of the City of London, who would advise him of the accepted practices, and he isolated as matters of law points of importance which had previously been submerged in the general issue of the defendant's liability. These points he then reserved for discussion by all the judges and saw that their rulings were properly reported.

The consequences for the law of contract were dramatic. In theory the model of a contract is still that of two private individuals settling all the terms of their obligation by patient negotiation. But most of the cases which decided disputed points of contract law for a century after Lord Mansfield arose out of the technicalities of commercial practice, and had to take account of the special features of negotiable instruments, charter-parties, bills of lading and the like. It has been said, with only slight exaggeration, that 'the incorporation of the Law Merchant in the Common Law turned the whole English law of contract into commercial law'.[2] By contrast with the law of tort, which appears to be concerned with familiar everyday occurrences,

1. Baker, pp 107ff.
2. F. H. Lawson *Common Lawyer* p 90.

such as street accidents, cases in the law of contract have an unfamiliar technical aspect which makes them difficult for the student who is not at home in commerce to understand the issues.

This commercialisation of English contract law did not permanently dispel the commercial community's suspicion of the common law courts. For although the law was more attuned to their needs, the protracted procedure and requirements of evidence – especially the need for cross-examination of witnesses in public – meant that litigation in the courts has not been attractive. To avoid the need to instruct judges in commercial practices and to provide a more flexible procedure, certain judges of the Queen's Bench Division have specialised in commercial cases, and since 1970 a section of that court has been designated as the Commercial Court, but it has not overcome businessmen's preference for informal arbitration. In 1962 it was reported that a trial cost ten times as much as arbitration,[3] so that this is hardly surprising.

In civil law countries the story has been different. The law merchant became a separate system which the civil law could not assimilate. This was due first to the authority of Roman law. Although in its formative period Roman law had incorporated some mercantile customs, the law as set out in Justinian's codification was regarded as essentially a closed system.[4] Some concessions had to be made to accommodate feudal law in regard to land ownership, but the merchants as a class did not have the kind of influence wielded by the feudal landowners. The commentators of the civil law looked with disdain on the rather primitive collections of mercantile customs and considered them as alien to the civil law that they professed. Secondly, in most countries there was no single strong legal system, as in England, but a series of relatively weak localised courts unable to expand their jurisdiction on their own initiative. So the merchant community fended for itself and developed its own customary rules that were applied in relatively informal courts set up at the regular international fairs and markets or in the seaport towns in which merchants congregated.

When the French monarchy sought to counteract the centrifugal tendencies of French law, by enacting ordinances settling particular fields of law for the whole country, the most important was the *Ordinance of commerce* (1673), the result of a collaboration between Colbert and a successful business man, Jacques Savary. It was an almost complete statement of the rules for the conduct of commercial transactions and provided merchants throughout France with an authoritative law. It was supplemented by an *Ordinance of*

3. *Report of Commercial Court Users' Conference* 1962, Cmnd 1616 p 23.
4. A. Watson *The Making of the Civil Law* (1981) pp 158ff.

maritime commerce (1681), which summarised with equal clarity and precision the law of the sea. These ordinances were used not just in France but also in other countries as statements of enlightened commercial practice. Lord Mansfield, for example, cited them with approval. They also ensured that commercial law remained independent of the civil law. Napoleon's Code Civil of 1804 was supplemented by a separate commercial code, published in 1807, whose compilers relied heavily on the two ordinances. Germany in the nineteenth century resembled France in the seventeenth century in that the multiplicity of local jurisdictions was seen as a hindrance to commerce. A general commercial code, *Handelsgesetzbuch*, applicable to most German states, was enacted in 1861, 40 years before the BGB, and the separation of civil and commercial law has been maintained.

Whereas in England the designation commercial law is a convenient description for a group of rules of private law and nothing more, in France and Germany it means a distinct body of law, applicable to a particular kind of transaction, which may actually conflict with the civil law.[5] For example, the BGB requires that a guarantee should be in writing but under the commercial code (HGB 350) a guarantee is enforceable even if it is made orally. Furthermore cases of commercial law are heard by different courts from those that deal with civil cases. In both France and Germany civil cases are heard exclusively by professional judges but commercial cases come to courts which include experienced business-men who need not be lawyers. It is therefore crucial to know when civil law applies and when commercial law. French law takes as the test the nature of the transaction. If the parties have entered into a business transaction (*acte de commerce*), the commercial law applies.[6] German law prefers to look rather at the character of the parties to the transaction. If they are businessmen, then it comes under commercial law.[7] There are manifestly difficulties of definition in both systems.

There are also variations in civil law countries as to what topics are included in commercial law. In most countries problems relating to business corporations, bills of exchange, industrial property, banking and bankruptcy are matters of commercial law. In some insurance is a commercial matter, whereas in others it is not. At the same time, commercial law is not wholly self-sufficient. Its institutions presuppose the framework of civil law rules and where there is no express provision of commercial law, the civil law applies.

5. C. Szladits, IECL II.2.78.
6. B. Nicholas *French Law of Contract* (1982) p 26.
7. Horn, Kötz, Leser, pp 211ff.

It is a matter of debate whether the distinction between civil and commercial law continues to have value and should be maintained. And in some countries, such as Italy, one unified code has replaced previously separate civil and commercial codes.

Consumer law

A recent outgrowth of commercial law, which has become known as consumer law, is designed to strengthen the protection offered by the traditional private law to consumers. The problem arises because the manufacturers of products and providers of services are typically large organisations wielding considerable economic power, whereas consumers as a class are normally not organised and have to claim their rights individually. Consumer law seeks to counteract this disparity. Commercial law, although to some extent modifying the ordinary rules of private law, mainly regulates specialist forms of arrangement that exist only in business activity, such as bills of lading and negotiable instruments. Consumer law operates more by altering the effect of the ordinary law in the transactions to which it applies.

In Britain, the Fair Trading Act 1973 set up the Office of Fair Trading which reviews the supply of goods and services to consumers. A consumer is defined as a 'person, not himself acting by way of business, who receives goods or services from a person who is' (s 137(2)). The Office can recommend that the relevant minister make statutory orders regulating trade practices which are found to be unfair to the consumer. It can refer potential monopoly situations, caused by the take-over of one company by another, to the Monopoly and Mergers Commission, with a view to finding whether they operate against the public interest by unduly restricting competition. The Restrictive Trade Practices Acts regulate agreements, between persons or organisations supplying goods or services, which are against the public interest, for example, because they maintain prices at an unduly high level or restrict suppliers to the market.

Apart from this machinery of governmental control, both the private law and the criminal law have been modified in the interests of the consumer. This has been achieved partly by statutes, such as the Unfair Contract Terms Act (p 202), and partly by judicial imposition of liability.[8] By implying terms in contracts and by recognising new duties of care in tort, the judges have provided a counterbalance to the fact that the consumer, who wishes to be

8.   G. H. Samuel *Cases in Consumer Law* (1979).

supplied with goods and services, is usually not able to negotiate the terms on which he receives them, but must take them on the supplier's terms. The Consumer Credit Act 1974, supplemented by subsequent regulations, provides an elaborate scheme, too complex to be discussed here, designed to give the consumer the maximum information about the obligations that he is undertaking and a chance to change his mind and withdraw from the agreement within a short period – usually 14 days – after entering into it. In particular, attention has been focused on a particular form of contract which was originally devised to safeguard the interests of suppliers of goods on credit. Mortgages of movables had been severely curtailed by the Bills of Sale Act 1878 and the Moneylenders Acts had restricted the conditions on which credit could be given. So the lawyers invented the hire-purchase contract, under which the consumer does not acquire ownership of the goods until he has paid all the instalments of the debt, which because of interest and expenses may considerably exceed the sale price. The terms of this hybrid contract were originally heavily weighted in favour of the creditor, who is often not the supplier of the goods but a finance company. Statute has now, to a large extent, restored the balance.

In certain instances the machinery of criminal prosecution has been harnessed to protect the consumer, thus dispensing the individual from taking any action other than the provision of relevant information to the appropriate local authority to enable it to prosecute. Thus the Trade Descriptions Acts make it an offence for anyone to apply, in the course of a trade or business, a false description to any goods or supply goods to which such a description is applied. The Consumer Safety Act 1978 creates offences relating to goods that are not safe or are accompanied by inappropriate information as to their use. These statutes may be seen as generalising the long-established forms of control of Weights and Measures and of Foods and Drugs.

Labour law

We have seen that law has long taken account of the special legal requirements of businessmen and has recently accepted the need to protect consumers as a class. We turn now to contracts of workers. In antiquity most menial work was done by slaves. Craftsmen were usually not employed by those for whom they worked but were independent contractors working simultaneously for a number of customers. They were independent of the latter's control and agreed to produce a given result. Contracts of employment were rarely needed. As late as the eighteenth century Adam Smith pointed out that slavery was still the norm in the world as a whole, and that its abolition in the small corner which was Western Europe was exceptional.[9] In his day the model of employment was that of the domestic servant and the contract of employment – known as 'master and servant' – was regarded as more part of family law than of the law of contract. It was bracketed with the relations between husband and wife and parent and child as 'domestic' and so not fully subject to legal regulation. In the nineteenth century, the emphasis on the individual and the autonomy of his will resulted in the removal of the master and servant relationship from the law of personal status and its transfer to that of contract. The contract between employer and worker was thought of as the product of individual negotiation. The worker undertook to serve the employer in return for an agreed remuneration. If he accepted the conditions offered by the employer, he was bound by them. The fact that in practice the worker had no alternative but to accept those conditions was not regarded as relevant. The inequality of bargaining power was a fact of life of which the law should not take account.

The situation changed as a result of gradual pressure from organised labour and humanitarian sentiment in the public, resulting in a series of statutes in all industrialised countries aimed at restricting the power of the parties to a contract of employment to include whatever terms they (ie, normally the employer) thought fit.[10] In Britain the earliest statutes were concerned with the protection of classes of workers considered to be in special need, such as women and young persons, or with ensuring the safety of workers in industrial processes. In the next stage, the law ensured minimum wages and minimum provision for holidays and holiday pay for particular classes of workers. More recently, legislation has strengthened the framework of rules which govern all contracts of employment, by providing increased security of employment to workers and giving them special remedies against unfair dismissal. If these statutes tend to have a similar appearance in most industrial countries in Europe, it is partly due to the influence of the various conventions prepared by the International Labour Organisation, which have been accepted by many countries.

These statutes provide a minimum platform of basic rights for workers. Universally they have been supplemented by collective agreements reached by trade unions on one side and associations of employers (or occasionally one large employer) on the other. Collective bargaining is the main feature of all modern industrial relations and has advantages for both sides of industry.

9. *Lectures in jurisprudence* (ed R. L. Meek, D. D. Raphael and P. G. Stein, 1978) pp 451–452.
10. O. Kahn-Freund *Labour and the Law* (2nd edn, 1977) pp 24ff.

'By bargaining collectively with organised labour, management seeks to give effect to its legitimate expectation that the planning of production, distribution etc, should not be frustrated through interruptions of work. By bargaining collectively with management, organised labour seeks to give effect to its legitimate expectations that wages and other conditions of work should be such as to guarantee a stable and adequate form of existence and as to be compatible with the physical integrity and moral dignity of the individual, and also that jobs should be reasonably secure.[11]

There are different forms of collective bargaining and its legal implications differ from country to country. These differences are not as much the product of differing legal traditions as of the fact that 'the labour law of a country tends to be much more deeply marked by national history and social mores than its law of contract or tort'[12]. In Britain both sides of industry have been traditionally suspicious of the legal process. The attitude of the unions in particular has been affected by the history of their legal status and their legal liability, which have been altered dramatically by successive statutes, apparently according to the political whims of different governments. Neither they nor the employers are keen to be confined by 'rigid' legal institutions and take care that any agreements that are reached in their name are not intended to create legal relations and so do not create contracts binding on the parties. In other countries, such as Germany and the USA, employers and unions quite readily accept that any agreement that they reach is a binding contract, imposing enforceable obligations on the parties, who may go to court and obtain damages or an injunction if it is broken.

The differences may also be partly due to differences in the organisation of industrial relations and in the nature of the legal process. In Britain unions represent workers in a particular trade or craft, so that in any one industry the workers are represented by several different unions. In Germany unions represent all the workers in a particular industry, so that the question which union represents a worker's interests depends not on what kind of work he does but on which industry his employer is engaged in, and one union can negotiate for all the workers in that industry. In Britain the legal process, even before a specialised tribunal, is perceived as a public contest, a trial of strength which might well exacerbate a strained situation. Elsewhere legal proceedings are often a protracted series of meetings which put less emphasis on 'winning and losing'.

11. O. Kahn-Freund, op cit, p 51.
12. Horn, Kötz, Leser, p 310.

The relations between the individual worker and his employer are governed by his employment contract, which defines the wages to be paid, holiday entitlement, sick pay, pension arrangements and hours of work. Apart from these matters, of which the employer in Britain is obliged to give the worker a summary in writing, the ordinary effects of the employment contract are dominated by the combined impact of the regulating statutes and collective agreements. There has been much debate on how far collective agreements entered into by an association confer rights on individual members of the association. The worker is not a party to the agreement. Does the union negotiate as his agent or is it rather a principal and therefore itself responsible as a body? Can individual workers or employers be regarded as third party beneficiaries where the law of contract allows that? Can a collective agreement properly provide for a 'closed shop', by which the employers agree not to employ anyone who is not a member of the relevant union? Such undertakings have been common in Britain, but in Germany the provision in the constitution of the Federal Republic (Basic Law, art 9), guaranteeing to workers the right to form associations, has been interpreted as giving an individual worker the right not to join one; so that a closed shop agreement would be unconstitutional.

These matters are of theoretical importance compared with the 'normative' effect of collective agreements in creating a set of agreed practices. Whether or not the agreement is itself a binding contract, these practices are by implication incorporated into each worker's contract of employment. Even though the individual worker is not a party to the collective agreement, it lays down a code of practice which applies to every contract of employment between those affected by the agreement.

Since the maintenance of industrial peace is dependent on the reaching of and adherence to collective agreements, most countries offer a range of institutions for mediation and arbitration in labour disputes that bear a close similarity to the institutions noticed in regard to stateless societies. The state can establish a service of conciliators and arbitrators, which is always available to advise, mediate and assist the two sides in finding common ground, but has no powers of compulsion, such as the British Advisory Conciliation and Arbitration Service (ACAS); or it can require those involved in a dispute to submit it to arbitration and collective agreements often provide for arbitration in the event of dispute. The law can provide a more congenial environment for the reaching of agreement by compelling the production of relevant information to both sides. German law requires the establishment of Works Councils at plant level which have statutory rights to be involved in management decisions. The extent to which such legal machinery can assist in reducing industrial friction depends very much on the prevailing climate of industrial relations and traditional attitudes die hard.

Most countries now provide specialised labour courts composed, at least in part, of members who are not lawyers but have relevant industrial experience. The latter are usually nominees in equal numbers of employers' federations and of trade unions. Usually, as in Britain and Germany, there is a legally qualified chairman. In many countries such courts have taken over all labour matters from the jurisdiction of the regular courts. Where collective agreements are binding, they are enforced against employees' associations or trade unions not by the ordinary courts but by the labour courts. Britain has, as usual, adopted a more piecemeal approach, and lets some claims go to the regular courts and others to the industrial tribunals. Thus when an individual worker, as opposed to workers as a group, has a claim against his employer arising out of his employment, the type of claim determines which court deals with the case.

Until relatively recently, a worker who was dismissed could do very little about it. Most contracts of employment contained provisions for giving the worker notice to terminate the employment without giving reason. In Britain, until 1965, a worker who was dismissed without proper notice could sue the employer, but the damages that he received would normally be limited to what he would have received if he had been given valid notice. Such an action for 'wrongful dismissal' in breach of the employment contract, may still be brought in the regular courts, and is worth bringing when highly paid employees are dismissed with substantial periods of their contracted service still to run. So also a claim in tort for personal injuries suffered at the place of work would be brought before the ordinary courts.

Now, however, workers are given much greater security of employment. In Britain a worker is entitled to compensation if he is made redundant because of contraction in the industry, the amount being based on his age, pay and length of service, or if he is 'unfairly dismissed'. Such claims are dealt with not by the regular courts but by industrial tribunals. If an employee has shown that he has been dismissed, the employer has to give a reason which is fair, such as that the employee is not capable of doing the work or has committed misconduct. Before the case is brought to a tribunal, ACAS is automatically notified with a view to reaching a settlement without a hearing, but if a hearing is necessary, it is more informal than in a regular court. In applying the standard of fairness the tribunal must be satisfied that the reason offered by the employer was sufficiently serious to justify dismissal and, in deciding that, the tribunal will be concerned to see that he has followed the terms of any relevant collective agreement. If in all the circumstances he has not acted reasonably, the tribunal must hold the dismissal to be unfair. The worker can then either ask for reinstatement in his old job, or for a new job with his old employer, or for financial compensation. The employer may refuse to take him back but in that case the damages that he must pay will be higher. The damages are composed of two elements: the basic award calculated, like redundancy payments, on age and length of service, and compensation for losses incurred by the dismissal. There is an appeal on points of law to an Employment Appeal Tribunal, consisting of a high court judge and two laymen.

German law protects workers' employment to a similar extent but in a somewhat different manner.[13] As in Britain, an employer may dismiss a worker, even without notice, if he has an 'important reason', normally based on the worker's misconduct. An employer who does not claim to have such a justification for dismissal and gives the worker notice must consult the local Works Council, to try to get their agreement. Although such agreement is not legally necessary, an employer would not normally want to risk a conflict with his council. Even if he gets their agreement, he may still be required to show to the satisfaction of the labour court that the dismissal was not 'socially unjustified'. This means that he must prove reasons either based on the person or conduct of the worker or on 'imperative business necessity'. The latter corresponds roughly to grounds for redundancy in Britain, and provision for it is usually covered by collective agreements.

13. Horn, Kötz, Leser, pp 322ff.

Epilogue

Legal institutions in simple societies arise out of society's need to settle disputes that might disturb the peace of the community. In complex modern societies they still fulfil that function, and the range of disputes that are settled by legal rather than by other methods is continually being extended. Recourse to law is much commoner in some countries than in others. It has been suggested, for example, that the United States is fast becoming a 'litigation society', in that the courts are being asked to resolve many social questions that are hardly susceptible of a judicial remedy.[1] In 1977 a group of irate fans of the Washington Redskins football team started an action in the US federal court to overturn a referee's call that had given a game to the St Louis Cardinals, and since then legal actions have been used to try to control sporting contests.

The prevalence of litigation is related to its cost and to the procedural arrangements for dealing with such cost. It is obvious that in any system the availability of legal aid for litigants must affect the number of actions that are brought to court. But the incidence of litigation may also be affected by less obvious procedural considerations. In most countries, including England and the other countries of Western Europe, the loser of a legal action is normally ordered by the court to pay the winner's legal costs, but in the United States such an order is not normally made. Further, in most countries a lawyer may not agree to represent a litigant on terms that he will not be paid if he loses the case, and will receive an agreed share of the damages if he wins. In the United States such a 'contingent fee' arrangement is allowed and is common in certain types of litigation. These factors mitigate the financial risks of litigation, and in a doubtful case the continued availability of civil jury trial in the United States encourages litigants to believe that if they engage an eloquent advocate, he may persuade the jury to overlook the weaknesses of his case in law.

Today the functions of law in society have moved beyond dispute settling. Many legal institutions have a preventive role, to facilitate the achieving of certain aims in such a way that disputes will not arise. For example, the law provides a framework of rules

1.   A. E. Dick Howard 'A litigation society?' (1981) The Wilson Quarterly 98.

within which a company or partnership can readily be formed or property transferred or a will made and much of a lawyer's work is 'non-contentious' in that he gives effect to his client's intentions through such institutions and ensures that he stays within them. But more than with the relations between the individuals within the group, the law is now concerned with relations between the individual and the group itself. It imposes duties on the citizen, such as to register births and deaths, to send children to school, to make returns of income, and it regulates certain kinds of activity, for example, to ensure that industrial production is carried on safely and does not cause environmental pollution, or to maintain fair competition in the market. In such areas of activity, although the law provides sanctions for non-compliance with the regulations, there is often more reliance on persuasion and negotiation between officials and those involved than on formal legal actions to achieve compliance. The sanctions are a last resort if the aims cannot be achieved in other ways.

Such duties imposed by the state on its citizens are all designed to achieve certain shared social aims. They may form the basis for the distribution of social benefits as well as burdens. Thus, as Professor Milsom has pointed out, today there are two intersecting systems in the law. 'There are the horizontal relationships between citizens, in which private rights are conceived of as having some absolute existence. And there is the vertical system of social regulation and dependant benefits, in which the citizen can have only claims or expectations as against authority rather than abstract rights', and probably 'the vertical system is superseding the horizontal'.[2]

The more legal institutions are seen as instruments by which society achieves certain goals, the more the traditional institutions of substantive law will be changed, and, as the examples of consumer law and labour law show, new categories will be created out of old. The traditional institutions of private law were developed when the law was primarily concerned with horizontal relationships. Now they are in the process of being adapted to accommodate the social aims of society as a whole as well as the interests of individuals and it is difficult to foresee how they will look when the process has proceeded further.[3] They will not disappear but their configuration will be modified. An understanding of how they have developed in the past and of their parallels in other systems than our own may help us to redraw their outlines with proper regard to their character and to their relation to other institutions.

2. 'The nature of Blackstone's achievement' (1981) 1 Oxford Journal of Legal Studies 3.
3. N. E. Simmonds 'The changing face of private law: doctrinal categories and the regulatory state' (1982) 2 Legal Studies 257.

Index

Accusatorial procedure. *See* ADVERSA-
RIAL PROCEDURE
Acquisitive prescription
civil law systems, in, 157, 158
English law, not recognised under (for
land), 168
Roman law, under (*usucapio*), 148,
149, 157
Administration of Estates Act 1925 . . .
182
Administrative law
constitutional law and, distinguished,
111
England, in—
common law, under, 116–119
judicial review, 118, 119, 120, 121
field covered by, 115
France, in, 114, 115
Nazi Germany, in, 114, 115
United States, in, 116, 117
Adoption
France, in, 143
Germany, in, 143
Roman law, under, 133, 134
Adultery
stateless societies, in, 7
Adversarial procedure
features of, 36–38, 68
**Advisory Conciliation and Arbitration
Service (ACAS)**
role of, 217, 218
Agricultural Holdings Act 1948 . . . 52
Albanian community
Yugoslavia, in, survival of the blood-
feud, 22, 23
Appeal
courts—
England, in, 48, 86
role of, 43
felony, of, 60
magistrates' courts, from, 65
matrimonial cases, discouraged in,
49
Roman law, under, 43, 55
tribunals, from, 50

Arbitration
advantages of, 53
Advisory Conciliation and Arbitration
Service (ACAS), 217, 218
alternative to process of law, as an, 51–
53
ancient Athens, in, 17, 18
award, 52
English law, under, 52, 217, 218
French law, under, 52
labour iaw, in, 217, 218
place for, in law, 15, 16
Roman law, under, 51, 52
stateless societies, in, 5–7
Arbitration Act 1950 . . . 52
Arbitration Act 1979 . . . 52
Aristotle
democratic doctrine, views on, 17
Arson
Roman law, under, 194
Athens, ancient. *See* GREECE, ANCIENT
Australia
aborigines, dispute settlement among,
11
constitution of, 110, 111

Bail
magistrates' powers as to, 64, 65
Battle. *See also* CONTESTS
formal, under early English law, 31,
60
Beaumanoir, Phillipe de
writings of, 78, 81, 86
Bentham, Jeremy
writings, of, 90, 91
Bills of Sale Act 1878 . . . 214
Blackstone, William
writings of, 86, 90, 125
Blood-feud
early English law, not tolerated under,
30, 60
stateless societies, in, 10–12
survival of, 18–23
Bracton, Henry de
treatise of, 81, 125

223

Britain. *See* ENGLISH LAW; SCOTTISH
LAW
Bubble Act 1720 . . . 137

Canada
constitution of, 110, 111
Canon law
contract, law of, origins in, 199
development of, 34
influence of, on law of persons, 135,
136
marriage, as to, 135, 140, 141
Case law
continental Europe, in, history of, 93–
96
England, in, 85–89, 93. *See also*
COMMON LAW, ENGLISH
Chancery, Court of
equity, principles of, in, 169
judges' powers, 48
role of, 32, 46, 47, 83
Children. *See* MINORS
China, imperial
criminal jurisdiction under, 56, 57
Church courts. *See* CANON LAW
Civil action. *See also* CIVIL LAW SYSTEMS
claims in criminal procedure, 66–68.
See also DAMAGES
criminal prosecution and, distinction
between, 54
Civil Evidence Act 1968 . . . 47
Civil law systems. *See also* FRENCH LAW;
GERMAN LAW
acquisitive prescription in, 157, 158
civil wrongs, as to, 206, 207, 208
codification, 97–103, 109
commercial law in, 211, 212, 213
contract, law of, 198–205
delictal obligations in, 205, 206, 207,
208. *See also* DELICTAL OBLIGA-
TIONS
history of, 77–80, 93–96
immovable things, law of property as
to, 164, 165
ownership under, 157, 158
right of retention, 163
Roman. *See* ROMAN LAW
succession in, 178–181
Civil wrongs
liability for—
civil law, in, 206, 207, 208
England, in. *See* TORT, ENGLISH
LAW OF
France, in, 206, 207, 208
Germany, in, 207, 208

Classical model of the legal process.
See PROCEDURAL MODELS
Coke, Sir Edward
writings and views of, 87, 90
Colbert
Ordinances of, 96, 98, 211
Commentators
work of, 78, 79, 93, 94
Commercial law
civil law countries, in, 211, 212, 213
commercial company as a legal person,
136–138
consumer law and, compared, 213.
See also CONSUMER LAW
English law, 210, 211
France, in, 211, 212
Germany, in, 212
Italy, in, 213
law merchant, position of, 210, 211
Roman law—
commercial contracts under, 185,
186
influence of, on, 209, 210, 211
topics included in, 212, 213
Common law, English
administrative law under, 116–119
development of, 85–89, 93
husband and wife, as to property of,
142
land law, 165–168
middle ages, in, 80–84, 85
plea rolls, 82
public and private law under, 116–
119, 122
trust, 162
Common Pleas, Court of
medieval England, in, 32, 81
Compensation. *See also* DAMAGES
acceptance of, history of, 19–23, 54
civil claims in criminal procedure, 66–
68
dismissal, for, 218, 219
orders, 67, 68
Roman law, under, 26, 27
Constitutional law
administrative law and, distinguished,
111
prominence of, 109, 110
protection of the individual, 111–114
written, 110–112
Consumer Credit Act 1974 . . . 214
Consumer law. *See also* COMMERCIAL
LAW
Britain, in, 213, 214
commercial law and, compared, 213

Consumer Safety Act 1978 . . . 214
Contests. *See also* BATTLE
stateless societies, in, 9, 10
Continental Europe. *See* EUROPE, CON-
TINENTAL
Contract, law of. *See also* COMMERCIAL
LAW; CONSUMER LAW; LABOUR LAW
agency, as to, 203, 204
breach of, damages for—
modern law as to, 205
Roman law, under, 195
civil law systems, in, 199–205
employment, as to. *See* LABOUR LAW
English law, under. *See* ENGLISH LAW
French law, under, 199, 200, 201, 202
German law, under, 201, 202
history of modern law of, 198–200
privity of contract—
abandoned as to agency, 203
English law, under, 203, 204
Roman law, under, 192, 193
quasi-contract—
modern law, under, 205, 206
Roman law, under, 193, 194
Roman law, under. *See* ROMAN LAW
validity of contract—
modern law, under, 202, 203
Roman law, under, 193
variants of, 209–219
Conveyances
Roman law, under, 147
English land law, in, 171–172
Courts
appeal, 43, 48, 86
Church courts, influence of, 135, 136
English—
appeal, 48, 86
Assizes, 62
Chancery. *See* CHANCERY, COURT OF
Church courts, influence of, 135,
136
Common Pleas, 32, 81
Crown, 63
development of, 31–34, 60
Exchequer, 32
High Court, 86
House of Lords, 86, 87, 89
Inns of Court, 82, 83
King's. *See* royal, *below*
King's Bench, history of, 32
local, 24, 32, 80
magistrates'. *See* MAGISTRATES
medieval times, in, 30–34, 36, 46,
60, 80–84, 135, 136, 168
Quarter Sessions, 62

Courts—*cont.*
English—*cont.*
royal, in medieval times, 31–33, 36,
46, 80, 81, 168
See also TRIALS, ENGLISH
French—
Chamber of Inquests, 35
Conseil d'Etat, 114, 115
history of, 24, 34, 35
local courts, 24
Parlement de Paris, 34, 35, 36, 79
Tribunal des Conflits, 115
German—
Grosse Strafkammer, 59
Reichskammergericht, 79
Schöffen, 24, 57, 58, 76, 79, 80
popular, of ancient Athens, 17, 18, 24
regular, introduction of—
blood-feud, influence of, on, 18–23
classical model, 14–16. *See also*
under PROCEDURAL MODELS
conclusions, 23, 24
generally, 13, 14
kinship, influence of, on, 18–23
popular feeling and, 16–18
Session, Court of, in Scotland, 83
Criminal Justice Act 1967 . . . 62, 63
Criminal Justice Act 1982 . . . 68
Criminal procedure. *See also* CRIMINAL
PROSECUTION
civil claims in, 66–68
continental Europe, in, 57–59
England, in—
generally, 60–63
summary trial today, 63–66
trial by jury today, 63
France, in, 58, 59
Germany, in, 59
Scotland, in, 59, 60
Criminal prosecution. *See also*
CRIMINAL PROCEDURE
civil action and, distinction between,
54
imperial China, in, 56, 57
Roman law, under, 55, 56
Crown Court
trial in, 63
Crown Proceedings Act 1947 . . . 116

Damages. *See also* COMPENSATION
award of, in England—
judges, by, 47, 48
jury, by, 44, 46
breach of contract, for—
modern law as to, 205

Damages—*cont.*
breach of contract, for—*cont.*
Roman law, under, 195
civil claims in criminal procedure, 66–
68
Roman law, under, 44–46, 55, 197,
198
Death penalty
felonies, for, 61, 62
Debt
early English law, under, 31
early Irish law, under, 18
Roman law, under, 28, 41, 154, 155,
191
security for—
modern law, under, 162, 163
Roman law, under, 154, 155
Delictal obligations. *See also* TORT,
ENGLISH LAW OF
civil law, development of, under, 205,
206
contributory   negligence,   where,
207
employers, liability of, 207, 208
English   law,   under.   *See*   TORT,
ENGLISH LAW OF
French law, under, 206, 207, 208
German law, under, 207, 208
industrial accidents, for, 208
Roman law, under, 194–198
Deposit of Poisonous Wastes Act 1972
. . . 66
Discretion
judge's powers of, 48, 49, 58, 62
tribunal's powers of, 50
Dispute settlement
stateless societies, in, 3–12. *See also*
STATELESS SOCIETIES
Divorce. *See* FAMILY LAW
Divorce Reform Act 1969 . . . 142

Employment.   *See*   LABOUR   LAW;
WORKERS
English law
administrative law, 116–122. *See also*
ADMINISTRATIVE LAW
arbitration under, 52, 217, 218
benefit of clergy, history of, 61
bill of indictment, 61, 62
case law, 85–89
commercial law—
cases of, 210, 211
commercial companies, recognition
of, 137
history of, 210, 211

English law—*cont.*
common   law.   *See*   COMMON   LAW,
ENGLISH
constitutional law—
complaints to European Commission of Human Rights, 112,
113
European Economic Community,
effect of, on, 113, 114
no single document of, 111, 112
consumer law, 213, 214
contract, of—
agreements deprived of contractual
force, 200, 201
breach, damages for, 205
covenants under seal, 200
frustration, 204
meaning of contract, 200, 201
privity of contract, 203, 204
quasi-contract, 205, 206
courts. *See* COURTS
criminal procedure, 60–66. *See also*
CRIMINAL PROCEDURE
damages, award of—
judge, by, 47, 48
jury, by, 44, 46
divorce, as to—
canon law, 140
today, 142, 143
See also FAMILY LAW
felony, history of, 60–62
industrial relations, as to. *See* LABOUR
LAW; WORKERS
judges. *See* JUDGES
jury. *See* JURY
labour law—
arbitration, 217, 218
collective bargaining, 216
contracts of employment, 218
dismissal of workers, 218, 219
history of, 214, 215
trade unions, 216, 217
See also LABOUR LAW
land law. *See* LAND LAW
lay model in, 30–34
lien, 163
marriage, as to, 140, 141, 142. *See also*
FAMILY LAW
medieval—
contract, law of, in, 200
De legibus et consuetudinibus Angliae,
81
felony, 60, 61
formal battles, 31
land law, 165–168

English law—*cont.*
  medieval—*cont.*
    local courts in, 24, 32, 80
    Norman influence, 30, 31, 80, 81
    ordeals, 30, 31
    persons, law of, in, 135, 136
    plea rolls, 82
    wager of law, 31
    written law and unwritten law, 80–84
    year books, 82, 85
  origins of, 30
  partnerships under, 136, 137
  persons, of, 135–143. *See also* PERSONS, LAW OF
  property, as to—
    generally, 157, 158
    land. *See* LAND LAW
    movable things, 159, 160, 161, 162, 163
    See also PROPERTY, LAW OF
  Reports, establishment of, 86
  statute law, growth of, 89–93
  succession under—
    capital transfer tax provisions, 183
    generally, 178
    history of, 181, 182
    intestate, 182
    surviving spouse, rights of, 182
    testamentary, 182, 183
    wills, provisions as to, 169, 182, 183
    See also SUCCESSION
  torts, of, 206, 207, 208. *See also* TORT, ENGLISH LAW OF
  trade unions. *See* labour law, *above*
  trials. *See* TRIALS, ENGLISH
  trust, 162, 169
Equity
  property, as to—
    English land law, in relation to, 168–170
    Roman law, under, 155–157
Eskimo
  dispute settlement among, 10, 11
Europe, continental. *See also under individual countries*
  case law in, history of, 93–96
  civil law in. *See* CIVIL LAW SYSTEMS
  codification—
    background to, 93–96
    civil law, of, 97–103
  criminal procedure in, history of, 57–59
  legal persons, laws as to, 136, 138

Europe, continental—*cont.*
  medieval—
    Commentators, 78, 79, 93, 94
    common law in, 77
    criminal procedure in, 57, 58
    Glossators of Bologna, 75, 77, 78, 81
    land law in, 164
    public law in, 108, 109
    Reception, 77, 79, 80
    written law and unwritten law in, 75–80
  natural persons, law as to, 138, 139
European Commission of Human Rights
  complaints to, by British citizens, 112, 113
European Communities Act 1972 . . . 113
European Convention on Human Rights 1953 . . . 112, 113
European Economic Community
  law of member states, effect on, 113, 114
Evidence
  admissibility of, in England, 47
  adversarial procedure, in, 37, 68
  circumstantial, 57, 58
  civil claims, in, 68
  continental criminal prosecutions, in, 58
  hearsay, 37
  indicia, 58
  inquisitorial procedure, in, 37, 38, 68
  jury and, 62
  law and fact, distinction between, 39–44
  Scottish law, in, 60
Exchequer, Court of
  history of, 32
Extortion
  Roman law, under, 56

Fact
  law and, distinction between, 39–44
Fair Trading Act 1973 . . . 213
Family. *See also* FAMILY LAW; KINSHIP GROUP
  Roman law, under, 26, 27, 132–135, 173–177
  succession. *See* SUCCESSION
Family law
  adoption. *See* ADOPTION
  adultery in stateless societies, 7

228 *Index*

Family law—*cont.*
divorce—
 canon law, under, 140
 Divorce Reform Act 1969 . . . 142
 England, in, 140, 142, 143
 France, in, 142, 143
 Germany, in, 142, 143
 Roman law, under, 133, 140, 143
guardians—
 modern law as to, 143
 Roman law, under, 134, 135
marriage—
 bride price, in stateless societies, 5
 dowry, under Roman law, 156
 England, in, 140, 141, 142
 France, in, 141
 Germany, in, 141
 husband and wife, property rela-
  tions of, 141, 142
 Roman law, under, 132, 133, 140
 matrimonial cases, judge's discretion
  in, 48, 49
 Matrimonial Causes Act 1973 . . .
  49*n*, 142
 surviving spouse, rights of, *See* SUC-
  CESSION
Federal Tort Claims Act 1946 . . . 116
Felony
 appeal of, 60
 benefit of clergy, 61
 English law, under, 60–62
Feud. *See* BLOOD-FEUD
Finance Act 1978 . . . 183
Frankish kingdom
 Salic law, 20, 76
 survival of blood-feud in, 21
French law. *See also* CIVIL LAW SYSTEMS;
  EUROPE, CONTINENTAL
 administrative law, 114, 115
 adoption under, 143
 arbitration under, 52
 civil claims in criminal procedure, 67
 civil wrongs, liability for, under, 206,
  207, 208
 codification of civil law, 98–103
 Colbert, Ordinances of, 96, 98, 211
 commercial law, 211, 212
 Conseil d'Etat, 114, 115
 constitution, 111, 112
 contract, law of, 199, 200, 201, 202
 criminal procedure, 58, 59
 delictal obligations under, 206, 207,
  208
 divorce, as to, 142, 143. *See also*
  FAMILY LAW

French law—*cont.*
 judges, application of civil code by,
  101–103
 jury under, 58, 59
 land law, 164, 165
 local courts, 24
 marriage, as to, 141. *See also* FAMILY
  LAW
 medieval—
 courts, development of, 34, 35
 criminal procedure in, 58
 Parlement de Paris, 34, 35, 36, 79
 Reception of Roman law, 79, 80
 written law and unwritten law, 78,
  79
 ownership under—
 definition of, 157
 transfer of movables, 159, 160
 See also PROPERTY, LAW OF
 persons, of, 139. *See also* PERSONS,
  LAW OF
 private law, derivation of, 125. *See also*
  CIVIL LAW SYSTEMS; PRIVATE LAW
 property, as to. *See* PROPERTY, LAW OF
 public law under, 109. *See also* PUBLIC
  LAW
 quasi-contracts, 205
 security for debt under, 163
 succession under—
 fideicommissary substitutions, 180,
  181
 generally, 177, 178
 intestate, 178
 surviving spouse, rights of, 178, 179
 testamentary restrictions, 179
 wills, provisions as to, 179–181
 Tribunal des Conflits, 115

Gaius
 Institutes of, 127, 128
German law. *See also* GERMANIC PEOPLES
 administrative law in Nazi Germany,
  114, 115
 adoption under, 143
 Bürgerliches Gesetzuch (BGB),
  development of, 100–103
 civil wrongs, liability for, 207, 208
 codification of civil law, 100–103
 commercial law, 212
 constitution, 110
 contract, law of, 201, 202
 criminal procedure, 59
 delictal obligations under, 207, 208
 divorce, as to, 142, 143. *See also*
  FAMILY LAW

German law—*cont.*
judges, application of civil code by, 101–103
labour law, 216, 217, 218, 219. *See also* LABOUR LAW
land law, 165
marriage, as to, 141. *See also* FAMILY LAW
medieval—
criminal procedure, 57, 58
Reception of Roman law, 79, 80
written law and unwritten law, 79, 80
ownership under—
definition of, 157
transfer of movables, 158, 159, 160
See also PROPERTY, LAW OF
persons law of, 138, 139. *See also* PERSONS, LAW OF
private law, derivation of, 125. *See also* CIVIL LAW SYSTEMS; PRIVATE LAW
property, as to. *See* PROPERTY, LAW OF
quasi-contracts under, 205
Schöffen, 24, 57, 58, 76, 79, 80
security for debt under, 162, 163
succession under—
generally, 177, 178
intestate, 178
legitim, rights as to, 179, 180
substitutions, 180, 181
surviving spouse, rights of, 178, 179
wills, provisions as to, 179–181
trade unions, 216. *See also* LABOUR LAW
Germanic peoples. *See also* GERMAN LAW
ancient—
advent of professionalism, 24
blood-feud, survival of, 19–21
kinship groups, role of, 19–21
Roman law of the Visigoths, 73, 78
medieval, written law and unwritten law of, 75, 76, 77
Prussian law, codification of, 97, 98, 100
Glanvill, Ranulf de
treatise of, 81
Glossators of Bologna
Justinian's *Corpus Iuris Civilis*, on, 75, 77, 78, 81
Greece, ancient
arbitration in, 17, 18
democratic doctrine in, 17, 18
influence on Rome, 125, 126
popular courts in Athens, 17, 18, 24

Guardians
modern law as to, 143
Roman law, under, 134, 135
High Court
role of, 86
Hire, contract of
Roman law, under, 186, 188, 189
House of Lords
role of, as a court of law, 86, 87, 89
Husband. *See* FAMILY LAW
Indictment
bill of—
meaning of, 61
proceedings under, 61, 62
trial on, in Crown Court, 62, 63
Inheritance (Provision for Family and Dependants) Act 1975 . . . 182
Inns of Court
establishment of, 82, 83
Inquisitorial procedure
continental Europe, in, for criminal prosecutions, 57, 58
evidence for civil claims in, 68
features of, 36–38
Ireland
judgment debt, enforcement in early middle ages, 18
land rights on Tory Island, 16
Italy
commercial law in, 213
medieval, written law and unwritten law in, 75, 77, 78
Jewish law
Maimonides's account of, 15
Judges
adversarial procedure, in, 37
civil codes, application of, by, 101–103
discretionary powers of, 48, 49, 58, 62
English courts, of—
case law, in relation to, 85–89
Crown Court, 63
medieval, 32, 33, 34, 36, 80, 81, 82
statute law, in relation to, 90–93
trial by judge alone, 47–49
French courts, of—
application of civil code, 101–103
criminal cases, role as to, 58, 59
medieval France, in, 36
German courts, of—
application of civil code, 101, 102
criminal cases, role as to, 58, 59

Judges—*cont.*
  inquisitorial procedure, role in, 37, 38
  Scottish law, under, 59, 60
Judicature Acts 1973–75 . . . 86
Jury
  English law, under—
    damages awarded by, 44, 46
    grand jury, 61, 62
    history of, 39, 41, 42, 43, 46
    petty jury, 62
    trial by, 61–63
  French criminal cases, in, 58, 59
  role of, generally, 39
  Scotland, in, 59, 60
Justices of the Peace. *See also*
    MAGISTRATES
  history of, 61
Justinian's law. *See under* ROMAN LAW

King's Bench
  history of, 32
King's courts. *See* ROYAL COURTS
Kinship group. *See also* FAMILY; FAMILY
    LAW
  blood vengeance by, in stateless
    societies, 10, 11
  early Roman law, under, 26, 27
  meaning of, in stateless societies, 4
  survival of blood-feud and, 18–23
  transfer of function to state from, 54–
    68

Labour law. *See also* WORKERS
  arbitration, role of, in, 217, 218
  collective agreements, 215, 216, 217,
    218, 219
  collective bargaining, 215, 216
  contracts of employment—
    features of, today, 217, 218
    historically, 214, 215
  dismissal of workers, 218, 219
  England, in. *See* ENGLISH LAW
  Germany, in, 216, 217, 218, 219
  history of, 214, 215
  trade unions—
    Britain, in, 216, 217
    Germany, in, 216
    USA, in, 216
  tribunals, role of, 218, 219
  workers, as to protection of, 215
Land law
  English—
    common law, under, 165–168
    conveyance—
      history of, 167

Land law—*cont.*
  English—*cont.*
    conveyance—*cont.*
      registered land, of, 171, 172
      unregistered land, of, 171, 172
    easements, 171, 172
    equitable principles, under—
      history of, 168, 169
      since 1925 . . . 169, 170
    fee simple, 166, 170
    generally, 165
    mortgages, 171, 172
    profits à prendre, 171
    real actions for land, history of, 167,
      168
    restrictive covenants, 171, 172
    rights in another's land, 171, 172
  France, in, 164, 165
  Germany, in, 165
  medieval Europe, in, 164
  Roman law. *See under* ROMAN LAW
Lands Tribunal Act 1949 . . . 52
Law. *See also* ROMAN LAW *and under
    individual countries*
  dispute-settlement, institutions for, 3
    et seq.
  fact, and, distinction between, 39–44
  finding, institutions of, 3 et seq.
  role of today, 220, 221
  written law and unwritten law. *See*
    WRITTEN LAW AND UNWRITTEN
    LAW
Laymen. *See also* JURY; JUSTICES OF THE
    PEACE; MAGISTRATES
  arbitrators, as, 51–53
  French criminal procedure, in, 58
  German law, in—
    criminal procedure, 59
    Schöffen, role of, in medieval
      Germany, 24, 57, 58, 76, 79,
      80
  lay model of procedure. *See* PROCEDU-
    RAL MODELS
  professional lawyers and, procedures
    involving both—
    generally, 39
    law and fact, distinction between,
      39–44
    remedies, 44–47
    tribunals, 49, 50
Lease
  Roman law, under, 146, 148, 152, 153
Legal process
  classical model of, 14–16. *See also
    under* PROCEDURAL MODELS

Liberia
  Loma, ordeals among, 9
Limitation Act 1975 . . . 49
Loans
  Roman law as to, 191, 192

Magistrates. *See also* JUSTICES OF THE
    PEACE
  court—
    appeal from, 65
    bail, powers as to, 64, 65
    clerk to, role of, 64
    compensation orders made by, 67,
      68
    role of, 63–66
  lay—
    praetor, under Roman law. *See
      under* ROMAN LAW
    role of, 64–66
    numbers of, 64
    sentencing by, 65, 66, 67, 68
    stipendiary, in England and Wales,
      role of, 64
Magistrates Courts Act 1980 . . . 68
Mandate
  Roman law, under, 186, 189, 190
Marriage. *See* FAMILY LAW
Matrimonial cases. *See* FAMILY LAW
Matrimonial Causes Act 1973 . . . 49*n*,
    142
Mediation. *See* ARBITRATION
Minors. *See also* FAMILY LAW
  adoption of—
    modern law as to, 143
    Roman law, under, 133, 134
  guardians of—
    modern law as to, 143
    Roman law, under, 134, 135
  parents of—
    care by, 143
    power of, under Roman law, 26, 27,
      132, 133
Mischief rule
  application of, 92
Models of procedure. *See* PROCEDURAL
    MODELS
Moneylenders Acts . . . 214
Mucius Scaevola
  treatise of, 126, 127
Murder
  Albanians in Kosovo, committed by,
    23
  early societies, in, 11, 20, 21, 22
  felony, a, 61
  Roman law, under, 55, 194

Murder—*cont.*
  stateless societies, in, 10, 11

New Guinea
  shaming in, 8
New Zealand
  constitution of, 111
  family protection in, 182
**New Zealand Family Protection Act
    1908** . . . 182

Obligations. *See also* CONTRACT, LAW OF
  contractual—
    modern law, under, 198–205
    Roman law, under, 184–193
    See also CONTRACT, LAW OF
  delictal. *See* DELICTAL OBLIGATIONS
  generally, 184, 198
  quasi-contractual—
    modern law, under, 205, 206
    Roman law, under, 193, 194
  tort, 206–208. *See also* TORT, ENGLISH
    LAW OF
Ordeals
  ancient Germanic law, under, 19
  early English law, under, 30, 31
  stateless societies, in, 9
Ownership. *See* LAND LAW; PROPERTY,
    LAW OF; ROMAN LAW

Parlement de Paris
  development of, 34, 35, 36, 79
Partnerships
  English law, under, 136, 137
  Roman law, under, 136, 186, 190
Persons, law of
  commercial companies, applied to,
    136–138
  equality before the law, 139, 140
  family law, 140–143. *See also* FAMILY
    LAW
  history of, 135, 136
  legal persons, 136–138
  natural persons, 138–140
  Roman law, under, 130–135
Philippines
  dispute-settlement among Ifugao, 10
Possession. *See* PROPERTY, LAW OF;
    ROMAN LAW
Powers of Criminal Courts Act 1973
    . . . 67*n*
Private law. *See also* CONTRACT, LAW OF;
    OBLIGATIONS; PERSONS, LAW OF;
    PROPERTY, LAW OF; SUCCESSION
  codification of, 97, 98, 99

Private law—*cont.*
history of, 125–129
public law and, distinction between—
England, in, 116, 119, 120, 122, 123
generally, 107–109, 122–124
Roman law—
influence of, 125–129
under, 107, 108
Procedural models
adversarial procedure, 36–38
classical model of the legal process—
acceptance of, 14–16
arbitration and, 15, 16
effects of non-acceptance of, 23, 24
limitations of, 16
meaning of, 14
effects of—
arbitration as an alternative, 51–53
generally, 39
law and fact, 39–44
remedies, 44–47
trial by judge alone in England, 47–49
tribunals, 49, 50
generally, 25
inquisitorial procedure, 36–38
lay model—
English law, in, 30–34
professional model and, compared, 36
Roman law, in, 25–30
professional model—
late Roman and French law, in, 34–36
lay model and, compared, 36
English law, in, 46–47
Procurator-fiscal
Scottish law, under, 59
Professional lawyers. *See also* JUDGES; PROCEDURAL MODELS
adversarial and inquisitorial procedures, 36–38
growth of a class of, 24
law and fact, role as to, 39–44
laymen and, procedures involving both—
generally, 39
law and fact, distinction between, 39–44
remedies, 44–47
tribunals, 49, 50
professional model in late Roman and French law, 34–36

Professional model. *See* PROCEDURAL MODELS
Property, law of
choses in action, meaning of, 161
damage to property, under Roman law, 196, 197
English land law. *See* LAND LAW
immovable things—
civil law countries, in, 164, 165
English land law. *See* LAND LAW
intellectual property, 161
modern law as to, generally, 157, 158
movable things, as to—
fund, 162
non-physical movables, 161
physically movable, where, 158–160
security for debt, 162, 163
things joined together, 160, 161
trust, in England, 162
usufruct, 152, 153, 162, 176
ownership—
definitions of, 157, 158
possession and, distinguished, 145, 157
Roman law as to. *See under* ROMAN LAW
simple societies, in, 40, 41, 144
stateless societies, in, 5
possession and ownership distinguished, 145, 157
Roman law as to. *See* ROMAN LAW
stocks and shares, 161
Public law
administrative law, 114–122. *See also* ADMINISTRATIVE LAW
constitutional law, 109–114. *See also* CONSTITUTIONAL LAW
private law and, distinction between—
England, in, 116, 119, 120, 122, 123
generally, 107–109, 122–124
Roman law, under, 107, 108

Race Relations Act 1968 . . . 66
Race Relations Act 1976 . . . 140
Reasonableness
role of laymen as to, 42–44
Rent assessment tribunals
role of, 50
Restrictive Trade Practices Acts . . . 213
Retaliation
ancient Germanic laws, under, 19, 20
Roman law, tolerated under early, 26
stateless societies, in, 10–12

Roman law
adoption under, 133, 134
appeals under, 43, 55
arson under, 194
civil law—
 classification of, 126–129
 criminal acts, as remedy for, 55, 56
 ius civile, meaning of, 26
 ius commune, influence of, in Europe, 77, 93–96
cognitio procedure, 34, 46, 73
commercial law, 185, 186, 209, 210, 211
compensation under, 26, 27
contract—
 breach of, 195
 commercial, 185, 186
 consensual, 186–191
 conveyance and, distinguished, 147
 hire, of, 186, 188, 189
 land, as to, 152, 153
 loans, as to, 191, 192, 194
 mandate, of, 186, 189, 190, 194
 not binding, where, 184, 185
 partnership, of, 186, 190
 privity of, 192, 193
 quasi-contracts, 193, 194
 sale, of, 186, 187, 188
 stipulation, of, 185, 186, 193
 terms of, 192, 193
 validity of, 193
conveyances, 147
Corpus Iuris Civilis, 74, 77, 94
criminal jurisdiction under, 55, 56
customary practices under early, 25, 26
damages under, 44–46, 55, 197, 198
delictal obligations. *See* obligations, *below*
disputes under early, 27, 28
emphyteusis, 153, 156
extortion under, 56
family under, 26, 27, 132–135, 173–177
Gaius' Institutes, 127, 128
guardians under. *See* tutors, *below*
history of, 28, 29, 70–75
iudex—
 damages awarded by, 44–46
 meaning of, 27
 role of, 27, 28, 29, 30, 34, 39, 41, 42–44, 55, 186, 197, 198
ius, meaning of, 70, 71
ius civile, 26

Roman law—*cont.*
ius commune, 77, 93–96
ius dicere, 71
Justinian's law, 74, 75, 77, 81, 84, 93, 95, 98, 99, 127–129, 148, 150, 157, 175, 177, 198, 211
kinship group in early, 26, 27
land, as to—
 praedial servitudes, 151, 152, 153, 171
 transfer of land, 147, 148
 usucapio, 148
lay model in, 25–30
leases, 146, 148, 152, 153
legal persons, 136
lex, meaning of, 71
lex Aquilia, 196, 197, 206, 207
magistrate. *See* praetor, *below*
marriage under, 131, 132, 133, 140
Mucius Scaevola, treatise of, 126, 127
murder under, 55, 194
obligations—
 contractual, 184–193. *See also* contract, *above*
 delictal, 194–198
 generally, 184
 quasi-contractual, 193, 194
ownership—
 acquisition of—
  occupation, by, 149
  things joined together, where, 149, 150, 160
  usucapio, by, 148, 149
 early law, under, 26, 27, 41
 equitable principles, 155–157
 possession and, distinguished, 145
 rights less than—
  personal servitudes, 152, 153
  praedial servitudes, 151, 152, 153, 171
  security for debt, 154, 155
  usufruct, 152, 153, 162, 176
 transfer of—
  land, as to, 147, 148
  physical delivery (*traditio*), by, 146, 147, 158, 159
 treasure, of, 151
 See also possession, *below*
partnerships under, 136, 186, 190
persons, as to, 130–135
possession—
 occupation, by, 149
 ownership and, distinguished, 145
 possessory interdicts, 145, 146
 stolen things, 148, 151

Roman law—*cont.*
possession—*cont.*
transfer of, 146, 147
usucapio, for, 148, 149, 157
See also ownership, *above*
praetor, role of, 27, 28, 29, 30, 45, 46,
51, 71, 72, 146, 155, 156, 175,
186, 191
private law—
influence on, of, 125–129
under, 107, 108
Proculians, 72, 73, 150
property, as to—
damage to, under *lex Aquila*, 196,
197
equity, 155–157
generally, 144, 145
ownership and possession, 145–151.
See also ownership, *above;* possession, *above*
rights less than ownership, 151–
155. *See also* ownership, *above;*
possession, *above*
public law under, 107, 108
Reception of, 77, 79, 80
Sabinians, 72, 73, 150
Sabinus, treatise of, 126–127
succession under—
generally, 173
intestate, 173–175
legacies, 176, 177
objections to will, 176, 177
testamentary, 175–177
widow, position of, 175, 176
theft under, 26, 45, 55, 148, 151, 195,
196, 206
Theodosian Code, 73, 74
tutors under, 134, 135, 174
Twelve Tables, 26, 27, 28, 70, 71,
134, 150, 173, 175, 197
usucapio, 148, 149, 157
usufruct, 152, 153, 162, 176
Visigoths, of, 73, 78
written law and unwritten law, 70–75
Royal courts
medieval England, in, 31–33, 36, 46,
80, 81, 168

Sabinus
treatise of, 126–127
Sale, contract of
Roman law, under, 186, 187, 188
Salic law
payment of *wergild* under, 20, 76
prologue to, 76

Schöffen
Germany, in, 24, 57, 58, 76, 79,
80
Scottish law
Court of Session, 83
criminal procedure under, 59, 60
feudal land law in, 166
history of, 21, 22
judge under, 59, 60
jury under, 59, 60
procurator-fiscal, 59
sheriff, 59
Security for debt
modern law, under, 162, 163
Roman law, under, 154, 155
Self-help. *See* RETALIATION
Sex Discrimination Act 1975 . . . 140
Shaming
stateless societies, in, 7–9
Sheriff
Scottish law, under, 59
Sorcery
stateless societies, in, 7–9
Stateless societies
adultery in, 7
bride price in, 5
dispute settlement in—
arbitration, by, 5–7
contest, by, 9, 10
generally, 3, 4
mediation, by, 5–7
ordeal, by, 9
retaliation and feud, by, 10–12
shaming and sorcery, by, 7–9
wrongdoing, coping with, 7–12
Statute law
growth of—
continental Europe, in, 95, 96
England, in, 89–93
Statute of Westminster I of 1275 . . . 31
Statute of Wills 1540 . . . 169
Stocks and shares
law of property as to, 161
Succession
civil law as to, 178–181
English law, under. *See* ENGLISH LAW
French law, as to. *See* FRENCH LAW
German law, as to. *See* GERMAN LAW
intestate—
civil law, under, 178, 179
English law, under, 182
Roman law, under, 173–175
modern law generally, 177, 178
Roman law, under, 173–177. *See also*
under ROMAN LAW

Succession—*cont.*
 surviving spouse—
  civil law, rights under, 178, 179
  English law, under, 182
  Roman law, under, 152, 175, 176
 testamentary—
  civil law, under, 179–181
  English law, under, 182, 183
  fideicommissary substitutions, 180, 181
  legitim, rights as to, in Germany, 179, 180
  restriction, in France, 179
  Roman law, under, 175–177
Supernatural forces
 control by, in stateless societies, 8, 9
Supreme Court Act 1981 . . . 117*n*

Tanzania
 dispute-settlement in, 6, 7
Theft
 Roman law, under, 26, 45, 55, 148, 151, 195, 196, 206
 stateless societies, in, 7, 9
 trial for, 65
Tort, English law of
 employers, liability of, 207, 208, 218
 examples of, 206
 industrial injury, as to, 208
 negligence—
  contributory, 207
  liability for, 207
Torts (Interference with Goods) Act 1977 . . . 158
Trade Descriptions Acts . . . 214
Trade unions. *See* LABOUR LAW
Treasure
 entitlement to, under Roman law, 151
 under French and German law, 161
 under English law, 161
Trials, English. *See also* COURTS
 judge alone, by, 47–49
 jury, by—
  damages awarded by, 44, 46
  history of, 61–63
  today, 63
  See also JURY
 summary trials, 63–66. *See also* MAGISTRATES
Tribunals
 administrative, 118
 appeals from, 50
 Council on, role of, 50
 industrial relations disputes, for, 218, 219

Tribunals—*cont.*
 role of, 49, 50
 types of, 50
Tribunals and Enquiries Act 1971 . . . 118*n*
Tribunals and Inquiries Act 1958 . . . 118
Tutors
 Roman law, under, 134, 135, 174
Twelve Tables. *See* ROMAN LAW

Uganda
 Lugbara, consultation of oracle by, 9
Unfair Contract Terms Act 1977 . . . 202, 213
United States
 administrative law in, 116, 117
 constitution of, 110, 111, 112
 recourse to law in, 220
 trade unions in, 216
Unwritten law. *See* WRITTEN LAW AND UNWRITTEN LAW
Usufruct
 meaning of, 152
 modern law, in, 162
 Roman law, under, 152, 153, 162, 176

Wergild
 payment of, 20
 written texts as to, 76
Wife. *See* FAMILY LAW
Will. *See also* SUCCESSION
 English law, under, 169, 182, 183
 French law, under, 179–181
 German law, under, 179–181
 Roman times, in, 152, 173, 175–177
Witnesses. *See also* EVIDENCE
 adversarial procedure, in, 37
 civil claims, as to, 68
 continental criminal procedure, under, 57, 58
 English courts, in—
  early, 33
  magistrates' courts, 65
  trials by judge alone, in, 47
 fact, question of, 40
 inquisitorial procedure, in, 37, 38
 Roman law, under, 27
 Scottish trials, in, 60
Workers. *See also* LABOUR LAW
 contracts of. *See* LABOUR LAW
 dismissal of, 218, 219
 employers liable for servants' torts, 207, 208
 industrial accidents, 208

Workers—*cont.*
  statutory protection of, 215
Written law and unwritten law
  ancient Rome, in, 70–75
  case law, 85–89, 93
  generally, 69, 70
  medieval—
    continental Europe, in, 75–80

Written law and unwritten law—*cont.*
  medieval—*cont.*
    England, in, 80–84
  statute law, 89–93

Yugoslavia
  Albanian community, survival of
    blood-feud among, 22, 23